BUSINESS PRINCIPLES and MANAGEMENT

STUDENT ACTIVITIES GUIDE

Kenneth E. Everard, Ed.D.
The College of New Jersey

James L. Burrow, Ph.D.
North Carolina State University

SOUTH-WESTERN
CENGAGE Learning

Australia · Canada · Mexico · Singapore · Spain · United Kingdom · United States

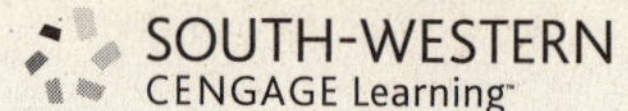

Business Principles and Management
by Kenneth E. Everard and James L. Burrow

Executive Editor Eve Lewis	**Manufacturing Coordinator** Kevin Kluck	**Cover** Bill Spencer
Project Manager Carol Sturzenberger	**Editorial Assistants** Linda Adams; Stephanie White	**Composition/Prepress** Lewis Editorial Services
Marketing Manager Nancy A. Long	**Production Assistant** Deb Roark	**Printer** Mazer
Marketing Coordinator Christian L. McNamee	**Consulting Editor** Cinci Stowell, Stowell Editorial Services	
Production Manager Patricia Matthews Boies		
Manufacturing Manager Carol Chase		

About the Authors:

Kenneth E. Everard, Ed.D., is Professor Emeritus at The College of New Jersey, where he served as professor of management and as developer and administrator of graduate programs in business education, office administration, human resources management, and management. Earlier he taught business education at the secondary level and also taught accounting and management at the University of Maryland in College Park, Europe, and the Far East.

James L. Burrow, Ph.D., is the coordinator of the graduate Training and Development Program at North Carolina State University in Raleigh, North Carolina. He has been a faculty member at the community college and university levels in marketing and human resource development as well as a consultant to business and public organizations.

CONTENTS

PREFACE TO WORKBOOK

A variety of activities appear in this workbook to help you learn the material you have studied in the Eleventh Edition of *Business Principles and Management*. Follow your teacher's instructions as you select workbook activities to complete. After completing your assigned tasks, you should have an excellent understanding of the principles that appear in the textbook. Four types of exercises are provided: Study Guides, Controversial Issues, Problems, and a Small Group Activity.

The Study Guide activities allow you to check your understanding of basic facts by involving you in answering yes-no, multiple choice, and matching or fill-in questions for each chapter. The Controversial Issues exercises challenge you to look at two questions that may be answered "yes" or "no." After studying each issue, you should provide reasons to support your answers. The Problems section requires you to study and solve realistic business problems and, in some situations, to perform calculations to arrive at sound decisions. The Small Group Activity is the last activity in each chapter. This project will likely provide you with one of the most valuable ways to learn about business.

Each of the four types of activities—Study Guides, Controversial Issues, Problems, and Small Group Activity—will provide you with a different way to review and learn the textbook material. Enjoy working through the exercises assigned by your teacher as you acquire new business knowledge by applying critical-thinking skills.

Kenneth E. Everard
Jim Burrow

<table>
<tr><td rowspan="3">Chapter 1

Characteristics of Business</td><td rowspan="3">Name ___________________

Date ___________________</td><td colspan="4" align="center">Scoring Record</td></tr>
<tr><td></td><td>Part A</td><td>Part B</td><td>Total</td></tr>
<tr><td>Perfect score</td><td>20</td><td>15</td><td>35</td></tr>
<tr><td>My score</td><td></td><td></td><td></td></tr>
</table>

Study Guide

Part A—*Directions:* Indicate your answer to each of the following questions by circling either yes or no in the Answers column.

		Answers	For Scoring
1.	Do more than 22 million businesses currently exist in the United States?	yes no	1. _______
2.	Do businesses vary in size from one employee to thousands of employees?	yes no	2. _______
3.	Is an organization that produces or distributes a good or service for profit called a store?	yes no	3. _______
4.	Do service firms produce goods?	yes no	4. _______
5.	Does marketing deal with money matters related to running a business?	yes no	5. _______
6.	Does the supply of a product refer to the number of similar products that will be bought at a given time and at a given price?	yes no	6. _______
7.	Do industrial businesses produce goods that other businesses use to make things?	yes no	7. _______
8.	Are banks and investment companies classified as industrial types of businesses?	yes no	8. _______
9.	Because a government provides fire and police protection, can it be considered an industry?	yes no	9. _______
10.	Are service businesses growing faster than production businesses?	yes no	10. _______
11.	Does effectiveness occur when an organization produces needed goods or services quickly and at low cost?	yes no	11. _______
12.	Are firms that are extremely efficient always very effective?	yes no	12. _______
13.	Is the concept of total quality management a commitment to excellence that is accomplished by teamwork and continual improvement?	yes no	13. _______
14.	Is the Malcolm Baldridge Award presented to companies from any country?	yes no	14. _______
15.	Does output refer to the quantity, or amount, produced within a given time?	yes no	15. _______
16.	Does the productivity rate in the U.S. currently exceed that of all other countries?	yes no	16. _______
17.	Do innovations refer only to the invention of new products?	yes no	17. _______
18.	Has reengineering increased customer satisfaction for most firms that have done it?	yes no	18. _______
19.	Is the franchisor the distributor of a franchised product or service?	yes no	19. _______
20.	Does risk in business involve competition from new products?	yes no	20. _______

	Answers	For Scoring

1. The business activity that is involved with how goods or services are exchanged between producers and consumers is (a) production, (b) marketing, (c) finance, (d) manufacturing. .... ______ 1. ______

2. Which is an example of a commercial business firm? (a) mining, (b) construction, (c) banking, (d) manufacturing. .... ______ 2. ______

3. Which industry employs the most workers in the U.S.? (a) wholesale and retail trade, (b) government, (c) manufacturing, (d) general services. .... ______ 3. ______

4. Which industry had the greatest increase in number of businesses from 1980 to 1995? (a) manufacturing, (b) wholesale trade, (c) retail trade, (d) services. ...... ______ 4. ______

5. Which of the following refers to a commitment to excellence? (a) ESOP, (b) TQM, (c) GDP, (d) T&I. .... ______ 5. ______

6. Which of the following is NOT a result of mass production? (a) effectiveness, (b) higher cost of goods manufactured, (c) fewer workers, (d) large numbers of items produced. .... ______ 6. ______

7. Which nation had the most productive workers in 1996? (a) United States, (b) Canada, (c) Japan, (d) England. .... ______ 7. ______

8. What effect does advanced technology usually have on the cost of each item produced by a business? (a) cost stays about the same, (b) cost increases, (c) cost decreases, (d) revenue and cost break even. .... ______ 8. ______

9. How does the GDP of $8.8 trillion appear when written out? (a) $8,800, (b) $8,008,000, (c) $8,000,800,000 (d) $8,800,000,000,000. .... ______ 9. ______

10. In the typical franchise business, the franchisee does NOT receive (a) help in selecting a location for the business, (b) special training in how to operate efficiently, (c) guaranteed profit, (d) exclusive rights to sell in a specified geographic area. .... ______ 10. ______

11. Which of the following best describes risk? (a) insurance, (b) possibility of failure, (c) net losses a business suffers, (d) protection. .... ______ 11. ______

12. Approximately what percentage of all businesses cease operations within six to seven years of startup? (a) 10%, (b) 20%, (c) 35%, (d) 50%. .... ______ 12. ______

13. The two primary reasons for business failures are (a) inadequate planning and experience, (b) overexpansion and neglect, (c) economic and finance causes, (d) disaster and fraud. .... ______ 13. ______

14. An employee who is given funds and freedom to create a special unit or department within a company in order to develop a new product, process, or service is called an (a) apprentice, (b) entrepreneur, (c) intrapreneur, (d) investor. .... ______ 14. ______

15. A business that strives in all its operations to promote general welfare and observe laws is fulfilling its obligation to (a) the public, (b) its workers, (c) its investors, (d) its managers. .... ______ 15. ______

Directions: Study each controversial issue carefully. Follow the advice of your teacher before listing in the columns provided reasons why people might answer Yes or No. Your teacher may want you to work with a classmate, talk with others in your community to gather information, or use the library or Internet to gather facts.

1-1. In order to protect U.S. businesses from foreign competitors, should the federal government provide financial aid that would enable troubled businesses to survive?

Reasons for "Yes"	Reasons for "No"

1-2. Because the failure rate among new businesses is high, should potential entrepreneurs be required to pass a test on how to run a business?

Reasons for "Yes"	Reasons for "No"

PROBLEMS

1-A. Check the column that correctly classifies whether each business listed below is an industrial business or a commercial business.

	Commercial	Industrial
1. Crushed stone mill	____	____
2. Credit card business	____	____
3. Sporting goods shop	____	____
4. Home building firm	____	____
5. Health care center	____	____

1-B. For each of the activities listed below, check the column that indicates whether the activity applies primarily to effectiveness or efficiency. Assume your company operates a lawn-mowing service and must compete with four other companies.

	Effectiveness	Efficiency
1. Ask customers what they like most and least about your service.	____	____
2. Buy new equipment to prevent lost mowing time from breakdowns.	____	____
3. Mow all lawns located near each other on the same day.	____	____
4. Add new services such as fertilizing and watering lawns.	____	____
5. Lower your operating costs by buying gas in quantity at lower prices.	____	____
6. Sharpen blades more often to improve appearance of grass.	____	____
7. Train your workers in customer courtesy.	____	____

1-C. The wealth of a nation can be shown in rates per thousand persons owning selected appliances. From the information shown below, answer the questions provided.

Appliance	U.S.	Denmark	Germany	Japan	China
Radio	2115	1146	946	957	195
Computer	407	360	256	202	6
Television	805	592	564	684	319
Mobile Phone	206	273	99	304	10

Source: Statistical Abstract of the United States, 1999

1. Based on the appliances owned, in which country is the standard of living the highest? __________________

   the lowest? __________________

2. Based on the appliances owned, which country has the second-best standard of living? __________________

3. Which appliance is the most popular in most countries? __________________

4. Given the "rates per thousand people," how would you explain why the number of radios shown for the U.S. and Denmark exceeds one thousand?

   ____

   ____

   ____

1-D. Place a check in the column that shows the form of business ownership that best identifies the situation of a firm with 100 employees.

	Employee Stock Ownership Plan	Entrepreneur	Intrapreneur
1. Each year all 100 workers buy 20 ownership shares of the firm.	____	____	____
2. One of these workers sells all her shares to the remaining workers in order to start a business of her own.	____	____	____
3. Three of the workers agree to work separately from the others to create new processes for increasing output and improving quality.	____	____	____
4. Two workers quit to form their own business making a special product they have agreed to sell to their old firm.	____	____	____

1-E. Are you the kind of person who could start a business and make it go? Here is a way to find out. For each question below, check the answer that says what you feel or comes closest to it. Be honest with yourself.

1. *Are you a self-starter?*
____ I do things on my own. Nobody must tell me to get going.
____ If someone gets me started, I keep going all right.
____ Easy does it. I do not put myself out until I have to.

2. *How do you feel about other people?*
____ I like people. I can get along with just about anybody.
____ I have plenty of friends—I do not need anyone else.
____ Most people irritate me.

3. *Can you lead others?*
____ I can get most people to follow when I start something.
____ I can give the orders if someone tells me what we should do.
____ I let someone else get things moving. Then I go along if I feel like it.

4. *Can you take responsibility?*
____ I like to take charge of things and see them through.
____ I will take over if I have to, but I would rather let someone else be responsible.
____ There are always some "eager beavers" around wanting to show how smart they are. I say let them be responsible.

5. *How good an organizer are you?*
____ I like to have a plan before I start. I am usually the one to get things lined up when the group wants to do something.
____ I do all right unless things get too confused. Then I quit.
____ I get all set and then something comes along and presents too many problems. So I just take things as they come.

6. *How good a worker are you?*
____ I can keep going as long as I need to. I do not mind working hard for something I want.
____ I will work hard for a while, but when I have had enough, that's it.
____ I do not believe that hard work gets you anywhere.

7. *Can you make decisions?*
____ I can make up my mind in a hurry if I have to. It usually turns out okay, too.
____ I can make decisions if I have plenty of time. If I have to make up my mind quickly, I think later I should have decided the other way.
____ I do not like to be the one who has to decide things.

8. *Can people trust what you say?*
____ You bet they can. I do not say things I do not mean.
____ I try to be honest most of the time, but sometimes I just say what is easiest.
____ Why bother if the other person does not know the difference?

9. *Can you stick with it?*
____ If I make up my mind to do something, I do not let anything stop me.
____ I usually finish what I start—if it goes well.
____ If it does not go right at the start, I quit. Why beat your brains out?

10. *How good is your health?*
____ I never run down!
____ I have enough energy for most things I want to do.
____ I run out of energy sooner than most of my friends seem to.

Count the checks you made. They should add to 10.

How many checks are there beside the first answer to each question? _______

How many checks are there beside the second answer to each question? _______

How many checks are there beside the third answer to each question? _______

If most of your checks are beside the first answers, you probably have what it takes to run a business. If not, you are likely to have more trouble than you can handle by yourself. Better find a partner who is strong where you are weak. If many checks are beside the third answer, you should not consider going into business for yourself. You will be better off working for someone else as an employee.

1-F. Many newly opened active businesses are started each year. Study the information given for a year. Then answer the questions below.

No. of Employees	No. of Firms	Percent of Firms
2 or fewer	135,010	______________
3 to 5	53,230	______________
6 to 10	24,902	______________
11 to 20	11,204	______________
21 or more	9,364	______________
Totals	______________	______________

1. How many businesses were started during the year? Record your answer in the space provided above.
2. For the number of employees in each category shown, what is the percent of new startups involved? Record your answers in the space provided above.
3. What percent of the total businesses that start have fewer than six employees? ________________________
4. Based upon the figures above and your answers to the questions asked, place a check on the line provided ONLY if the statement is correct.

   a. The majority of newly started businesses have two or fewer employees. ____________________________

   b. Less than one percent of the newly started businesses have six or more employees. ____________________

   c. Over eighty percent of the newly started businesses have five or fewer employees. ____________________

1-G. Ten years ago Raul and Sangita Patel started a small restaurant that sold mostly seafood. The high quality of the food, fair prices, and an attractive dining room caused the business to become very successful. Two years ago after the first restaurant was opened, they opened an identical restaurant for their oldest daughter to operate in a nearby community. This restaurant is also successful. Today the Patels have five restaurants, and each is doing well.

The Patels would like to continue opening restaurants in other nearby communities. However, they know they cannot operate any more restaurants because even now their time is much too limited. For that reason they have been thinking of other ways to expand their business. A friend, Jason Johnson, suggested that they start a franchise and he be given the first chance to operate one of the restaurants in a nearby state.

1. Do you think operating under a franchise arrangement will work for the Patels? Yes _______ No _______

2. If the Patels gave Jason Johnson the opportunity to open a restaurant under a franchise agreement, who

    would be the franchisor? _______________________________

3. Who would be the franchisee? _______________________________

4. List some of the kinds of help that the Patels might provide Jason Johnson under a franchise agreement.

    ____

    ____

    ____

5. How will the Patels benefit by franchising their restaurants to people such as Jason Johnson? _______________

    ____

    ____

6. How can the Patels control the way others run their franchised restaurants? _______________

    ____

    ____

    ____

    ____

SMALL GROUP ACTIVITIES

Businesses have spent a great deal of time and money attempting to become more effective and more efficient. They have tried new approaches as described in the chapter, including the empowering of workers. Could schools empower students to become more effective and efficient? In this exercise you are being empowered to assist your school in making the learning process more effective and efficient.

With instructions from your teacher, form groups of four students. Each group of four should further divide into pairs. One pair of students in each group will focus on identifying effective and efficient ways to improve learning about business *in school.* The other pair in each group will focus on effective and efficient ways to improve learning about business *at home.* Follow the steps below.

Group Activity 1

1. With your partner, create two lists on separate sheets of paper. Label the first list *Effectiveness* and the second *Efficiency.*
2. Decide which pair of students in your group will focus on learning in school and which will focus on learning at home.
3. With your partner, offer specific suggestions for how learning could be improved. Do not discuss the ideas at this point—just record them on the list that best characterizes the idea: Effectiveness or Efficiency. Your goal is to generate as many ideas as possible within the time allotted by your instructor. Some examples for school-learning and home-learning ideas appear below.
4. When you complete your list, record the number of items you generated.

School-Learning Examples:

1. "I think one businessperson should be invited to answer student questions after students have learned the material in each chapter." Action: Don't discuss this now, but record it on the *Effectiveness* list.
2. "I don't think the teacher should waste class time dealing with unimportant things—things we may already know or have no interest in knowing." Action: Don't discuss, but record it on the *Efficiency* list.

Home-Learning Examples:

1. "I think all study should be done at home in a quiet place without interruptions from anyone." Action: Don't discuss, but record it on the *Effective* list.
2. "I want to limit my textbook study to one hour per day or less." Action: Don't discuss, but record it on the *Efficiency* list.

Group Activity 2

1. Each pair of students should now meet with the other pair in their group of four. Together, discuss your group's *Effectiveness* lists and combine them into one list for the group. First, decide whether each item is correctly classified as *effective* or *efficient.* You may have to move some items from one list to the other. If necessary, improve the wording to clarify the idea.
2. Now rank the items on your group's combined list into these categories: most important, somewhat important, and least important. Provide reasons for your answers.
3. Repeat Steps 1 and 2 above for the *Efficiency* list.
4. After completing Steps 1 through 3, report to the class the "most important" items on your *Effectiveness* and *Efficiency* lists with reasons for your answers.

Chapter 2		Scoring Record				
Social and Ethical Environment of Business	Name ________________ Date ________________		Part A	Part B	Part C	Total
		Perfect score	20	10	5	35
		My score				

Study Guide

Part A—*Directions:* Indicate your answer to each of the following questions by circling either yes or no in the Answers column.

		Answers	For Scoring

1. Does the United States have the world's largest economy? .... yes no 1. ______
2. Do changes in population as well as changes in lifestyles directly affect business operations? .... yes no 2. ______
3. In order for living standards to improve, must the country's population grow at a faster rate than its GDP? .... yes no 3. ______
4. Must a business consider both the size of the population and the characteristics of the population during its planning process? .... yes no 4. ______
5. Is a country's population growth rate controlled mostly by its birth, death, and immigration rates? .... yes no 5. ______
6. Did the "baby bust" period create an increased supply of workers? .... yes no 6. ______
7. Will a business that specializes in selling goods for a particular age group be affected if the number of people in that age group greatly increases or decreases? yes no 7. ______
8. Is the labor force defined as most people aged 16 or over who are available for work, whether employed or unemployed? .... yes no 8. ______
9. In the last three decades, did the labor participation rate for women decrease? yes no 9. ______
10. Has one of the problems of America's economy been its inability to create new jobs? .... yes no 10. ______
11. Has the demand for skilled workers been falling? .... yes no 11. ______
12. Were recent high school graduates particularly deficient in math, computer, and communication skills? .... yes no 12. ______
13. Has the United States Bureau of the Census found that about 25 percent of the population live in poverty? .... yes no 13. ______
14. Is the invisible barrier to job advancement referred to as the glass ceiling? ..... yes no 14. ______
15. If male carpenters and female construction workers require the same level of training and responsibility, should the pay scale be higher for males with families? .... yes no 15. ______
16. Does productivity tend to drop when employees regularly switch jobs within the organization? .... yes no 16. ______
17. Are resources such as natural gas, oil, and iron ore in unlimited supply? .... yes no 17. ______
18. When a business changes from natural gas to coal, does it meet environmental goals but violate conservation goals? .... yes no 18. ______
19. Does "ethics" refer to standards of moral conduct that individuals and groups set for themselves? .... yes no 19. ______
20. Does the American Civil Liberties Union examine workplace discrimination practices? .... yes no 20. ______

Part B—*Directions:* For each of the following statements, select the word, or group of words, that best completes the statement. In the Answers column, write the letter corresponding to the answer selected.

For
Answers   Scoring

1. The north central and northeastern states where manufacturing firms once dominated is known as the (a) frost belt, (b) sun belt, (c) rust belt, (d) snow belt. ...   1. ______

2. In a recent year, the Bureau of Labor Statistics reported that the size of the American labor force was almost (a) 140 million, (b) 115 million, (c) 90 million, (d) 65 million. ....   2. ______

3. By 1999, the labor participation rate for women reached about (a) 50%, (b) 60%, (c) 70%, (d) 80%. ....   3. ______

4. Over the years, the labor participation rate for men has (a) increased greatly, (b) increased slowly, (c) stayed about the same, (d) dropped greatly. ....   4. ______

5. With improved technology in recent years, the demand for qualified workers has (a) increased, (b) decreased a little, (c) remained about the same, (d) decreased a great deal. ....   5. ______

6. Which statement about the workforce is *incorrect?* (a) Women and racial minorities sometimes find it hard to be promoted above a certain level. (b) Many states have passed laws that promote using comparable worth for determining wages in government jobs. (c) Wages tend to be lower in jobs that employ lots of men than in jobs held primarily by women. (d) The rapid growth in the computer industry has led to high wages for those with the necessary education and skills. ....   6. ______

7. Which of the following is NOT a factor in determining comparable worth? (a) Requiring special skills for a job. (b) Requiring certain educational backgrounds for a job. (c) Requiring certain physical ability for a job. (d) Requiring males or females for a job. ...   7. ______

8. Which of the following is an *incorrect* statement regarding what employers are doing to attract and retain competent workers? (a) Improve the way work is done. (b) Assure healthier and safer working conditions. (c) Help workers deal with personal problems. (d) Train workers to like repetitive jobs. ....   8. ______

9. Which statement about the human factor in business is *false?* (a) Employees want more variety in their work. (b) Employees want more opportunity to participate in decisions that affect their working lives. (c) Employees do not want to work in teams. (d) Employees want more on-the-job responsibility. ....   9. ______

10. Which statement is *incorrect* about ethical issues? (a) One good approach for handling ethical issues is to select the behavior that does the most good for the most people. (b) Notions of what is right and wrong do not change over time. (c) Ethical issues arise when firms must choose ethical practices of a foreign country or of their own country. (d) Ethical issues arise when it is not clear whether a particular action is legal or illegal. ....   10. ______

Part C—*Directions:* Below are listed several kinds of pollution. Indicate how each type of pollution should be classified by placing a check mark in the appropriate column.

	Water Pollution	Air Pollution	Land Pollution	For Scoring
1. Exhaust being discharged by automobile engines.				1. ______
2. Chemicals being dumped from a house into a sewer line.				2. ______
3. Oil being spilled while being transported by an ocean liner.				3. ______
4. A town's trash being dumped into an abandoned stone quarry.				4. ______
5. Fish being killed by waste from a factory.				5. ______

Directions: Study each controversial issue carefully. Follow the advice of your teacher before listing in the columns provided reasons why people might answer Yes or No. Your teacher may want you to work with a classmate, talk with others in your community to gather information, or use the library or Internet to gather facts.

2-1. Because most jobs require more skills than in the past, should the minimum amount of education be raised to 18 years or a high school diploma?

Reasons for "Yes"	Reasons for "No"

2-2. Should all firms be required to use the CERES Principles rather than practicing the principles only on a voluntary basis? (The CERES Principles appear in the textbook on page 43.)

Reasons for "Yes"	Reasons for "No"

PROBLEMS

2-A. Assume that there are 92 million people who work in or near cities in the United States. Study the categories of jobs held by these people and answer the questions that follow. The figures are shown in millions of workers.

Clerical	15.8
Professional	13.6
Managerial	12.2
Sales	11.2
Precision crafts	9.9
Service	9.9
Machinists	5.5
Technicians	3.6
Transportation	3.4
Laborers	3.4
Others	3.4

1. What percent of the workforce applies to each of the top four job categories?

    a. Clerical _____________________

    b. Professional _____________________

    c. Managerial _____________________

    d. Sales _____________________

2. About what percent of the workforce do the top four job categories represent? _____________________

3. Which one job do you believe would be *most* likely to be held mainly by females? _____________________

4. Which one job do you believe would be *least* likely to be held mainly by females? _____________________

5. Which one job is *most* likely to be held by people with the fewest job skills? _____________________

2-B. Assume the "baby busters" (busters) who were aged 18-29 in a recent year were compared with the entire population. The estimated breakdown by race is shown. Study the statistics and answer the questions that appear below the table. Note: Hispanics are also classified as white; therefore, totals will exceed 100%.

	Baby Busters	Total Population
White	81.2%	83.5%
Black	14.0	12.4
American Indian	.9	.8
Asian	3.9	3.3
Hispanic	12.3	9.5

1. What is the percentage difference of white busters in relation to the total white population? _____________

2. What is the percentage difference of black busters in relation to the total black population? _____________

3. Which race has the greatest percentage difference? _____________________

    What is the percentage difference? _____________________

4. What conclusion can be made about the difference between white busters and other busters?

____

2-C. Assume that the percent of the entire United States population living below the poverty level was 14.2 percent. Shown below are poverty levels for a sample of states. Study the figures and answer the questions.

Michigan	14.1%
Mississippi	23.3%
Montana	15.4%
Nevada	11.4%
New Hampshire	7.3%
New Mexico	22.4%
Wisconsin	9.9%

1. Which states are in the Frost Belt? ________________________________

    ____

2. Which states are in the Sun Belt? ________________________________

    ____

3. Which one state can be most considered a Rust Belt state? ________________________________

4. What is the average poverty level for the states shown? ________________________________

5. How many times greater is the poverty level in Mississippi compared to New Hampshire's poverty level?

    ____

6. For the states shown, is the poverty level higher in the Frost Belt or the Sun Belt? ________________________________

2-D. Assume the yearly differences in pay between men and women with college degrees by age groups differ as shown below. Study the figures and answer the questions.

Age Group	Men	Women	Percent of Women's Pay to Men's Pay
18-24	$22,300	$20,500	_________
25-34	33,900	25,500	_________
35-44	44,700	28,900	_________
45-54	50,200	29,600	_________
55-64	54,600	29,600	_________

1. Calculate the percent of women's pay to men's pay and record your answers in the column shown above.
2. Provide three major reasons why the percent of women's pay to men's drops throughout one's working life.

    a. ________________________________

    b. ________________________________

    c. ________________________________

2-E. How aware are you of your environment? Answer the following questions as truthfully as possible about yourself and your family. Circle yes or no for each question. When you finish, check your environmental awareness score following the test.

1. Does your home or apartment have storm windows? .... yes no 1. _______
2. Do your doors and windows have weather stripping or caulking? .... yes no 2. _______
3. Is the thermostat lowered to 65 degrees or less when you go to bed? .... yes no 3. _______
4. Do you turn off unnecessary lights when they are not being used? .... yes no 4. _______
5. Is the thermostat in your home set no higher than 68 or 70 degrees when some-
   one is there during the day? .... yes no 5. _______
6. Do you turn the water off while you brush your teeth? .... yes no 6. _______
7. Do you drink a glass of water immediately without running the water awhile
   first? .... yes no 7. _______
8. Are you aware that less water is used in a quick shower than in a bath? .... yes no 8. _______
9. Are you aware that a self-defrosting refrigerator costs 25 percent more to operate? yes no 9. _______
10. Is there usually someone watching your television set while it is on? .... yes no 10. _______
11. Do you place plastic containers, tins, newspapers, and magazines in recycling
    containers instead of throwing them in the garbage? .... yes no 11. _______
12. Do you use a regular blanket rather than an electric blanket? .... yes no 12. _______
13. Is your family car (or cars) regularly maintained? .... yes no 13. _______
14. Do you use sand rather than salt on icy roads, driveways, or sidewalks? .... yes no 14. _______
15. When you take out fast food, do you regularly put the waste packaging such as
    wrappers and paper cups in waste containers? .... yes no 15. _______
16. Do you compost leaves, grass clippings, and kitchen vegetable waste? .... yes no 16. _______
17. When you buy your first car (or next car), will it be an economy car? .... yes no 17. _______
18. Are you upset when you see litter, such as bottles, cans, and paper strewn about
    in your community? .... yes no 18. _______
19. Do you discourage excessive purchase of food, clothes, and other items that you
    do not need? .... yes no 19. _______
20. Do you, or would you, car pool to work? .... yes no 20. _______

Count the number of *yes* answers and place your total score here. ______

If your total score is 16-20, you are *very alert* to your environment.
If your total score is 12-15, you are *fairly alert* to your environment.
If your total score is 8-11, you are *somewhat alert* to your environment.
If your total score is 0-7, you are *not alert* to your environment.

2-F. Businesses must be ethically responsible. For each situation, decide whether each business is "ethical" or "unethical." Circle your answer and give a reason for your decision.

1. Because the cost of hiring a firm to dispose of waste liquids from a paint manufacturing firm is so high, a company daily dumps a small amount into a nearby large river. The president knows that a very large business nearby also does this. "If they can do it, so can we," he says.

   Decision: Ethical Unethical

   Reason: ____

   ____

2. A large company that sells apple juice and advertises it as "fresh" finds itself in financial difficulty. It decides to keep running the same ad but use imitation rather than real apple juice because people cannot tell the difference in taste. This action would allow the business to make enough profit to survive without having to fire some workers and cut other costs.

   Decision: Ethical Unethical

   Reason: ____

   ____

3. Each December a small entrepreneur gives a sizable cash Christmas gift to key city officials with the hope that when special favors are needed, these officials will readily grant them. This is fairly common practice in this community.

Decision: Ethical Unethical

Reason: ____

____

2-G. Read the following story and answer the questions that follow:

For years the Gumshoe Company has been doing rather well making house slippers for distribution by a large department store chain. Its 200 workers come from the small city of 75,000 in which the plant is located. Over 150 of the workers are women, most of whom work in the plant's cutting, sewing, and packaging departments. About 25 men work in the receiving and shipping department. There are about ten supervisors and managers, all of whom are males. The rest of the employees are office, maintenance, and design people. Last week the plant manager, Barry Danziger, received the following typewritten message:

```
Sir: For too long this company has been run by men who keep women in
their place. Sexist comments are heard frequently and, worst of all, not
a single woman holds a management position. None of us is ever considered
for a supervisory position when an opening occurs. Someone from the
shipping and receiving department always gets it. We expect the next
supervisory position that opens to be filled by a woman, or you will
immediately see that we mean business.
                                          Women's Rights Committee
```

Mr. Danziger asked the present supervisors what they knew about the matter. None had heard anything. Some of the more outspoken women workers were also contacted. All remained silent. Barry Danziger was puzzled. All management openings are announced through a newsletter and posted on plant bulletin boards. When the last opening occurred, not a single woman had applied.

1. What action could the women take to show management that they "mean business"? ________________

____

2. Give two possible reasons why no woman applied for the last supervisory position. ________________

____

____

____

____

3. If no women from the plant apply for the next position, what should the plant manager do? ___________

____

____

____

____

2-H. Assume you are an employee in a company where the business situations described below have occurred. Check your decision in the ethical or unethical column that appears on the right and give a reason for your decision.

Ethical Unethical

1. A co-worker was absent from work yesterday to visit a friend but plans to report it as an illness. .... ______ ______

   Reason: ____

   ____

2. Your boss plans to overstate your department's output so that she will win the Manager of the Month award. .... ______ ______

   Reason: ____

   ____

3. You learn that the business has an old warehouse that is no longer needed for storage. Management has decided to make offices there for fifty clerks. The building's walls have asbestos that could harm workers over time. .... ______ ______

   Reason: ____

   ____

4. A product your firm makes is dangerous to users but the firm plans to take no action to make the item safe. .... ______ ______

   Reason: ____

   ____

5. Another employee has been using illegal drugs on the job and the supervisor does not know about it. .... ______ ______

   Reason: ____

   ____

6. A salesperson has the use of a company car but you have seen the car used on weekends for personal use. .... ______ ______

   Reason: ____

   ____

7. A highly qualified African American worker applied for an opening as a supervisor but was rejected in favor of a less qualified white candidate. .... ______ ______

   Reason: ____

   ____

8. A less qualified black male was promoted to a managerial position over a more highly qualified white female. .... ______ ______

   Reason: ____

   ____

SMALL GROUP ACTIVITIES

QUILT: A Game About Diversity

To Win: Have the highest number of squares initialed by the end of the game.

Rules:
1. In the center square, write your own definition of *diversity*.
2. Read the statements in the gray boxes and put your initials in the ones that apply to you.
3. Ask someone around you to put his or her initials in the white boxes that apply. Each person should initial no more the three squares. Then move on to ask another person.

Someone in the group who. . .

1. Has a close friend from a different race.	2. I have visited a church, temple, mosque, or synagogue different from mine.	3. Works in a male dominated occupation.	4. Has received a large amount of money from a lawsuit.	5. Has been married at least twice.
6. Has been a victim of sexual harassment.	7. Knows someone who has died of AIDS-related illness.	8. Owns and uses a gun for recreation.	9. Has parents of mixed religions.	10. I would not object to my son or daughter marrying someone of a different race.
11. I speak a language other than English at home.	12. Has a relative who is 70 years old or older and is still in the work force.	13. [make up your own statement about diversity]	14. Went to a religious school.	15. Would not like to have children.
16. Has lived abroad for more than six months.	17. Has a child in the family with a physical deficiency.	18. Has experienced racial discrimination.	19. I have a friend who is gay or lesbian.	20. Has a family member who has been in jail.
21. Comes from a multiracial family.	22. Has fought in a war.	23. I prefer a female boss.	24. Is a vegetarian.	25. Interacts with someone who is blind.

<table>
<tr><td rowspan="3">Chapter 3

Economic Environment of Business</td><td rowspan="3">Name _______________

Date _______________</td><td colspan="4" align="center">Scoring Record</td></tr>
<tr><td></td><td>Part A</td><td>Part B</td><td>Total</td></tr>
<tr><td>Perfect score</td><td>20</td><td>15</td><td>35</td></tr>
<tr><td></td><td></td><td>My score</td><td></td><td></td><td></td></tr>
</table>

Study Guide

Part A—*Directions:* Indicate your answer to each of the following questions by circling either yes or no in the Answers column.

		Answers	For Scoring
1.	Is "economics" the body of knowledge that relates to producing and using goods and services to satisfy human wants?	yes no	1. _______
2.	Does the school cafeteria provide for an economic want?	yes no	2. _______
3.	Does our economic system satisfy all the wants of the people?	yes no	3. _______
4.	Does a retail grocer provide both time utility and place utility?	yes no	4. _______
5.	Is a robot on a car assembly line an example of a consumer good?	yes no	5. _______
6.	Are capital goods needed to produce consumer goods and services?	yes no	6. _______
7.	Can a country produce as many capital goods as it wishes to produce at any one time?	yes no	7. _______
8.	If the production of consumer goods increases, must the production of capital goods and services also increase?	yes no	8. _______
9.	Are countries that adopt a market economy often dictatorships?	yes no	9. _______
10.	Does privatization occur when a government provides a good or service that was formerly provided by a business?	yes no	10. _______
11.	As the demand for a product decreases, does the price of the product usually increase?	yes no	11. _______
12.	Can a change in the demand or the supply of a product cause a change in the price of a product?	yes no	12. _______
13.	Do consumers help decide what will be produced as well as how much will be produced?	yes no	13. _______
14.	Is competition among businesses limited mainly to price competition?	yes no	14. _______
15.	Is it necessary to expand only the production of goods and services for economic growth to occur?	yes no	15. _______
16.	Does production decrease and unemployment increase occur during recessions?	yes no	16. _______
17.	Is a recession a decline in the GDP that continues for three months or more?	yes no	17. _______
18.	Does inflation result in a decline in the purchasing power of money?	yes no	18. _______
19.	During inflation, does the dollar buy more than it did before inflation?	yes no	19. _______
20.	Does the lowering and raising of taxes by the federal government aid in controlling recession and inflation?	yes no	20. _______

	Answers	For Scoring

1. Which of the following is NOT considered an economic want? (a) want for a television set, (b) want for medical attention, (c) want for friendship, (d) want for new clothing. .... _______ 1. _______

2. A shoe manufacturer creates (a) form utility, (b) time utility, (c) place utility, (d) economic utility. .... _______ 2. _______

3. The basic factors of production are (a) land (natural resources) and labor; (b) land (natural resources), labor, and capital goods; (c) land (natural resources), labor, capital goods, and entrepreneurship; (d) capital goods and labor. .... _______ 3. _______

4. When the production of consumer goods decreases, the production of (a) capital goods increases, (b) capital goods decreases and services increases, (c) capital goods decreases, (d) capital goods and services decreases. .... _______ 4. _______

5. Machines used to make automobiles are classified as (a) consumer goods, (b) capital goods, (c) consumer services, (d) domestic goods. .... _______ 5. _______

6. In which type of economy do individual buying decisions in the marketplace together determine what, how, and for whom goods and services will be produced? (a) communistic, (b) command, (c) market, (d) mixed. .... _______ 6. _______

7. What type of economy is China attempting to move toward? (a) capital, (b) command, (c) market, (d) mixed. .... _______ 7. _______

8. The term that best describes our present economic/political system is (a) socialism, (b) communism, (c) capitalism, (d) privatization. .... _______ 8. _______

9. Approximately what percent of total receipts represents the average net profit of all business firms? (a) 5%, (b) 10%, (c) 15%, (d) 25%. .... _______ 9. _______

10. Demand for a product is the (a) same as want, (b) price at which the product will sell most readily, (c) number of products that will be bought at a given time at a given price, (d) number of future customers. .... _______ 10. _______

11. Prices are determined by the forces of (a) supply only, (b) demand only, (c) both supply and demand, (d) business cycles. .... _______ 11. _______

12. Non-price competition occurs when a firm (a) takes business away from its competitors by lowering prices, (b) conducts an extensive advertising campaign to convince the public that its product is better than all other brands, (c) does not have to compete with other sellers for consumer dollars, (d) occurs only when service is provided. .... _______ 12. _______

13. Economic growth occurs when a country produces goods and services at (a) the same rate the population is increasing, (b) a faster rate than the population is increasing, (c) a slower rate than the population is increasing, (d) the same rate unemployment is increasing. .... _______ 13. _______

14. The Consumer Price Index (CPI) is (a) the total market value of all goods produced and services purchased in a year, (b) the total of all the products that are purchased at a given time, (c) a measure of the average change in prices of consumer goods and services, (d) the same as the Economic Index of Leading Indicators. .... _______ 14. _______

15. Which of the following is NOT likely to occur during a recession? (a) decreased production, (b) increased unemployment, (c) increased demand for goods and services, (d) decline in GDP. .... _______ 15. _______

Directions: Study each controversial issue carefully. Follow the advice of your teacher before listing in the columns provided reasons why people might answer Yes or No. Your teacher may want you to work with a classmate, talk with others in your community to gather information, or use the library or Internet to gather facts.

3-1. Should the federal government privatize the U.S. Postal Service?

Reasons for "Yes"	Reasons for "No"

3-2. To encourage savings and, in turn, capital formation, should the interest earned by individuals on savings and other investments NOT be taxed by the federal government?

Reasons for "Yes"	Reasons for "No"

PROBLEMS

3-A. In economics, *utility* is the ability of a good or service to satisfy a want. For each of the four common types of utility shown in the columns below, check the one type of utility that best fits the situation described.

	Types of Utility			
	Form	Place	Time	Possession
1. You go to a nearby store to buy a canvas walking shoe, but the store carries leather only.	____	____	____	____
2. You have just completed signing the rental form for the use of a portable computer to take on a business trip.	____	____	____	____
3. You dash into a bookstore on your lunch hour and ask for this week's best-selling novel by name, which the clerk has in stock.	____	____	____	____
4. You were planning to walk home after a movie, but it is raining so you look for a taxi. One pulls up as you leave the theater.	____	____	____	____

3-B. For each item listed below, determine whether it is a capital good or a consumer good. Check the appropriate column.

	Capital Good	Consumer Good
1. Bulldozer for building contractors	____	____
2. Garden hose	____	____
3. Home	____	____
4. Factory	____	____
5. Machines for making bicycles	____	____

3-C. On the line provided, write the name of the economic system that best represents each statement.

1. Resources are allocated by government only. ________________________________

2. Marketing decisions are made by market conditions. ________________________________

3. China is a good example of this economic system. ________________________________

4. Businesses and individuals own natural resources and capital goods. ________________________________

5. Government controls business decisions extensively for the allocation of some resources, but little over distribution. ________________________________

3-D. For each economic-political system listed, check the column that best fits its characteristics.

	Capitalism	Socialism	Communism
1. Freedom to own land and other property.	___	___	___
2. Usually a shortage of consumer goods.	___	___	___
3. Some industries owned by government but often allows some private ownership.	___	___	___
4. Nearly any individual may start a business.	___	___	___
5. Government decides how and what goods are to be produced	___	___	___

3-E. Below are a few average prices shown in Year 3 dollars for goods and services for three different time periods. Study the figures and answer the questions.

In Year 3 Dollars

	Year 1	Year 2	Year 3
Gallon of gas	1.55	1.26	1.12
Movie ticket (New York City)	2.75	5.74	5.05
Television (color)	1,432*	1,466	220
Hospital cost for one day	108	332	752
Eggs (one dozen)	3.77	2.54	.89
Postage (first-class letter)	.16	.26	.29

Only available in black and white.

1. Which items declined in price from Year 1 to Year 3? _______________________________

2. What economic factors might have most influenced the price of the items that declined in price?

   ____

3. Provide a possible reason why the price of movie tickets went up in Year 2 but dropped in Year 3.

   ____

4. If car manufacturers produce engines that use half as much gas, what might happen to the price of gas

   twenty years from now? ____

5. By what percent did the cost of eggs decrease from Year 1 to Year 3? _____________________

   ____

6. By what percent did the cost of postage on a first-class letter increase from Year 1 to Year 3? _____________

   ____

3-F. Study the Consumer Price Index figures below for two different years. Then answer the questions below.

	Year 5*	Year 15*
Food and beverages	188.0	302.0
Housing	164.5	349.9
Apparel and upkeep	142.3	206.0
Transportation	150.6	319.9
Medical care	168.6	403.1
Entertainment	152.2	265.0
Other goods and services	153.9	326.6

*In Year 1, the CPI was 100.

1. Which item had the greatest increase in the CPI during the ten-year period? _______________

2. Which item had the least increase in the CPI during the decade? _______________

3. As the CPI increases, does the purchasing power of the dollar increase, decrease, or stay about the same?

____

4. What types of people are hurt most by rapid increases in the CPI? _______________

5. Are increases in the CPI a measure of the rate of inflation, recession, or depression? _______________

3-G. If the national economy grows too fast, the result may be inflation. But if it grows too slowly, a recession or a depression is likely to occur. The federal government may take different actions that can help control the economy by controlling the rate of growth. Place a check in one of the columns on the right to show the expected effect of each governmental action on the economy.

		Speeds Economic Growth	Slows Economic Growth	No Effect on Economic Growth
1.	Raising federal income taxes	_____	_____	_____
2.	Lowering federal income taxes	_____	_____	_____
3.	Increasing government spending for transportation	_____	_____	_____
4.	Reducing government spending for defense	_____	_____	_____
5.	Launching a new satellite to the planet Venus	_____	_____	_____
6.	Passing a new law to lower the voting age	_____	_____	_____

3-H. Most nations experience business cycles. Check the appropriate business cycle phase shown in the columns on the right with the situation described on the left.

		Expansion	Peak	Contraction	Trough
1.	A period when unemployment is at its worst.	_____	_____	_____	_____
2.	A period of high employment and rising wages and prices.	_____	_____	_____	_____
3.	A period called depression.	_____	_____	_____	_____
4.	A period just before the unemployment rate starts to climb.	_____	_____	_____	_____
5.	A period of runaway inflation.	_____	_____	_____	_____
6.	A period when prices stop rising and graduates begin to find it more difficult to land jobs.	_____	_____	_____	_____

3-I. Obtain three brands of ballpoint pens, or some other low-priced product that most people buy from time to time. Select brands that differ in price, color, size, or shape. Ask ten people which item they would buy if they needed a pen and if these were the only choices. Once each person has selected the brand, ask for the main reason for the selection. Record the information below and answer the questions that follow.

	Brand A	Brand B	Brand C
Brand or product preference:	____	____	____

Main reason for selecting Brand A, Brand B, or Brand C

	Brand A	Brand B	Brand C
Price	____	____	____
Color	____	____	____
Size	____	____	____
Shape	____	____	____
Quality	____	____	____
Reputation of company	____	____	____
Other (write in) ___________________	____	____	____

1. Which brand was the most popular? _______________________________________

2. Which brand was the least popular? _______________________________________

3. What was the main reason for selecting the most popular brand? _______________________________________

____

4. Did price or nonprice competition most often influence potential buyers? _______________________________________

SMALL GROUP ACTIVITIES

Group Activity 1

In this activity you will compare current prices of common household products with prices ten years ago. Your instructor will place you into small groups of two to three students. Your task is for each group to select three common household products used by the typical family. Each group member is to pick a different store to obtain product prices. The group should then average the prices from the different stores.

Using the Internet or the library, find what those same or similar products cost today and ten years ago. Now compare the prices and calculate the percent of increase or decrease. Each group is to report its "inflationary rates" for its products for the ten-year period to the class.

Group Activity 2

Your teacher will place you in one of three groups. Each group will represent one of the three fictitious nations that are described below. Each nation will experience economic conditions during different time periods. As members of your nation's top economic council, your group must make recommendations to your government leaders and provide them with reasons for your suggestions. Here are the groups:

Group A: This group represents the country of Algoon. It is a struggling third-world communistic agricultural nation. Algoon has only a few manufacturing firms. Its population is relatively poor and a dictator rules this command economy. Your group aids the ruler in declaring economic policy.

Group B: Bazoon is a somewhat backward but fast-growing country economically. Bazoon has plenty of natural resources, and many developed countries want those resources. Its government is socialistic and its economic system is mixed. Your group helps the government make economic decisions.

Group C: This nation, named Capsoon, is large in size with a variety of industrial and service firms. Its population is economically well off. While it has many citizens who are poor, even the poor are much better off than those in Algoon and Bazoon. It is a democratic nation that is primarily a market economy. Your group advises your government in economic matters.

Problems and Decisions:

Each country's economic council will offer advice, with reasons, to its nation's leaders for how to accomplish the following tasks in keeping strictly with its economic and political system.

1. A recession has existed during the last six months. Offer the leader advice on what to do to turn your economy around. Why does your council feel this is good advice?

2. The unemployment rate is so high that some people are dying of starvation or freezing to death because they cannot afford heat, food, and winter clothing. Recommend immediate corrective economic measures that will get your country out of a major depression.

3. Runaway inflation is creating problems for everyone, especially retirees. The value of their retirement savings has diminished greatly. What can your council do to stabilize your economy?

Study Guide

Part A—*Directions:* Indicate your answer to each of the following questions by circling either yes or no in the Answers column.

		Answers	For Scoring

1. Have trade patterns on an international level shifted from services to goods? . — yes no 1._______
2. Is buying goods and services made in other countries called *importing*? .... — yes no 2._______
3. Do Americans export goods from France when they buy French perfume? ...... — yes no 3._______
4. Is a *parent firm* a business that owns or controls production or service facilities in more than one country? .... — yes no 4._______
5. Are most of the world's smallest corporations multinationals? .... — yes no 5._______
6. Is one reason for imposing tariffs to earn revenue for the country? .... — yes no 6._______
7. Does dumping lower the price of goods sold in a foreign market? .... — yes no 7._______
8. Do quotas limit the number of goods permitted to enter a country? .... — yes no 8._______
9. Do tariffs raise the price of foreign products? .... — yes no 9._______
10. Do non-tariff barriers increase the number of imports that enter a country? ... — yes no 10._______
11. Are governments allowed to restrict investments made by foreigners? .... — yes no 11._______
12. Is profit usually the main reason why firms sell abroad? .... — yes no 12._______
13. Does the WTO create and enforce rules governing trade within the United States? .... — yes no 13._______
14. Does a trading bloc discourage free trade among its members? .... — yes no 14._______
15. Is the IMF's main purpose to provide low-cost loans for roads and electric power plant development in less-developed countries? .... — yes no 15._______
16. Do sales level off during the maturity stage of a product? .... — yes no 16._______
17. Do American companies move to foreign countries when sales at home begin to grow? .... — yes no 17._______
18. Does a balance of payments deficit exist when more money leaves a country than comes in? .... — yes no 18._______
19. Might countries with prolonged trade deficits have to restrict the activities of foreign businesses in their countries? .... — yes no 19._______
20. When the demand for foreign currency decreases, does the value of the dollar increase? .... — yes no 20._______

		Answers	For Scoring

1. Which method is likely to be the least costly and risky way to expand abroad? (a) franchising, (b) licensing, (c) dumping, (d) exporting. .... _______ 1. ______

2. Two or more firms sharing the costs of doing business in foreign countries and also sharing the profits are (a) joint ventures, (b) strategic alliances, (c) wholly-owned subsidiaries, (d) licensed enterprises. .... _______ 2. ______

3. If the United States sets a tariff of 15 percent on $150 cameras that are made in Germany, the cost of the camera in the U.S. will rise to (a) $155.50, (b) $165, (c) $172.50, (d) $175. .... _______ 3. ______

4. How do tariffs affect the prices of foreign goods? (a) Prices increase. (b) Prices decrease. (c) Prices remain the same. (d) Prices fluctuate at a quick pace. .... _______ 4. ______

5. Non-tariff barriers (a) increase the number of imports that enter a country, (b) increase the value of one currency to another, (c) protect domestic producers, (d) protect foreign producers. .... _______ 5. ______

6. In a high-context culture such as Japan, communication would NOT likely be (a) direct, (b) gestures, (c) indirect, (d) vague. .... _______ 6. ______

7. If a U.S. company overproduces, the best way to dispose of its surplus goods profitably is to (a) advertise widely to attract buyers, (b) drop the price of the surplus goods to attract buyers, (c) create a trading bloc to create demand for the goods, (d) sell the surplus goods abroad. .... _______ 7. ______

8. In order to gain a trade advantage, a country specializes in a product it can provide more efficiently than can other countries. What theory is that country practicing? (a) balance of trade theory, (b) comparative advantage theory, (c) product life cycle theory, (d) balance of surplus theory. .... _______ 8. ______

9. The first two stages that a product goes through are the (a) introductory and growth stages, (b) introductory and decline stages, (c) growth and maturity stages, (d) growth and decline stages. .... _______ 9. ______

10. If the Canadians keep increasing the number of American cars purchased, (a) American products will become more expensive for Canadians, (b) Canadian products will become more expensive for Americans, (c) American products will become less expensive for Canadians, (d) Canadian products will become less expensive for Americans. .... _______ 10. ______

Column I	Column II	Answers	For Scoring
A. Culture	1. An example of a trade bloc.	_______	1. ______
B. Dumping	2. Restrictions on quantities permitted to enter a country.	_______	2. ______
C. EU			
D. Exports	3. Selling goods below cost in a foreign market.	_______	3. ______
E. Free trade	4. Goods and services purchased from other countries..	_______	4. ______
F. Imports	5. Customs, beliefs, values, and patterns of behavior of the people of a country or group.	_______	5. ______
G. Quotas			

Name ____

Directions: Study each controversial issue carefully. Follow the advice of your teacher before listing in the columns provided reasons why people might answer Yes or No. Your teacher may want you to work with a classmate, talk with others in your community to gather information, or use the library or Internet to gather facts.

4-1. Should South America form a trading bloc that might be called SAFTA (South American Free Trade Association)?

Reasons for "Yes"	Reasons for "No"

4-2. Because of the growing importance of international trade and relations, should all students be required to study a foreign language and take a course dealing with world cultures?

Reasons for "Yes"	Reasons for "No"

PROBLEMS

4-A. Listed below are the names of ten of the world's largest firms. Use the library, the Internet, or other sources to name the home country and the main industry or product for each.

Company	Country	Industry
Aerospatiale	__________	__________________
Bayer	__________	__________________
Citizens Watch	__________	__________________
E. I. DuPont de Nemours	__________	__________________
Electrolux	__________	__________________
Hyundai Motor	__________	__________________
Northern Telecom	__________	__________________
Petrofina	__________	__________________
Siemans	__________	__________________
Smithkline Beecham	__________	__________________

4-B. Listed below is the value of exports shown in millions of dollars for three fictitious countries for selected products. Study the figures and answer the questions that follow.

	Galafo	Minion	Ungwa
Lumber	$1,350	$ 700	$ 0
Coffee	50	7,000	850
Rice	920	250	6,900
Fish	530	610	490

1. Which country is likely to have the competitive advantage for each of the following products?

   a. Lumber ____

   b. Coffee ____

   c. Rice ____

2. How could Galafo best trade with Minion? ____

3. How could Minion best trade with Ungwa? ____

4. If Ungwa had an embargo on Galafo's lumber, what might Ungwa do to obtain lumber? ____

____

____

____

4-C. Assume that the following chart shows the cost for selected products available to customers in four major world cities in a recent year. Study the chart and answer the questions below.

	New York	London	Tokyo	Mexico City
Compact disc	$12.99	$14.99	$22.09	$13.91
Movie	7.50	10.50	17.29	4.55
Sony Walkman (mid-range)	59.95	74.98	211.34	110.00
Cup of coffee	1.25	1.50	2.80	.91
Designer jeans	39.99	74.92	79.73	54.54
Nike Air Jordans	125.00	134.99	172.91	154.24

1. If you lived in Japan, which city would you most like to visit to get the best buys for your money?

____

2. If you did not live in any of the countries represented by these cities, which city would you least like to visit

if you decided to go on a shopping spree to buy some of the items listed above? _______________

3. What percentage more would an American pay for a movie in London than in New York? _______________

____

4. What percentage less would a New Yorker pay for a movie in Mexico City? _______________

____

5. What purchasing advice would you give to an American who wants to travel to London?

____

____

4-D. Indicate whether each situation described below is an embargo, tariff, quota, sanction, or non-tariff barrier.

	Embargo	Tariff	Quota	Sanction	Non-Tariff Barrier
1. The United States limits the number of Japanese cars that may be imported each year. ..	____	____	____	____	____
2. The Japanese do not permit the importing of certain American products.	____	____	____	____	____
3. The U.S. government forbids U.S. companies from conducting business with Cuba.	____	____	____	____	____
4. France places a tax on alcoholic beverages imported from the United States.	____	____	____	____	____
5. Some countries do not buy VCRs from many producers because they are made mostly in black, which is the color of death.	____	____	____	____	____
6. Action the U.S. government might take if a foreign firm attempted to dump its products here.	____	____	____	____	____

4-E. Assume that the U.S. Department of Commerce reported the following figures on imports and exports of selected products in millions of dollars. Study the figures and answer the questions that follow.

	Exports	Imports
Coffee	$ 9.8	$1,735.6
Rice	752.2	80.3
Wheat	3,348.1	66.1
Clothing	3,211.6	26,205.8
Motorcycles/bicycles	1,302.6	1,635.9
Scientific instruments	13,487.6	6,757.4
Total	_______	_______

1. Calculate the total exports and imports and record each total in the space provided.

2. By how much did the imports exceed the exports? _______________________________________

3. Which goods are imported in greater quantity than exported? _______________________________

4. Which goods are exported in greater quantity than imported? _______________________________

5. Based on these products only, does a balance of trade surplus or deficit exist? ________________

6. Which one item most contributed to the difference between the total imports and exports? __________

4-F. Assume that the following exchange rates for four countries equals one American dollar.

	Year 1	Year 2
Canadian dollar	$1.28	$1.37
French franc	5.69	5.56
Japanese yen	1.06	1.12
Mexican peso	3.35	3.13

1. Assume you bought the following products while vacationing over the last two years. Determine how much you paid in American dollars in the currency of the country you visited.

   a. Camera for 150 Canadian dollars (Year 1) _______________________________________

   b. Perfume for 110 French francs (Year 2) _______________________________________

   c. Jewelry for 50 Mexican pesos (Year 1) _______________________________________

2. Assume you bought binoculars in Japan in Year 1 for 87 yen and in Year 2 you returned to Japan for a second visit and you saw the item at the same store for 115 yen.

   a. In Year 1, what were the binoculars worth in American dollars? _______________________

   b. What was the dollar price in Year 2? _______________________________________

4-G. Many countries belong to trading blocs. Place a check mark in the column at the right to indicate whether the country is a member of the European Union (EU), North American Free Trade Association (NAFTA), or neither.

	EU	NAFTA	Neither
1. Greece	____	____	____
2. Britain	____	____	____
3. Mexico	____	____	____
4. Japan	____	____	____
5. Canada	____	____	____
6. Brazil	____	____	____
7. Italy	____	____	____

4-H. Assume that you have been working in an American company for several years and you now have the opportunity to work in one of its branch offices located in another country. Answer the following questions before you leave for your new job abroad.

1. Provide the name of the country to which you wish to be assigned. ______________________________

2. Why did you select this country? ______________________________

   ____

3. What is the currency and how many units of that currency are equal to one American dollar? __________

   ____

4. Assume that your salary in the United States is $25,000 a year. What is it worth in the currency of your

   new country? ______________________________

5. What are two main products that this country exports? ______________________________

6. What are two main imports of this country? ______________________________

7. What is the language of your new country? ______________________________

8. Write the following sentence in the language of the country: "My name is ... and I live in the United States

   of America." ______________________________

   ____

9. What are the average temperatures for the following months:

   June __________   October __________

   January __________   March __________

10. Identify several different customs practiced in this country regarding such items as being on time

    for appointments, working hours, table etiquette, popular food dishes, eye contact, dress, holidays, and

    religion. ______________________________

    ____

    ____

    ____

SMALL GROUP ACTIVITIES

Group Activity 1

Your instructor will place you into groups of two. With your partner, make a list of five non-book items in your possession. Examples might include watches, jewelry, wallets/purses, sneakers, backpacks, pens, beepers, personal digital assistants, and cell phones. Next to each item, identify the country of origin. Report your results to the class.

After all pairs have reported their findings and recorded them on the board, the class should answer these questions together:

1. What are the top three countries identified?
2. How many countries in all are identified?
3. Which continents or regions of the world are most represented?
4. Are any particular industries more dominant than others? Which ones?

Group Activity 2

Find someone who recently came to this country from another country either to live or as a visitor. Then ask that person the following questions and write notes summarizing their answers. Later you will be asked to share this information with your class.

1. When you first arrived in this country, what practices or behavior seemed most different from your country?
2. In your home country, if you need to tell someone on the job that you disagree with him or her, do you tell them directly or do you only imply or hint that you disagree?
3. What time do people go to work on day jobs in your country and what time do they leave at the end of the day? How long is their lunch period? When do they have breaks during the day?
4. What is the procedure for obtaining a pay increase in your country when you believe you have earned it?
5. In your country, if you have been improperly treated or discriminated against on the job by your supervisor or other employees, would you have the right legally to sue your employer?
6. If an American went to your country, what things would you tell him or her to avoid doing?
7. How do you greet someone in person in your country and on the telephone? How do you say good-bye?

After obtaining answers to the above questions, your teacher will place you into groups based upon the language, country, or region of the world that you selected. Compare your answers with those of other members of your group to see whether your answers are similar or different. Your group should select a leader to report your results to the entire class.

<table>
<tr><td rowspan="3">Chapter 5

Proprietorships and Partnerships</td><td colspan="2">Name ______________________</td><td colspan="5">Scoring Record</td></tr>
<tr><td colspan="2" rowspan="2">Date ______________________</td><td></td><td>Part A</td><td>Part B</td><td>Part C</td><td>Total</td></tr>
<tr><td>Perfect score</td><td>20</td><td>10</td><td>5</td><td>35</td></tr>
<tr><td></td><td></td><td>My score</td><td></td><td></td><td></td><td></td></tr>
</table>

Study Guide

Part A—*Directions:* Indicate your answer to each of the following questions by circling either yes or no in the Answers column.

		Answers	For Scoring
1.	Do most businesses start with several owners?	yes no	1. ______
2.	Is it typical for months and years to pass before a new business earns a profit?	yes no	2. ______
3.	Do new businesses often fail for financial reasons?	yes no	3. ______
4.	Do typical entrepreneurs give up quickly when they are not immediately successful?	yes no	4. ______
5.	In recent years, have an increasing number of women opened their own businesses?	yes no	5. ______
6.	Is the legal form of ownership one of the first decisions that a new owner must make?	yes no	6. ______
7.	Does the form of ownership selected depend upon the financial responsibility the owner is willing to assume?	yes no	7. ______
8.	Should the entrepreneur write a business plan soon after launching the business?	yes no	8. ______
9.	Is the corporation the most common form of ownership?	yes no	9. ______
10.	Can as few as two people form a sole proprietorship?	yes no	10. ______
11.	Does it usually take less time for decisions to be made in a proprietorship than in other forms of business ownership?	yes no	11. ______
12.	Can a sole proprietor be forced to use personal possessions to pay off debts if the business fails?	yes no	12. ______
13.	Is a business that provides personal services well suited to the proprietorship form of organization?	yes no	13. ______
14.	Is a partnership limited to a maximum of six partners?	yes no	14. ______
15.	Can a partnership usually borrow money more readily than a sole proprietorship?	yes no	15. ______
16.	If one person in a partnership is unable to pay business debts, are all other partners responsible for paying those debts?	yes no	16. ______
17.	Is it true that a partner can lose only the amount of money invested in the partnership should the business fail?	yes no	17. ______
18.	If a partner enters into a contract against the wishes of the other partners, are the other partners legally responsible for the contract?	yes no	18. ______
19.	Can the bankruptcy of any partner cause a sudden end to the partnership?	yes no	19. ______
20.	Must creditors be informed about the formation of a limited partnership?	yes no	20. ______

Part B—*Directions:* For each of the following statements, select the word, or group of words, that best completes the statement. In the Answers column, write the letter corresponding to the answer selected.

<table>
<tr><td></td><td></td><td>Answers</td><td>For
Scoring</td></tr>
</table>

1. New businesses mainly fail because (a) owners work short hours, (b) owners are too young, (c) owners lack financial resources, (d) owners would rather work for others. .... _______ 1. _______

2. Which statement is *true* about successful entrepreneurs? (a) Most successful entrepreneurs experienced early successful startups. (b) Most successful entrepreneurs do not enjoy working on their own. (c) Most successful entrepreneurs feel that it is not necessary to obtain work experience in the types of businesses they launch. (d) Most successful entrepreneurs learned from their mistakes during unsuccessful startups and started over. .... _______ 2. _______

3. To start your own business, you need (a) adequate funds; (b) adequate funds and a general knowledge about business; (c) adequate funds, a general knowledge about business, and some work experience; (d) adequate funds, a general knowledge about business, some work experience, and a business opportunity. .... _______ 3. _______

4. The form of ownership selected depends on (a) the capital needed and the financial responsibility the owner is willing to assume, (b) the nature and size of the business and the tax laws, (c) neither a nor b, (d) both a and b. .... _______ 4. _______

5. The terms *capital, net worth,* and *equity* are (a) interchangeable and defined as assets less liabilities, (b) not interchangeable but defined as assets less liabilities, (c) interchangeable and defined as assets plus liabilities, (d) interchangeable and defined as assets plus capital. .... _______ 5. _______

6. If a balance sheet shows cash as $118,000, liabilities as $115,000, and capital as $125,000, how much would the land and building be worth? (a) $122,000, (b) $233,000, (c) $240,000, (d) $243,000. .... _______ 6. _______

7. Approximately how many businesses are formed as proprietorships? (a) one out of two, (b) two out of three, (c) three out of four, (d) four out of five. .... _______ 7. _______

8. Which statement is *true* about proprietorships? (a) Owner must consult with others before making decisions. (b) Owner pays less income tax than corporations. (c) Owner shares all losses. (d) Owner shares all profits. .... _______ 8. _______

9. If one partner makes a contract that the other partners do not like, (a) only the partner making the contract is bound by it, (b) all partners are bound by it, (c) only the agreeing partners are bound by the contract, (d) the other partners can reject the contract. .... _______ 9. _______

10. The trade name of a business (a) does not reduce the owners' liability to creditors, (b) cannot be an artificial name, (c) cannot be listed as the Dixie Service Company, (d) does not have to be registered. .... _______ 10. _______

Part C—*Directions:* Below are descriptions of several types of business firms. Indicate which form of business ownership would be best for each business by placing a check mark in the appropriate column.

<table>
<tr><td></td><td>Proprietorship</td><td>Partnership</td><td>For
Scoring</td></tr>
</table>

1. The owner of a small grocery store wants to expand but does not have the capital. .... _______ _______ 1. _______

2. An accountant is opening an office in a small town. .... _______ _______ 2. _______

3. A farmer wants to sell fruits and vegetables from a roadside stand. .... _______ _______ 3. _______

4. A person who has worked as a repairer of large appliances wants to open a store to sell and service appliances. The person has had no experience in sales. .... _______ _______ 4. _______

5. A person who will be retiring in ten years wants an employee to begin taking over the business. .... _______ _______ 5. _______

          Name ________________________________

Directions: Study each controversial issue carefully. Follow the advice of your teacher before listing in the columns provided reasons why people might answer Yes or No. Your teacher may want you to work with a classmate, talk with others in your community to gather information, or use the library or Internet to gather facts.

5-1. Should states pass requirements, such as reaching a minimum age of 21 or obtaining a license, that individuals must meet in order to form a partnership?

Reasons for "Yes"	Reasons for "No"

5-2. In a partnership of three or more people, should all major decisions require only a majority vote of the partners?

Reasons for "Yes"	Reasons for "No"

PROBLEMS

5-A. Below are statements about entrepreneurs.
   a. Read each statement and indicate whether you agree or disagree.
   b. Ask two adults to answer these same statements.
   c. Decide whether you would change any of your answers based on the responses of the adults you talked to. Then ask your teacher for the results of a study of entrepreneurs.

	Agree	Disagree
1. Entrepreneurs are most commonly the oldest children in their families.	____	____
2. The large majority of entrepreneurs are married.	____	____
3. Three out of four entrepreneurs have college degrees.	____	____
4. The primary reason entrepreneurs start their own businesses is that they don't like working for others.	____	____
5. Entrepreneurs are risk takers but not high-risk takers.	____	____
6. The majority of entrepreneurs are from families where one or both parents were at one time entrepreneurs.	____	____

5-B. Prospective business owners whould make a business plan before starting the business. The plan is usually divided into the sections shown below. Study each of the following statements from a business plan and indicate in which section of the plan it would best belong.

Section I:	Nature of the Business
Section II:	Goals and Objectives
Section III:	Marketing Plan
Section IV:	Financial Plan
Section V:	Organizational Plan

1. "Money from my savings accounts and from an uncle—amounting to $9,000—will be used to launch the business." ____________________

2. "By the end of one year, I plan to make no profit but neither do I expect to incur any losses; but by the end of the second year, I expect to make a net profit of $8,000." ____________________

3. "My oldest brother, Tom, will handle the marketing and hiring of workers and I will handle the buying of merchandise and all money matters." ____________________

4. "The business will be located at 19 Chestnut Street, which should be a good location in relation to competitive businesses." ____________________

5-C. In 1983, John Sortino started selling teddy bears from a cart in downtown Burlington, Vermont. He made them of high-quality materials and did reasonably well. He later added two partners to his growing business. Because most teddy bears are sold from stores for children, John wanted to distinguish his bears from the store-bought bears. He decided to gift-wrap and personalize the bears in order to appeal to people of all ages. He also mailed them as gifts for special occasions, including birthdays and promotions. The idea of Bear-Grams caught on quickly. Ten years later, sales were $18 million. Sales have doubled each year. Because the Vermont Teddy Bear Company does not operate in many states, growth opportunities are still great.

1. What are the dollar sales predicted for the next year? ______________________________________

2. If Bear-Gram gifts are delivered by mail, how do you think the company finds its many customers?

    ____

3. Name four special occasions when someone might send a Bear-Gram.

    ____

    ____

    ____

    ____

4. Some of the employees recommended that to fulfill the firm's social responsibility, it should donate Bear-Grams to certain people or groups. What types of people or groups would you recommend if you were an employee?

    ____

    ____

5-D. Owning a business as a proprietorship offers several advantages to the owner. However, there are also many advantages of partnerships. For each of the items listed, indicate whether it is an advantage of a proprietorship or a partnership by placing a check mark in the appropriate column.

		Proprietorship	Partnership
1.	The owner has sole claim to the assets of the business.	_____	_____
2.	An individual is bound only to those contracts he or she has made.	_____	_____
3.	The management skills of more than one person are combined.	_____	_____
4.	Money needed for business operations is easier to obtain.	_____	_____
5.	An owner can more easily retire from management and keep the business operating.	_____	_____
6.	The management of the business is more flexible.	_____	_____
7.	If losses occur, one owner does not usually have to pay the entire amount.	_____	_____
8.	It is very easy to begin and end the business.	_____	_____
9.	Employees understand clearly where final responsibility and authority are located.	_____	_____
10.	Decisions about business problems are easier to make.	_____	_____

5-E. Below are listed possible businesses that one might consider starting. For each business, indicate whether you might be interested in it. Give reasons for your answers.

1. Physical fitness and tennis center ____

    ____

2. Personal shopping service for people who are too busy to do their own shopping ___________

    ____

3. Fresh flowers and plant shop ____

    ____

4. Recycled music store selling used records, cassette tapes, and compact discs

    ____

5-F. Read the following case situation and answer the questions that follow.

Drs. Johnson, Jenson, and Jacobi formed a medical services partnership. Dr. Johnson is an eye specialist, Dr. Jenson is a nose specialist, and Dr. Jacobi specializes in ear surgery. Each contributed an equal amount of capital to open the business and orally agreed to divide all profits equally. Two office workers and three medical assistants were hired. A meeting is held each month to discuss business matters and to make decisions.

Within a year, their medical practice was doing quite well. However, problems arose. There was much confusion in scheduling patients, paying bills, and dividing earnings. The office staff seemed to spend much more time doing Dr. Jenson's paperwork than anyone else's. And Dr. Jacobi generated far more income than Drs. Johnson and Jenson. As a result, Dr. Jacobi felt he should receive more of the profits than Drs. Johnson and Jenson. The nurses also believed they should be paid more for their services and overtime.

1. In the absence of any written partnership agreement, what percent of the profits should each receive according to the law? ____

    ____

    ____

    ____

2. If the partners were to decide to write a partnership agreement, what problem will be the most difficult to agree upon? ____

    ____

    ____

    ____

3. Assume that the three doctors decided that after all expenses are paid each year, the profit will be divided as follows: Dr. Johnson, 30%; Dr. Jenson, 30%; and Dr. Jacobi, 40%. For the year just ended, the profit was $350,000. How much will each partner earn?

a. Dr. Johnson ____

b. Dr. Jenson ____

c. Dr. Jacobi ____

5-G. Thomas W. Henry and Marie T. Shaw decide to form a partnership on November 1 of the current year for the purpose of operating a business that will repair electronic equipment such as televisions and VCRs. Henry will invest $40,000 and Shaw, $30,000. The business will be located at 640 Main Street, Centerville, New York, and will be known as the Frontier Television Shop. The partnership is to run for five years. Henry is to have general supervision of television repairs, and Shaw is to be in charge of all other electronic repairs. Each partner will draw a monthly salary of $2,000. Profits are to be shared in proportion to the investments of the partners.

Using the information given above, fill in the partnership agreement form that follows.

Partnership Agreement

THIS CONTRACT, Made and entered into on the day of (1.) _____ of (2.) 20___ by and between (3.) ____

WITNESSES: That the said parties have this day formed a copartnership for the purpose of engaging in and conducting (4.) ____

business under the following stipulations, which are made a part of the contract:

FIRST: The said copartnership is to continue for a term of (5.) _______________ from date hereof.

SECOND: The business shall be conducted under the firm name of (6.) _______________________________ at (7.) _______________________________

THIRD: The investments are as follows: (8.) ____

FOURTH: All profits or losses arising from said business are to be divided as follows: (9.) ____

FIFTH: Each partner is to devote his or her entire time and attention to the business and to engage in no other business enterprise without the written consent of the other.

SIXTH: Each partner is to have a salary of (10.) $___________ a month, the same to be withdrawn at such time or times as he or she may elect. Neither partner is to withdraw from the business an amount in excess of his or her salary without the written consent of the other.

SEVENTH: The duties of each partner are defined as follows. (11.) ____

EIGHTH: Neither partner is to become surety or bondsperson for anyone without the written consent of the other.

NINTH: (12.) ____

TENTH: (13.) ____

IN WITNESS WHEREOF, The parties aforesaid have hereunto set their hands and affixed their seals on the day and year above written.

(14.) ____

(15.) ____

5-H. Answer the following questions about the partnership of Thomas Henry and Marie Shaw in Problem 5-G:

1. After the salaries to the partners have been paid, the profits for a particular year amounted to $37,800. Henry's share will be $___________________.   Shaw's share will be $__________________.

2. Since Henry has the larger investment in the partnership, does he have more authority than Shaw in deciding how to operate the business? ____________________

3. Without Shaw's knowledge, Henry placed an order for ten television sets of a new make. Will the partnership be bound by this contract? ____________________

4. Is the partnership operating under a trade name? ___________________

5. Can the partnership be dissolved before the end of five years by mutual agreement of the two partners? __________________

SMALL GROUP ACTIVITIES

Group Activity 1

Your teacher will divide the class into groups of three to five students. Each group member is to select a small business—a sole proprietorship—and interview the entrepreneur. Ask the following questions:

1. Before starting your business, did you prepare a business plan? If yes, did you spend much time developing the plan?

   ____

   ____

2. If you needed to obtain a loan, did your bank or other lenders examine the business plan?

   ____

   ____

3. Did you own a business prior to this one? If so, what kind?

   ____

   ____

4. What were your biggest worries when you first got started?

   ____

   ____

5. Are your customers of the type you expected to attract?

   ____

   ____

6. Do you plan to enlarge your business, move to a new location, or open a new branch?

   ____

   ____

7. If you were to expand your business, would you form a partnership or a corporation?

   ____

   ____

8. If you could start your business over again, what would you do differently?

   ____

   ____

9. What do you like most and least about being an entrepreneur?

   ____

   ____

10. What advice would you give to a young person wanting to become an entrepreneur?

    ____

    ____

After all group members finish their interviews, the group should meet to share their answers. Your group should then prepare a brief written summary of the three businesses represented, and make a report to your class.

Group Activity 2

Your teacher will assign you to a three-person group of students, and your group will operate a partnership. Your business sells outdoor furniture in a small southern city in the U.S. Your products include such items as patio chairs, tables, and umbrellas. You and your two partners made an equal investment to get the business started. One of you has training and experience in marketing, another in accounting, and the third in managing people. Each person, however, is able to fill in for the others during busy times.

During your first year of operation, the problems listed below arise, and the partners need to agree on solutions. The partners must discuss and resolve each of the situations. Note your group's decisions in the spaces below and report them to the class.

1. At the outset the business needs a name that reflects the nature of the business.

   ____

2. The partners need to be assigned job responsibilities and titles.

   ____

3. Everyone agreed that the business should be open at least 6 1/2 days a week. The weekday hours approved by all were Monday through Friday, 10:00 a.m. until 6:00 p.m.; Saturdays, 10:00 a.m. until 8:00 p.m.; and Sundays, 1:00 p.m.–5:00 p.m. A big argument arises over who should work what days and hours, and the partnership needs to resolve this conflict.

   ____

   ____

4. One partner calculated that she had worked, on average, eight hours per week more than the other two partners did and demanded that her share of the profits be increased 20 percent. She was single and the two male partners were married with young children.

   ____

   ____

5. The new business did quite well for the first half of the year, and then sales started to decline. The business was not making enough money to satisfy one of the partners, who then suggested that they dissolve the business before they lose their shirts. The second partner disagreed, saying, "It takes time to build our reputation." The third partner was undecided.

   ____

   ____

<table>
<tr><td rowspan="3">Chapter 6

Corporate Forms of Business Ownership</td><td rowspan="3">Name ___________

Date ___________</td><td colspan="4" align="center">Scoring Record</td></tr>
<tr><td></td><td>Part A</td><td>Part B</td><td>Total</td></tr>
<tr><td>Perfect score</td><td>20</td><td>15</td><td>35</td></tr>
<tr><td>My score</td><td></td><td></td><td></td></tr>
</table>

Study Guide

Part A—*Directions:* Indicate your answer to each of the following questions by circling either yes or no in the Answers column.

		Answers	For Scoring
1.	Although a corporation is owned by a group of people, does it act as if it were a single person?	yes no	1. _______
2.	Is a corporation allowed to make contracts but not borrow money?	yes no	2. _______
3.	Is it possible for a corporation to be sued in its own name?	yes no	3. _______
4.	Can a person who buys only one share of stock become an owner of a corporation?	yes no	4. _______
5.	Is a dividend the amount of money a person pays to buy a share of stock?	yes no	5. _______
6.	Could a stockholder be responsible for all the debts of a corporation?	yes no	6. _______
7.	Can creditors collect from stockholders if the corporation fails?	yes no	7. _______
8.	Are the members of the board of directors elected by stockholders?	yes no	8. _______
9.	Can a corporation make important changes in the purpose of its business without changing its charter?	yes no	9. _______
10.	When shares are transferred, must the transfer of ownership be indicated in the records of the corporation?	yes no	10. _______
11.	Is the annual state tax rate for corporations based on profits?	yes no	11. _______
12.	Is it possible for some corporations to avoid double taxation?	yes no	12. _______
13.	Does a joint venture occur when two major contractors agree to connect two cities by building a tunnel under a river?	yes no	13. _______
14.	Do virtual corporations tend to be temporary relationships?	yes no	14. _______
15.	Is a limited liability company taxed as if it were a sole proprietorship or partnership?	yes no	15. _______
16.	Is a major strength of an LLC its limited liability feature?	yes no	16. _______
17.	Do large corporations and multinational firms usually qualify as LLCs?	yes no	17. _______
18.	Does a nonprofit corporation pay dividends to shareholders?	yes no	18. _______
19.	Is a "quasi-public corporation" operated only by state governments?	yes no	19. _______
20.	Does a cooperative provide members with both cost and profit advantages that they would not have individually?	yes no	20. _______

	Answers	For Scoring

1. Corporations tend to be (a) many in number and small in size, (b) many in number and large in size, (c) few in number and large in size, (d) few in number and small in size. .... _______ 1. _______

2. In a recent year, corporate sales of goods and services were about (a) four times more than sales from partnerships, (b) eight times more than sales from partnerships, (c) twelve times more than sales from partnerships, (d) sixteen times more than sales from partnerships. .... _______ 2. _______

3. An official document giving power to run a corporation is a (a) stock certificate, (b) charter, (c) proxy, (d) shareholder certificate. .... _______ 3. _______

4. Shareholders of a corporation are often called (a) boards, (b) officers, (c) owners, (d) buyers. .... _______ 4. _______

5. Net proceeds refer to the (a) cash received from the sale of all assets, (b) accumulation of capital, (c) payment of all debts, (d) cash received from the sale of all assets minus the payments of all debts. .... _______ 5. _______

6. Unissued shares are the (a) shares bought by the organizers, (b) shares bought by the shareholders, (c) shares that might be sold and used to expand the business at a later date, (d) shares bought by the board of directors. .... _______ 6. _______

7. Which statement is *true* about obtaining money in corporations? (a) Corporations have a more difficult time than proprietorships in raising capital. (b) Partnerships have an easier time raising money than do corporations. (c) Corporations can borrow money more easily than do partnerships. (d) Proprietorships and partnerships have an easier time raising money than do corporations. ...... _______ 7. _______

8. People who invest in a corporation are (a) legally liable for the debts of the corporation beyond their investment in the shares purchased, (b) not taxed on dividends received, (c) provided one vote regardless of the number of shares held, (d) financially liable up to the amount originally invested. .... _______ 8. _______

9. When an owner of a corporation dies, (a) the business automatically ends, (b) the corporation must be changed to either a partnership or a sole proprietorship, (c) the life of the corporation is not affected, (d) the corporation must be changed to a closely held corporation. .... _______ 9. _______

10. Taxes that are unique to a corporation are (a) a filing fee for a charter and an organization tax; (b) a filing fee and an annual state tax; (c) a filing fee, an organization tax, and an annual state tax; (d) a filing fee, an organization tax, an annual state tax, and a federal income tax. .... _______ 10. _______

11. A corporation with taxable earnings of $74,000 has a tax rate of 15% on the first $50,000 and a 25% tax rate on the next $25,000. The federal income taxes will amount to (a) $13,500, (b) $17,100, (c) $18,500, (d) $29,600. .... _______ 11. _______

12. An agreement that involves two or more businesses to make or sell a good or service is called (a) a corporation, (b) a joint venture, (c) a nonprofit organization, (d) an LLC .... _______ 12. _______

13. A virtual corporation (a) is not a form of joint venture, (b) does not include business partners who are competitors, (c) takes advantage of fast-changing market conditions, (d) operates solely on its own to take advantage of special opportunities. .... _______ 13. _______

14. In order to form an LLC, what is the maximum number of stockholders that the firm can have? (a) 5, (b) 15, (c) 25, (d) 35. .... _______ 14. _______

15. The TVA is an example of a (a) close corporation, (b) open corporation, (c) quasi-public corporation, (d) virtual corporation. .... _______ 15. _______

Directions: Study each controversial issue carefully. Follow the advice of your teacher before listing in the columns provided reasons why people might answer Yes or No. Your teacher may want you to work with a classmate, talk with others in your community to gather information, or use the library or Internet to gather facts.

6-1. Because many small stockholders do not cast their proxy ballots, should corporations be permitted to sell common stock without voting privileges at a somewhat lower price?

Reasons for "Yes"	Reasons for "No"

6-2. Should the dividends paid to stockholders of corporations be taxed by the federal government?

Reasons for "Yes"	Reasons for "No"

PROBLEMS

6-A. Corporations have to meet many more legal requirements than proprietorships or partnerships. The following list describes activities of a corporation. Write the letter *L* behind those activities that are legal; write the letter *N* behind those activities that are *not* usually legal.

1.   Three people start a corporation without obtaining approval of the state in which it will operate. ______

2.   A person who is not a shareholder is elected to the board of directors. ______

3.   An open corporation allows only relatives of current owners to buy its stock. ______

4.   After receiving permission to do business from only one state, the corporation operates in ten other states. ______

5.   A stockholder is sued by creditors for personal assets beyond the amount of the original investment. ______

6.   Everyone who has *ever* owned stock in the company is allowed to vote at the annual meeting. ______

7.   The name of the corporation is Tot Toy Company, Inc. ______

8.   Dividends are given only to the shareholders owning the most stock. ______

9.   Shareholders are required to pay taxes on the dividends they receive. ______

10.   One shareholder signs an authorization for the president of the corporation to cast the stockholder's vote at the annual meeting. ______

6-B. Assume there are 13.7 million proprietorships, 1.7 million partnerships, and 3.6 million corporations in the United States. However, corporations sell 90 percent of all goods and services. Proprietorships sell 6 percent and partnerships sell 4 percent. (*With your teacher's permission, the following activities may also be done on a computer.*)

1.   In the circle below on the left, construct a pie chart to show the percentage of businesses by the type of ownership.
2.   In the circle below on the right, construct a pie chart to show the percentage of sales by the type of ownership.

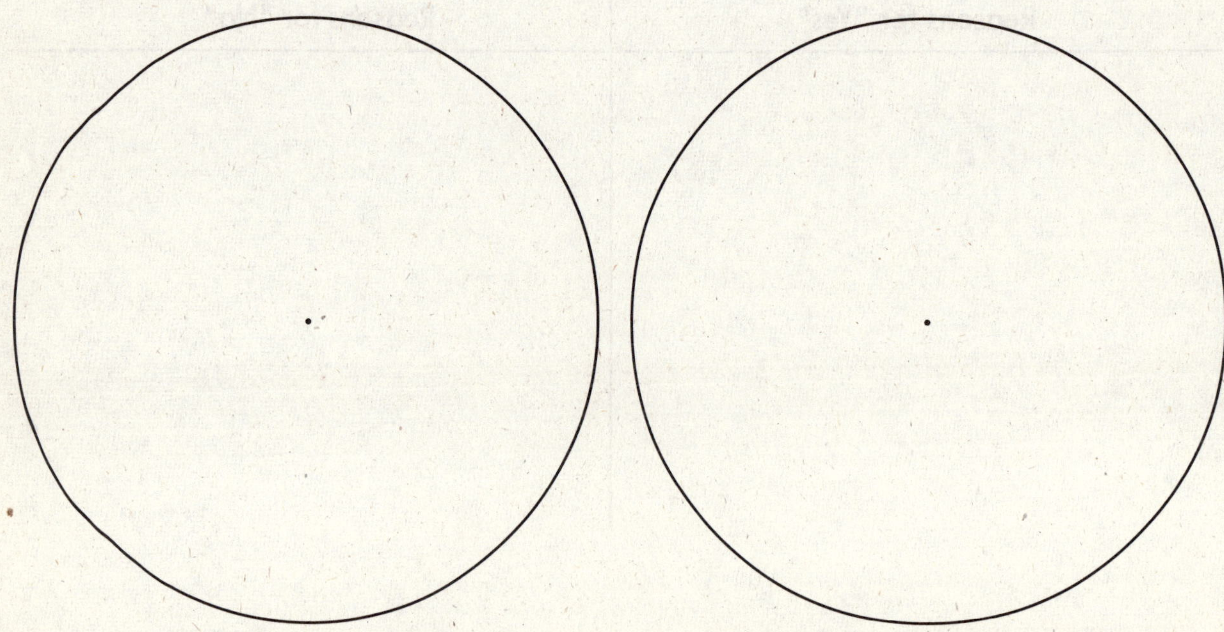

Percentage of U.S. firms
by type of ownership
Percentage of sales of goods and services
by type of ownership

3. What conclusions can you make from the two charts?

____

____

____

____

6-C. Which of the following statements are rights of stockholders and which are not?

	Right of Stockholders	Not a Right of Stockholders
1. To sell shares to other stockholders.	____	____
2. To vote for members of the board of directors.	____	____
3. To vote on who is hired as president.	____	____
4. To work as a manager in the corporation.	____	____
5. To receive notices of stockholders' meetings.	____	____
6. To vote on certain matters even if they cannot be present at stockholders' meetings.	____	____
7. To attend all meetings of the board of directors.	____	____

6-D. Study the following proxy and the accompanying explanatory notes that appear in the notice of the annual stockholders' meeting. Then complete the five activities that follow by recording your answers on the proxy.

<table>
<tr><td>

XYZ CORP.

Proxy No.

0   067   515

☐☐00000
11111☐1
2222222
3333333
4444444
5555☐5☐
66☐6666
777☐777
8888888
9999999

</td><td colspan="2">

XYZ's directors recommend a vote for the proposals numbered 1 and 2 and against the stockholder proposals numbered 3 and 4 and SHARES WILL BE SO VOTED UNLESS OTHER-WISE INDICATED:

</td></tr>
<tr><td rowspan="3"></td><td>

1. FOR ☐ NOT FOR ☐ election of directors
J. Smith, M. Jones, T. Benson, R. Juarez,
A. Bonini, C. Jackson
(*To withhold authority to vote for any individual nominee, strike out that nominee's name.*)

</td><td>

3. FOR ☐ AGAINST ☐ ABSTAIN ☐
Approve the authorization of 100,000 shares of preferred stock.

</td></tr>
<tr><td>

2. FOR ☐ AGAINST ☐ ABSTAIN ☐
Ratify appointment of Chen Accounting Inc. as auditing firm.

</td><td>

4. FOR ☐ AGAINST ☐ ABSTAIN ☐
Stockholder proposal to outlaw the use of live animals to conduct research that may lead to future company profits.

</td></tr>
<tr><td colspan="2">

X _______________________________________
PLEASE SIGN HERE AND RETURN PROMPTLY
Dated:
☐ Please send me a ticket for the St. Louis meeting

</td></tr>
</table>

1. Vote for all board of director nominees, except M. Jones.
2. Vote as the directors wish you to do for Chen Accounting Inc. as the auditing firm.
3. Vote as you personally desire for stockholder proposal No. 3.
4. Vote as you personally desire for stockholder proposal No. 4.
5. Sign and date the proxy.

6-E. A small corporation has calculated its taxable earnings for the year to be $120,000. Complete the table below to determine the total income taxes the corporation will pay.

	Tax Rate	Tax
Not over $50,000	15%	___________
Over $50,000, but not over $75,000	25%	___________
Over $75,000, but not over $100,000	34%	___________
Over $100,000, but not over $335,000	39%	___________
TOTAL TAX		___________

6-F. For each of the items below, indicate by letter in the space provided which of the following types of organizational structures is most suitable:

A. Cooperative
B. Corporation
C. Joint Venture
D. Nonprofit Corporation
E. Limited Liability Company (LLC)
F. Virtual Corporation

_____ 1. Three people who own a partnership wish to convert to some other type of structure that would limit their liability.

_____ 2. Twenty partners from three different countries run a highly successful partnership and need an extremely large amount of capital in order to expand.

_____ 3. Fifteen separate growers of cranberries located near each other meet regularly to discuss ways to improve growing and harvesting methods and now decide they wish to form a group that would handle sales of their product.

_____ 4. Three small competitors individually see an opportunity to produce and sell a new product but they must move quickly to succeed over larger competitors. None of them alone have the resources or expertise, but combined they do.

6-G. Study the table below and answer the following questions:

Some Top Farm Cooperatives	Products	Annual Sales (in millions)	Percent of Total Sales
Land O'Lakes	Butter	$2,200	_______
Sunkist	Oranges	855	_______
Ocean Spray	Cranberries	736	_______
Blue Diamond	Flavored Almonds & Butter	420	_______
Welch's	Grape Juice	282	_______
TOTAL		_______	_______

1. Calculate the total annual sales for the five farm cooperatives. Record your answer above.

2. Determine the percent of total sales for each company. Record your answers above.

3. If the two companies that produce butter were to merge, what percent of the total sales would they possess?____

6-H. After reading this case problem, answer the questions that follow.

The Snorkel Company was operated as a partnership for years by Ann Bird, Pat Rossi, and Ron Shaffer. Primarily to gain added capital, they converted their partnership to a corporation. It then became known as Snorkel Company, Inc. Five friends invested large sums of money by buying shares of stock in the new corporation. The company remained a close corporation.

All eight shareholders have been extremely satisfied with the profits over the last five years. But, as the firm continued to improve its profit picture, the owners became more upset. Ron Shaffer summed up the feelings of everyone when he said, "That double taxation is killing me." The eight shareholders have become so upset that they are seriously thinking about reorganizing again into a partnership.

1. Why was the *"Inc."* added to the title of the company?

   ____

   ____

2. What did Ron Shaffer mean by "double taxation"?

   ____

   ____

   ____

3. Explain how the company can avoid double taxation without going back to being a partnership.

   ____

   ____

   ____

   ____

6-I. The following chart describes several stock purchases and the dividends paid on those stocks. Fill in the missing values for each stock purchase to complete the chart. The first row has been completed as an example.

Number of Shares	Price per Share	Total Cost	Dividends per Share	Total Dividends	Total Dividends as a Percent of Total Cost (to nearest whole percent)
350	$26.00	$ 9,100.00	$1.25	$ 437.50	5%
125		437.50	0.50		
	10.50	2,100.00			10%
670	56.00			2,251.20	
20		675.00	0.80		
	45.00	2,925.00			13%

SMALL GROUP ACTIVITIES

Group Activity 1

Your instructor will place you into groups of three to five students for the purpose of forming a small corporation. Each member will invest $10,000. Your group tasks are to complete the three phases below.

Phase 1: Getting Started

1. Decide on what type of small corporation to form in your area.
2. State the general purpose of your corporation and the type of product or service you will provide.
3. Identify the type or types of customers you wish to serve.
4. List specific means by which you can promote your goods or services to your customers.
5. Determine which student members will serve as CEO, Vice President, and Secretary and Treasurer.

Phase 2: Getting Incorporated

6. Prepare a Certificate of Incorporation—see Figure 6-1 in your textbook.
7. Prepare a simple financial plan and a balance sheet.
8. Learn from library or Internet materials the procedures for incorporating a business.
9. Ask an attorney for incorporation papers, for an estimate of the time needed to incorporate, and for an estimate of the state and attorney's costs for forming a small corporation.

Phase 3: Reporting Results

10. Your group should prepare a report for the class that your officers will present.
11. After each officer reports to the class about the group's corporation, other class members may ask questions.

Group Activity 2

This activity is a question-answering game, and students will write questions and answer questions in groups. Here are the rules:

1. All students are to create five or more one-sentence questions in the time allowed that are based upon the material in the chapter. Answers may be yes-no, true-false, or a few words. Next to the question, write the answer and the text page number where the answer can be found.

2. Then your teacher will place the class into groups of three students each. An even number of teams is required. If there are students remaining, each can join a different team of three. Now each group will review the questions their members created. The group will select the 16 best questions, revising any that might need to be more clearly written.

3. Your teacher will select two teams to start the contest. One team asks the other team four questions and then decides whether the answers are correct. The teacher serves as the judge and handles disputes. The other team then poses four of its questions to the first team. For each correct answer, the answering team earns two points. If the question is not sufficiently clear, as decided by the teacher, the asking team loses two points. (Only one answer is allowed; no second guesses. The points can be recorded on the board.)

4. When both teams have completed asking and answering their four questions, the scores are added, and the team with the most points wins. If there is a tie, each team can ask another question until the tie is broken.

5. Two more teams now compete in the same manner as the first two teams until a winner is identified. This process should continue until all teams have competed.

6. The winning teams are now paired and compete against each other and the process continues until there is one final winner.

<table>
<tr><td rowspan="3">Chapter 7

Legal Aspects of Business</td><td rowspan="3">Name __________

Date __________</td><td colspan="5" align="center">Scoring Record</td></tr>
<tr><td></td><td>Part A</td><td>Part B</td><td>Part C</td><td>Total</td></tr>
<tr><td>Perfect score</td><td>20</td><td>10</td><td>5</td><td>35</td></tr>
<tr><td>My score</td><td></td><td></td><td></td><td></td></tr>
</table>

Study Guide

Part A—*Directions:* Indicate your answer to each of the following questions by circling either yes or no in the Answers column.

		Answers	For Scoring
1.	Does a monopoly exist as long as there are at least two producers?	yes no	1. _______
2.	When competition exists, are prices generally higher than when a monopoly exists?	yes no	2. _______
3.	Does competitive pricing cause less efficient companies to struggle for survival?	yes no	3. _______
4.	Does the Sherman Antitrust Act permit competitors to agree to set the same selling prices on goods?	yes no	4. _______
5.	Under the Clayton Act, can a business that produces computers require a buyer to also purchase supplies, such as paper and tapes, that are needed to run the computer?	yes no	5. _______
6.	Can owners of a firm get protection by filing for bankruptcy?	yes no	6. _______
7.	Do unpaid debts of a bankrupt firm stay on file for ten years?	yes no	7. _______
8.	Can a firm that filed for bankruptcy obtain credit easily for new startups?	yes no	8. _______
9.	Is it generally lawful to publish work that is protected by a copyright without permission of the author or publisher?	yes no	9. _______
10.	Is it illegal to copy computer programs to distribute to friends?	yes no	10. _______
11.	Is a trademark a type of monopoly?	yes no	11. _______
12.	Does research show that the majority of those who smoke when young die prematurely of smoking-related diseases?	yes no	12. _______
13.	Under the federal Warranty Act, must sellers specify what they will or will not do if their product is defective?	yes no	13. _______
14.	If a customer is refused a loan because a store gave an incorrect credit balance to a bank, are both the store that provided the incorrect information and the bank that refused credit liable?	yes no	14. _______
15.	Is it a crime for any unauthorized person to access a major computer system and view, use, or change data?	yes no	15. _______
16.	Does the federal government regulate interstate as well as intrastate commerce?	yes no	16. _______
17.	Do state and local governments use licensing to limit and control the number of certain types of businesses?	yes no	17. _______
18.	Is it possible to both copyright and license a software program?	yes no	18. _______
19.	Is a progressive tax a single tax rate that is the same for everyone?	yes no	19. _______
20.	Because a sales tax applies to purchases rather than to income, is it a regressive tax?	yes no	20. _______

Part B—*Directions:* For each of the following statements, select the word, or group of words, that best completes the statement. In the Answers column, write the letter corresponding to the answer selected.

	Answers	For Scoring
1. What is the name of the 1936 act whose main purpose was to prevent setting different prices for different customers? (a) Clayton Act, (b) Robinson-Patman Act, (c) Sherman Antitrust Act, (d) Wheeler-Lea Act.	______	1.______
2. Which act included outlawing unfair practices such as false advertising? (a) Clayton Act, (b) Robinson-Patman Act, (c) Sherman Antitrust Act, (d) Wheeler-Lea Act.	______	2.______
3. Which practice allows a business to sell its assets to pay it debts? (a) licensing, (b) zoning, (c) bankruptcy, (d) monopoly.	______	3.______
4. Once a business files for bankruptcy, under the law, (a) it must close its doors immediately, (b) it must close its doors within a six-month period, (c) it can continue to operate for a few months until it sells its assets, (d) it can create a survival plan that might enable it to recover.	______	4.______
5. Which of the following is NOT an illegal practice? (a) copying tapes and programs for distribution to others, (b) copying an employer's software program for personal use on a home computer, (c) using another firm's trademark to promote a product, (d) photocopying a copyrighted article for distribution in a classroom.	______	5.______
6. Under a federal Warranty Act, (a) sellers cannot set different prices for different customers, (b) cosmetic producers must show products will not be harmful when used, (c) sellers must specify what they will or will not do if their product is defective, (d) consumers cannot sue manufacturers.	______	6.______
7. A policy of taxation based on one's ability to pay is called (a) proportional taxation, (b) progressive taxation, (c) regressive taxation, (d) flat taxation.	______	7.______
8. A tax that is levied on the profits of businesses and on earnings of individuals is (a) a sales tax, (b) a federal excise tax, (c) an income tax, (d) a property tax.	______	8.______
9. The largest source of revenue for the federal government is the (a) sales tax, (b) income tax, (c) property tax, (d) progressive tax.	______	9.______
10. The main source of revenue for most local governments is the (a) property tax, (b) sales tax, (c) income tax, (d) assessed tax.	______	10.______

Part C—*Directions:* In the Answers column, write the letter of the word or expression in Column I that most closely matches each statement in Column II.

Column I	Column II	Answers	For Scoring
A. Copyright Office	1. Protects creators of software, novels, histories, poetry, and textbooks.	______	1.______
B. Federal Communications Commission	2. Regulates stocks and bonds.	______	2.______
C. Food and Drug Administration	3. Enforces laws dealing with unfair competition.	______	3.______
D. Federal Power Commission	4. Regulates radio, television, telephone, and satellite communications.	______	4.______
E. Federal Trade Commission	5. Grants property rights to inventors.	______	5.______
F. Securities and Exchange Commission			
G. Patent and Trademark Office			

                    Name _______________________________

Directions: Study each controversial issue carefully. Follow the advice of your teacher before listing in the columns provided reasons why people might answer Yes or No. Your teacher may want you to work with a classmate, talk with others in your community to gather information, or use the library or Internet to gather facts.

7-1. Should a federal law be passed that would prevent all organizations that collect information about individuals from selling or sharing that information with anyone else without their written approval?

Reasons for "Yes"	Reasons for "No"

7-2. Should the federal government substantially raise the so-called "sin taxes" on tobacco products and alcoholic beverages to increase federal revenues and to discourage the use of these products?

Reasons for "Yes"	Reasons for "No"

PROBLEMS

7-A. Place a check mark in the column at the right by the types of businesses that would most likely meet the qualifications for being considered a monopoly.

1. Automobile manufacturing business   _____
2. Gas utility company   _____
3. Nuclear power generation plant   _____
4. Cosmetic development laboratory   _____
5. Computer production plant   _____

7-B. Write the name of the main federal law that regulates each of the following business practices.

1. Prevents two competitors from agreeing to set the same prices in order that both might do well financially.

   ____

2. Forbids specifying goods that a buyer must purchase in order to get other goods.

   ____

3. Outlaws false advertising.

   ____

4. Stops competitors from charging different prices to different customers.

   ____

5. Prohibits the sale of unhealthful products that people eat, take as medicine, or apply to their bodies.

   ____

6. Stops businesses from selling non-food products that are found to be dangerous when used.

   ____

7-C. Study each business practice listed below, and place a check mark in the column at the right if the practice is prohibited by the Federal Trade Commission.

1. Putting "Made in the U.S.A." on a product that was made in South Korea. .... _____
2. Selling as "new" undamaged car parts that were obtained by buying late-model wrecked cars and removing undamaged parts. .... _____
3. A bookstore that does not regularly sell pens advertises in a local newspaper: "A free pen when you buy two or more books." .... _____
4. A small, new store uses a well-known trademark of a large, famous store. .... _____
5. A store sells jeans at the regular price, despite running a newspaper ad stating, "Big discounts on new designer jeans." .... _____
6. A store runs a newspaper ad stating, "50% discount on all small appliances in our downtown store only, but not in any of our five suburban branches" .... _____

7-D. Read the following article prepared by a government agency that regulates business activity, and answer the following questions.

Look for That Label*

    "Hey, mister, wanna buy a genuine seal fur coat for your wife? A real bargain. Look at the label—the real McCoy. Only $500. But, you gotta buy now."

    If anyone approaches you with a deal like this—BEWARE! You may be taken in by a fly-by-night operator. He or she has a label on the fur—but not a legal one. WHAT'S THIS ABOUT A LABEL?

When you buy a garment, a fur, or a fabric in a store, it often carries a label telling who made it or from which store it was purchased.

More important is the label that is attached to a wool, fur, or textile product that tells you of what the product is made.

This label is required by law. It should be written in plain English and be where you can find it easily. Either on or close to the label should be the name of the one responsible for the label's truth (either the person's name or code number, which is registered with the FTC).

Most shoppers today aren't expert enough to know exactly what kind of fur or material they buy. So, they must put their faith in the store that sells the product or in what the label says.

To be absolutely sure of what you buy, you would need a chemical laboratory and a microscope, and you would have to go through much training to learn to examine the fur or material to know the truth.

Congress passed laws assuring the consuming public it would get the kind of furs and textiles for which it paid.

The Federal Trade Commission was given the job of enforcing the laws. It is a tremendous task—one that would be far beyond the capacity of the FTC except for the fact that most sellers of these products are willing to abide by the laws.

Source: Adapted from FTC Buyer's Guide No. 6, "Look for That Label"

1. For what federal agency do the letters *FTC* stand? ____

2. If the product-content label on a piece of clothing is missing, has a federal law probably been violated?

   ____

3. Why were laws passed requiring sellers to reveal what materials were used in the manufacture of clothing

   products? ____

   ____

4. Examine two pieces of clothing, such as a coat and sweater, and provide the following:

Kind of Item	Is There a Label?	What Information is on the Label?

7-E. Use a check mark in the columns at the right to indicate whether the following statements are true or false under bankruptcy law.

	True	False
1. Businesses but not individuals may file for bankruptcy.	____	____
2. A record of unpaid debts stays on file for ten years.	____	____
3. If selling all the firm's assets doesn't result in enough cash to pay all its debts, the law excuses the business from paying the remaining debts.	____	____
4. All businesses that file for bankruptcy are declared permanently bankrupt.	____	____
5. Once a firm has been declared bankrupt, it will need to conduct all business forever thereafter for cash.	____	____
6. Any firm may file for bankruptcy again after five years.	____	____
7. A bankrupt firm that starts over again may apply for credit when buying goods.	____	____
8. Business owners declared bankrupt must serve three years or more in prison.	____	____

7-F. Collect examples of two different trademarks from package labels or advertisements. Paste them in the space below and indicate the company that owns the trademark.

Space for Trademark	Company Owning the Trademark

7-G. Place a check mark in the column at the right to indicate whether the item described would be eligible for a patent, copyright, or trademark.

	Patent	Copyright	Trademark
1. Created a computer program to help landscape lawns.	___	___	___
2. Wrote a ninety-page children's story for day-care center use.	___	___	___
3. Designed a bird-calling device to attract most types of song birds.	___	___	___
4. Created a specially designed pen that would allow a person without hands to write with a foot.	___	___	___
5. Created a new type of flower that always blooms.	___	___	___
6. Developed a new logo for a new firm.	___	___	___

7-H. Many businesses are required to secure a license from a local government (such as a city) before they can operate. Find out if a special license is required for as many of the businesses listed below as are found in your community. Make your report from the following form:

Type of Business	License Required	License Not Required
1. Automobile repair business	___	___
2. Bakery	___	___
3. Beauty salon or barber shop	___	___
4. Bowling alley	___	___
5. Dry cleaning business	___	___
6. Service station	___	___
7. Motel	___	___
8. Drug store	___	___
9. Restaurant	___	___
10. Grocery store	___	___

7-I. For the items listed below, indicate if each is primarily a progressive, regressive, or proportional tax.

1. Tax on gasoline for automobiles. ____

2. State income tax rate that rises with every additional $1,000 of annual income earned. _______________

3. State sales tax on all items except food, clothing, and home rental fees. _______________

4. Real estate taxes on assessed value of home. _______________________________________

7-J. Assume the average business tax rates for three countries are as shown below. Also shown is the taxable income for three firms. After studying the information, calculate the tax each business would pay in each country.

		Tax Rate for Countries		
Business	Taxable Income	Thailand (40%)	Nicaragua (54%)	Somalia (66%)
A	$ 50,000	__________	__________	__________
B	$ 275,000	__________	__________	__________
C	$2,400,000	__________	__________	__________

7-K. Study the year's information below regarding two individuals who live in a state that has a 6 percent sales tax. Then answer the questions that follow.

		Jennings	Sherrer
a.	Take-home pay	$20,000	$35,000
b.	Amount spent	20,000	26,000
c.	Amount saved	0	9,000
d.	Tax calculation	__________	__________
e.	Amount of tax	__________	__________
f.	Tax rate calculation	__________	__________
g.	Effective tax rate	__________	__________

1. Complete the information needed for lines d through g.

2. Did Jennings or Sherrer benefit most from the tax system?______________________________

3. Is this a progressive, regressive, or proportional tax?__________________________________

SMALL GROUP ACTIVITIES

Group Activity 1

After reading the following business case, personally decide whether the corporation is right or whether its competitors are right.

A large trucking company, named KOT (Keep On Trucking), has been buying up small trucking firms over the last several years. KOT now does about 75 percent of all interstate trucking but only 40 percent of the intrastate trucking. Because of its efficient means of operating a large fleet of trucks nationwide, smaller firms are complaining, saying that a monopoly exists. The Small Truckers Association (STA), however, plans to initiate a lawsuit shortly and will invite other smaller nationwide trucking firms to join them.

KOT has a large law firm representing it and feels quite certain that it can win such a lawsuit on the grounds that its goal is to offer businesses timely and efficient services that meet their heavy trucking demands on schedule. Small firms are often much slower. Also, the drivers of the small firms do not receive as much training and have a higher accident record. Further, KOT is doing nothing to block the small firms from competing more aggressively. KOT is not interfering with any of their rights or efforts to get larger. This morning STA served formal notice to KOT that it was filing a lawsuit against it.

Team Tasks:

1. Your instructor will form a legal team for KOT and another for STA. Each team of attorneys will have a staff of legal aides assisting it. Half of the remaining students will be assigned to the KOT team and the other half to the STA team. These teams will obtain whatever information the attorney groups need in order to help establish the legal grounds for their attorneys.

2. The KOT team will meet, organize its evidence that can be presented in its case, and delegate requests for information to its staff of legal aides. The STA team will organize to make a plan for winning the case and will request of its legal aides the ammunition to win its case.

3. The two legal aide groups should immediately dig up all the information possible that would allow their legal teams to win. Use any source available, such as reviews of the AT&T breakup of the country's long distance company some years ago and the more recent case against Microsoft. Read from library and Internet sources as much as possible about how judges decide such cases. For example, are there any guidelines the judges use for deciding when a company is a monopoly? (Many articles appear in business and other journals available in the library or on the Internet.)

4. When the evidence has been gathered and presented to the attorneys, the attorneys for each side will present their views to the judge, who may be your teacher or other designated person. The judge will make a decision, but the losing group may appeal to a federal court or accept the judge's verdict.

Group Activity 2

Many firms declare bankruptcy each year, but not all go out of business. After being assigned a partner by your teacher, your two-person team will need to find answers to these questions:

1. What are the basic procedures to be followed for most types of bankruptcy?
2. Explain why some businesses that have filed for bankruptcy may continue to operate for many years.
3. Identify five or more companies that operate in or near your state that have filed for bankruptcy.
4. Do any bankrupt firms ever recover and become successful?

To research your answers, use your library, the Internet, or a lawyer who handles bankruptcy cases. Prepare a written report for your teacher. Then you and your partner can present an oral report of your findings to your class.

<table>
<tr><td rowspan="3">Chapter 8

Technology and Information Management</td><td rowspan="3">Name ___________

Date ___________</td><td colspan="5" align="center">Scoring Record</td></tr>
<tr><td></td><td>Part A</td><td>Part B</td><td>Part C</td><td>Total</td></tr>
<tr><td>Perfect score</td><td>20</td><td>10</td><td>5</td><td>35</td></tr>
<tr><td colspan="2">My score</td><td></td><td></td><td></td><td></td></tr>
</table>

Study Guide

Part A—*Directions:* Indicate your answer to each of the following questions by circling either yes or no in the Answers column.

		Answers	For Scoring
1.	Does the term "information" refer to the original unprocessed facts and figures that businesses have generated?	yes no	1. ______
2.	Does application software manage the computer's file system?	yes no	2. ______
3.	Can the Internet be used as a substitute for phoning?	yes no	3. ______
4.	Do all Web addresses begin with "www."?	yes no	4. ______
5.	Is it possible to access the Internet without an ISP?	yes no	5. ______
6.	Does a search engine allow users to navigate and view Web pages?	yes no	6. ______
7.	Does a LAN usually cover a geographic area, such as a state?	yes no	7. ______
8.	Can e-mail be sent to the Internet through an intranet?	yes no	8. ______
9.	Can an extranet allow a supplier to track a company's inventory records without gaining access to other company data?	yes no	9. ______
10.	Do organizations violate business ethics when they sell information about people who use the Internet to browse or buy merchandise?	yes no	10. ______
11.	Does the FTC require that businesses notify buyers of their rights on how personal information will be used?	yes no	11. ______
12.	Are fingerprints and retina scanning examples of methods being tested to safeguard organizational information?	yes no	12. ______
13.	Is a computer system that processes data into meaningful information called an information system?	yes no	13. ______
14.	Is a system that helps managers consider alternatives in making decisions called a decision support system?	yes no	14. ______
15.	Can an EIS system be used to collect information about competitors or about government policies?	yes no	15. ______
16.	Is it *true* that managers cannot reduce or eliminate common complaints, such as eyestrain and backaches, by workers who use computers for long periods?	yes no	16. ______
17.	Are improper keyboard or chair heights likely to cause hand problems for computer operators?	yes no	17. ______
18.	Has the title for most secretaries changed to one like "administrative assistant" because their roles have changed?	yes no	18. ______
19.	Is it *true* that help desk employees need technical skills but not "people skills"?	yes no	19. ______
20.	Has the use of computers in business cut paperwork in addition to increasing worker productivity?	yes no	20. ______

Part B—*Directions:* For each of the following statements, select the word, or group of words, that best completes the statement. In the Answers column, write the letter corresponding to the answer selected.

<table>
<tr><td></td><td></td><td>Answers</td><td>For
Scoring</td></tr>
</table>

1. The typical office computer that most workers use is a (a) laptop, (b) notebook, (c) mainframe, (d) personal computer. .... _______ 1. _______

2. Spreadsheets are used primarily to create (a) written documents, (b) financial statements, (c) graphics, (d) business forms. .... _______ 2. _______

3. Which of the following can be shared on the Web? (a) printed text only, (b) text and videos only, (c) text and photographs only, (d) text, videos, and photographs. .... _______ 3. _______

4. A program that allows users to navigate and view Web pages is called a (a) Net-service program, (b) browser, (c) search engine, (d) telecommunications program. .... _______ 4. _______

5. Who created the World Wide Web? (a) Gordon Moore, (b) Tim Berners-Lee, (c) Intel, (d) Bill Gates. .... _______ 5. _______

6. Which statement is *false* about CIOs? (a) CIOs do not need management skills. (b) CIOs protect information from being improperly used. (c) CIOs must know what types of equipment to purchase to meet an organization's needs. (d) CIOs protect information from getting to people who should not have it. .... _______ 6. _______

7. A computer that stores data and application software for all PC workstations in a single building or building complex is called a (a) search engine, (b) server, (c) browser, (d) bus. .... _______ 7. _______

8. All of the following are types of information systems *except* (a) an MIS, (b) a DSS, (c) an ISP, (d) an EIS. .... _______ 8. _______

9. The ability to consider alternatives by analyzing "what if" scenarios is a key capability of (a) an MIS, (b) a DSS, (c) an EIS, (d) an ISP. .... _______ 9. _______

10. Which statement is NOT true about downsizing? (a) Many firms help employees get retrained. (b) Some firms help employees find new jobs with other firms. (c) Employees may become less productive. (d) Morale improves quickly. _______ 10. _______

Part C—*Directions:* In the Answers column, write the letter of the word or expression in Column I that most closely matches each statement in Column II.

Column I	Column II	Answers	For Scoring
A. Help desk	1. Assists workers with computer problems.	_______	1. _______
B. Network administrator	2. Creates and modifies software programs.	_______	2. _______
C. Programmer	3. Helps create and maintain an MIS.	_______	3. _______
D. Systems analyst	4. Manages and maintains a Web site.	_______	4. _______
E. Telecommuter	5. Uses electronic equipment to work at home.	_______	5. _______
F. Web page designer			
G. Webmaster			

Directions: Study each controversial issue carefully. Follow the advice of your teacher before listing in the columns provided reasons why people might answer Yes or No. Your teacher may want you to work with a classmate, talk with others in your community to gather information, or use the library or Internet to gather facts.

8-1. Would more people use the Internet to buy goods and services if the privacy of their personal information were better protected than it is today?

Reasons for "Yes"	Reasons for "No"

8-2. Has the extensive and increasing use of electronic technology, such as computers, cell phones, Web sites, and e-mail, reduced the interpersonal relationships in our society to an undesirable level?

Reasons for "Yes"	Reasons for "No"

PROBLEMS

8-A. Check whether the items listed below are more often associated with a traditional office or an electronic office.

Item	Traditional Office	Electronic Office
1. Filing cabinets	_____	_____
2. Compact disc	_____	_____
3. Facsimile machine	_____	_____
4. Typewriter	_____	_____
5. Cellular phone	_____	_____
6. Stenographer	_____	_____
7. Floppy disk	_____	_____
8. Laser printer	_____	_____

8-B. Listed below are components of a computer system. Indicate what type of device each component is by writing a check mark in the appropriate column.

	Input Devices	Central Processing Unit	Output Devices
a. Computer memory	_____	_____	_____
b. Mouse	_____	_____	_____
c. Monitor	_____	_____	_____
d. Digital camera	_____	_____	_____
e. Hard drive	_____	_____	_____
f. Digital video disk	_____	_____	_____
g. Keyboard	_____	_____	_____
h. Operating system software	_____	_____	_____
i. Scanner	_____	_____	_____
j. Printer	_____	_____	_____

8-C. After each task described, write the name of the type of computer software needed to perform each task.

1. Key a letter or other business document. _______________________________________

2. Create a newsletter for the business. _______________________________________

3. Prepare accounting financial statements. _______________________________________

4. Develop a bar or pie chart. _______________________________________

5. Store a variety of information about all employees in a business. _______________________________________

8-D. Assume that on an average day, 60 percent of people with Internet access are on the Net. According to the Pew Research Center, below is how Internet users spend time online. Study the information and answer the questions that appear below the table.

Activity		Percent	Activity		Percent
a.	Send e-mail	52	j.	Get travel information	7
b.	Get news	22	k.	Get health & medical information	7
c.	Surf the Web for fun	21	l.	Visit a government Web site	7
d.	Look for information on a hobby	18	m.	Play a game	6
e.	Check the weather	16	n.	Chat in a chat room	5
f.	Do research for a job	16	o.	Listen to or download music	5
g.	Get financial information	15	p.	Look for information about a job	5
h.	Look for political news or info.	10	q.	Participate in an online auction	3
i.	Look for information about movies, books, or other leisure activities	8	r.	Buy or sell stocks, bonds, and funds	3
			s.	Buy or make a reservation for travel	1

1. If you were a "typical" Internet user and you spent 20 hours online this week, how many hours did you spend sending e-mail? _______________________________

2. What total percent of the time do people "do research for a job" and also "look for information about a job?" _______________________________

3. What percent of the time do people spend in recreationally related activities online? _______________________________

____

____

4. What three items on the list most surprise you about how people use the Internet? _______________________________

____

____

5. Which five ways listed above do you most use the Internet or would use it if you had your own computer at home? _______________________________

____

____

8-E. Michael Armstrong, CEO of AT&T, reportedly made the following statement: "It took radio 30 years to reach its first 50 million Americans; it took TV 13 years. After only six years, the World Wide Web had 100 million users. With the next advance—broadband technology, which can transfer every issue of *The New York Times* from the last 100 years in just one second—the Web could reach millions even faster." Answer the following questions:

1. How does Moore's Law relate to Mr. Armstrong's statement? ______________________________

____

____

____

2. If Mr. Armstrong made his statement on June 15 of the year 2000, about when will *The New York Times* be

able to be transferred in half a second if Moore's Law is somewhat accurate? ___________________

____

____

3. Given the time for radio, TV, and the Web to reach large audiences, what general conclusion can you make

about the speed of technological change? ____

____

____

8-F. For each item listed, indicate whether it is part of telecommunications.

	Yes	No
1. An airmail letter sent to Argentina.	____	____
2. A message sent via computer from one floor in a building to another computer located on another floor in the same building.	____	____
3. A chart sent by facsimile from Chicago to Houston.	____	____
4. A contract sent from a manager's computer in Atlanta to a manager's computer in London, England.	____	____
5. A telephone message to a manager in another city was left with the receptionist because the line was busy.	____	____

8-G. Study the cost of installing a new computer system from the information provided. Then answer the questions below:

	Cost	Percent
1 Server computer	$15,000	__________
10 Desktop computers	12,000	__________
5 Laser printers	4,600	__________
8 Software programs	3,200	__________
Installation	3,800	__________
Training employees	5,200	__________
Total	__________	__________

1. In the column shown above, write the total cost of the computer system.

2. In the column provided, calculate the percentage cost of each component of the system.

3. To what activity should most of the training time be devoted? _____________________________

    ____

4. What is the total cost of the various pieces of hardware? $ _____________________________

5. What percent of the total cost is for hardware and what percent is for other costs?

    a. Hardware __________

    b. Other Costs __________

8-H. For each item listed below, indicate by a checkmark the appropriate computer network that would handle the task shown.

	Intranet	Extranet	Internet
1. Send a memo to another worker located in another building.	____	____	____
2. Send a request to a supplier to ship goods today.	____	____	____
3. An employee checks his health care benefits.	____	____	____
4. A manager searches for a competitor's similar product.	____	____	____
5. At lunch a worker sends a note to his daughter at home.	____	____	____
6. A firm processes weekly paychecks for a corporation that are sent by computer to the corporation each Friday.	____	____	____

8-I. Check the appropriate column to indicate which computer information system would provide the needed information for each item listed below.

	Management Information System	Decision Support System	Executive Information System
1. Find out the total daily sales from each of the eight point-of-sale terminals.	_____	_____	_____
2. Compare yearly total sales to major competitors.	_____	_____	_____
3. Get a breakdown of manufacturing costs for every quarter of the year and consider how to lower them.	_____	_____	_____
4. Obtain total hours worked for each assembly line worker for the last three weeks.	_____	_____	_____
5. Forecast sales for the next three years.	_____	_____	_____
6. What is the total cost of goods sold and operating expenses for each month during the past year?	_____	_____	_____
7. Set new product prices based upon the Consumer Price Index.	_____	_____	_____

8-J. Assume that within the next six months, a firm's chief information officer has announced to her managers that voice recognition software for all office workers will be installed that will enable them to dictate words and numbers into their computers with 99 percent accuracy. The managers will face certain problems from employees when they learn of this announcement. As the CIO or a manager, how would you answer the following two questions?

1. What problems will arise and how will you handle them if the task of keying data into computers using keyboards will no longer be necessary and will result in some workers no longer being needed?

____

____

____

____

____

____

2. How will you reorganize or redesign the many jobs that involve some keying of data?

____

____

____

____

____

____

SMALL GROUP ACTIVITIES

Group Activity 1

Background

A common term today is "sick building." It means that the building or objects in the building are causing employees to become ill. Those objects can be chairs, desks, carpets, or tobacco smoke. In addition, computers, keyboards, lighting, and the adjustability of chair height and backs may contribute to health problems. The construction material in buildings may also affect one's health. Factory equipment may injure some workers.

Employee lawsuits caused by dangerous equipment, dangerous smells, and unclean air circulating throughout buildings are increasing. Poor circulation is a primary contributor, because air with dangerous elements in it is often not adequately replaced by fresh air fast enough. The sad fact is that old as well as new buildings may be sick. But when managers address the problem, employee absences can decrease and productivity can climb. Evidence suggests that fixing sick buildings reduces accidents and illnesses.

Instructions

Your instructor will put you into small groups for the purpose of gathering information and conducting interviews about sick buildings in the work climate. Here are your tasks:

1. Each team member should obtain and report to fellow team members the key points made in a magazine article dealing with sick buildings. One example would be "Is Your Office Killing You?" by Michelle Conlin in *Business Week*, June 5, 2000.
2. Once your team has reviewed and shared information from the magazine articles, identify a profit- or not-for-profit organization with 10 or more employees. With the approval of the managers and your teacher, interview managers and workers at the organization. Or, interview people at shopping malls or in different neighborhoods about their workplaces.
3. Obtain answers to the following questions, and add other questions with your teacher's approval:
   a. Has your health or the health of other workers ever been affected by the building in which you work?
   b. What health problems have you or other employees experienced?
   c. What building conditions exist, or might exist, that you believe would cause or contribute to your health problems?
   d. Has your doctor indicated the possible cause or causes of your condition that might be related to the building in which you work?
   e. Have you informed your employer about the affect of the building on your health or that of other employees?
   f. Has any action been taken to improve the condition of the building, such as replacing or improving ventilation?

Final Action

Your team should summarize the information gathered from magazines and the surveys and then present an oral report to the class. If requested by your teacher, prepare a written group report. Include tables and diagrams in both your oral and written report.

Group Activity 2

Your teacher will place you into groups of three to five students. Your group is to find out from other students in your school or community what types and brands of software and hardware they own or use away from school. With your group, prepare a questionnaire. Select one of the following topics: operating system software, application software, input devices, output devices, or computer systems (Dell, Compaq, Apple, etc.). Once your group has selected its topic, obtain approval from your instructor.

Each questionnaire can be quite simple and should contain between five and ten questions. The questions can be of different types, such as yes/no, checklists, and fill-in-the-blanks. Each student should first individually create five questions for his or her group. The group should then meet to review the questions and to reduce and refine the list to not more than ten clear questions. Now test your questionnaire on about five students in order to improve the wording of questions. Revise the questionnaire as needed. You can administer the questionnaire orally and record student responses on your copy.

After collecting the answers, meet as a group and sort out the answers, prepare tables of answers, and calculate percentages. Use a graphics or presentation software, such as Power Point, to prepare tables and charts to show on a screen. Make an oral report to the class of your questionnaire answers. Draw conclusions about the popularity of what students use most and least.

<table>
<tr><td rowspan="3">Chapter 9

E-Commerce</td><td rowspan="3">Name _______________

Date _______________</td><td colspan="4" align="center">Scoring Record</td></tr>
<tr><td>Part A</td><td>Part B</td><td>Part C</td><td>Total</td></tr>
<tr><td>Perfect score</td></tr>
</table>

		Part A	Part B	Part C	Total
	Perfect score	20	14	5	39
	My score				

Study Guide

Part A—*Directions:* Indicate your answer to each of the following questions by circling either yes or no in the Answers column.

		Answers	For Scoring

1. Does the United States lead the world in Internet users with over 50% of all users? .... yes no 1. _______

2. Has the Internet allowed many small businesses to compete successfully with larger, established companies? .... yes no 2. _______

3. According to the U.S. Department of Commerce, does the total amount of U.S. Internet sales to consumers and businesses exceed $50 billion? .... yes no 3. _______

4. Does the dollar volume of consumer Internet sales exceed the dollar value of business to business sales? .... yes no 4. _______

5. Is internal and external communication the main use of the Internet by businesses? .... yes no 5. _______

6. Is an advantage of using e-mail the increased speed of communications? .... yes no 6. _______

7. Is much of the information on the Internet provided free by government agencies, colleges and universities, libraries, and private businesses? .... yes no 7. _______

8. Is it possible for businesses to benefit from promotion on the Internet without actually selling products online? .... yes no 8. _______

9. Must a company be either a bricks-and-mortar company or a dot-com company? yes no 9. _______

10. Does the interaction stage of e-commerce development allow customers to complete an entire sales transaction online? .... yes no 10. _______

11. Are the most frequently Internet-purchased consumer items books, computer hardware and software, and music? .... yes no 11. _______

12. Has the Consumer Product Safety Commission set Internet advertising standards to guard against pornographic and inappropriate advertising on Web sites? yes no 12. _______

13. Do most consumers still purchase most of their products from bricks-and-mortar businesses, even if they use the Internet to gather product information? ... yes no 13. _______

14. Are online shoppers proving to be less brand and store loyal? .... yes no 14. _______

15. Is the Webby award given to organizations with the most effective Web site designs? .... yes no 15. _______

16. Is security one of the main concerns of online shoppers? .... yes no 16. _______

17. Is the first step in establishing an e-commerce Web site to determine the purpose of the Web site? .... yes no 17. _______

18. Is it important to know the age of your customers before designing your Web site? .... yes no 18. _______

19. Must all domain names be registered? .... yes no 19. _______

20. Do consumers who pay by credit card online have any legal protection against fraud or theft? .... yes no 20. _______

		Answers	For Scoring

1. The Internet has allowed many small businesses to (a) compete with larger, established businesses, (b) reach customers all over the world, (c) exchange business-related information, (d) all of the responses. .... ________ 1. ______

2. What percent of all sales by businesses to consumers is completed using the Internet? (a) 1%, (b) 5%, (c) 50%, (d) 80%. .... ________ 2. ______

3. The Internet was first devised as (a) a method of sending personal e-mail messages, (b) a military and research tool, (c) a way to advertise products and services electronically, (d) all of the responses. .... ________ 3. ______

4. It is reported that in 1998, business-to-business sales on the Internet totaled approximately (a) $8 billion, (b) $45 billion, (c) $200 billion, (d) $1 trillion. ________ 4. ______

5. The Internet is used for (a) personal communications, (b) business-to-business communications, (c) business-to-customer communications, (d) all of the responses. .. ________ 5. ______

6. Salespeople who log onto a company Web site and check inventory levels are demonstrating what use of the Internet? (a) business communications, (b) information gathering, (c) business operations, (d) all of the responses. .... ________ 6. ______

7. When a customer completes a registration card, what use of the Internet is being demonstrated? (a) business communications, (b) information gathering, (c) business operations, (d) all of the responses. .... ________ 7. ______

8. A dot-com business (a) usually has a bricks-and-mortar headquarters, (b) is a company that does almost all of its business activities through the Internet, (c) is typically an outgrowth of a bricks-and-mortar business, (d) is always a small business. ________ 8. ______

9. If a business has a Web site where customers can search a product database, download a catalog, and print an order form to be mailed or faxed to the company, the Web site is (a) interactive, (b) integrated, (c) informational, (d) all of the responses. ________ 9. ______

10. A business Web site that allows consumers only to learn about the company and its products is (a) interactive, (b) fully integrated, (c) informational, (d) transactional. ________ 10. ______

11. Today, most consumers go online to (a) purchase products, (b) gather information, (c) view product advertisements, (d) communicate. .... ________ 11. ______

12. Which factor is the most important to consumers when shopping online? (a) a company telephone number, (b) lower prices than at bricks-and-mortar businesses, (c) an easy to use Web site with effective customer service, (d) online coupons. .... ________ 12. ______

13. When establishing an e-commerce Web site, which of the following steps should be the final one before opening the business? (a) determine the purpose of your Web site, (b) advertise the online business, (c) study your customers, their needs, and their Internet experiences, (d) obtain a Web server and a domain name. ... ________ 13. ______

14. A pixel is (a) an advertisement on the Web, (b) one or more dots on a video display screen, (c) another name for an e-commerce business, (d) a Web-hosting service. . ________ 14. ______

Part C—*Directions:* In the Answers column, write the letter of the word or expression in Column I that most closely matches each statement in Column II.

Column I	Column II	Answers	For Scoring
A. E-commerce	1. The address for locating an online business.	________	1. ______
B. Pixel	2. Doing business online.	________	2. ______
C. Dot-com	3. Stage of Web site development that allows customers to complete a product purchase online.	________	3. ______
D. Bricks-and-mortar			
E. Integration	4. Unit of measure used for determining the size of Internet advertisements.	________	4. ______
F. Interaction			
G. Domain name	5. Businesses that sell most of their products online.	________	5. ______

        Name ______________________________________

Directions: Study each controversial issue carefully. Follow the advice of your teacher before listing in the columns provided reasons why people might answer Yes or No. Your teacher may want you to work with a classmate, talk with others in your community to gather information, or use the library or Internet to gather facts.

9-1. Should businesses that gather information online by asking customers to fill out warranty or registration cards sell that information to other businesses without the customer's permission?

Reasons for "Yes"	Reasons for "No"

9-2. Should people be prevented from registering the name of a business, product, or celebrity if they plan to sell it for a profit rather than using it for an Internet business or a Web site?

Reasons for "Yes"	Reasons for "No"

PROBLEMS

9-A. In the year 2000, the number of regular Internet users worldwide was estimated at 500 million people. Using the following information showing the percentage of users by country taken from Figure 9-2 of the textbook, calculate the number of Internet users in each country. Then determine the number and percentage of users in all other countries.

Country	% of Users	Number of Users
United States	42.9%	_______________
Japan	6.9%	_______________
United Kingdom	5.4%	_______________
Canada	5.1%	_______________
Germany	4.7%	_______________
China	2.4%	_______________
All other countries	_______________	_______________

9-B. Both bricks-and-mortar and dot-com businesses maintain Web sites. However, by visiting a Web site, you should be able to identify which businesses have one or more physical locations where they sell products and which use e-commerce as the primary method of selling products. Using the Internet or business information and advertising in magazines, newspapers, or telephone directories, identify five bricks-and-mortar businesses and five dot-com businesses. In the column on the right, list the primary information you found that identified the appropriate classification for the business.

CATEGORY OF BUSINESS   **REASON FOR CLASSIFICATION**

Bricks-and-Mortar

1. _______________________   _______________________________________
2. _______________________   _______________________________________
3. _______________________   _______________________________________
4. _______________________   _______________________________________
5. _______________________   _______________________________________

Dot-Com

1. _______________________   _______________________________________
2. _______________________   _______________________________________
3. _______________________   _______________________________________
4. _______________________   _______________________________________
5. _______________________   _______________________________________

9-C. Businesses use the Internet for a number of purposes in addition to selling products and services to customers. Select a business that you might like to own and operate. Then answer the following questions to identify the ways you could use the Internet in that business.

The type of business I might like to own and operate is _______________________________

1. If you were going to use the Internet for communications in your business:
   With whom would you communicate?   For what purpose?

2. If you were going to use the Internet for information gathering in your business:
   What information would you need?   What information source would you use?

3. If you were going to use the Internet to improve the business operations of your business:
   What operations would you improve?   How would the Internet benefit your business?

9-D. Businesses using e-commerce will be in one of three stages of development—information stage, interaction stage, or integration stage. Search the Internet to identify three businesses in each of the stages. In the following chart, list the company name, the Internet address, and the evidence from the Web site you used to classify the business into the stage.

INFORMATION STAGE

Company Name	Internet Address	Evidence of Information
__________	__________	__________
__________	__________	__________
__________	__________	__________

INTERACTION STAGE

Company Name	Internet Address	Evidence of Interaction
__________	__________	__________
__________	__________	__________
__________	__________	__________

INTEGRATION STAGE

Company Name	Internet Address	Evidence of Integration
__________	__________	__________
__________	__________	__________
__________	__________	__________

9-E. The following spaces illustrate common sizes of Internet advertisements. Use an Internet browser to locate an example of a business advertisement for each of the sizes shown that you believe is particularly effective in promoting the business or product. Re-create each advertisement by drawing it in the appropriate space. For each size, write a short statement that identifies why you believe the ad design is effective.

Full Banner

Half Banner

Micro Button

Button

Vertical Banner

The reason I believe the advertisement is effective:

Full Banner ____

____

Half Banner ____

____

Vertical Banner ____

____

Button ____

____

Micro Button ____

____

9-F. The Internet allows businesses to direct their products and services toward very specific groups of customers. Search the Internet and identify two businesses that appear to be marketing their products and services to each of the identified groups. For each, list the products and services the business is selling on the Web.

Customer Group	Business	Products and Services Offered
New Parents		
Teenagers		
Musicians		
Other Businesses		
Travelers		

Now identify three other customer groups for which you have located e-commerce businesses that are marketing their products and services to the specific group.

9-G. The following steps allow you to make the initial decisions necessary to develop an online business. Answer each of the following questions to complete each step.

1. What is the purpose of your Web site? ______________________________

   ____

   ____

2. Who will be the primary customers you want to visit your Web site? ______________________________

   ____

3. What products and services will you offer? Will your site be informational, interactive, or integrated?

   ____

   ____

   ____

4. What domain name would you like to use for your Web site? (Check with an online registration service to see if it is available.) What Web-hosting service will you use? (Search the Internet to find a service.)

   ____

   ____

   ____

5. What electronic shopping cart software would you use? (Search the Internet to identify available software, features, and cost.) ______________________________

   ____

   ____

6. What will your business home page look like? (Develop a design using a computer-based drawing program or by hand-drawing.) ______________________________

   ____

   ____

7. What are two primary locations where you will advertise your business? Design one Internet advertisement that introduces your business. ______________________________

   ____

   ____

SMALL GROUP ACTIVITIES

Group Activity 1

A number of organizations recognize the top Internet Web sites with awards such as the Webby Awards, presented by the International Academy of Digital Arts and Sciences. Form a team with three or four other classmates to complete the following activities.

1. Each team will search the Internet to identify the best home page for an e-commerce business. When your team has agreed on the best site, print a copy of the home page using a color printer, if available.
2. Following your teacher's instructions, cooperate with the other teams to develop an exhibit of posters displaying all teams' printed home pages. Clearly identify each home page with the company name.
3. Display the exhibit in a central location in the school with a ballot box, copies of ballots that list each of the companies, and a blank space by each name on the ballot for voting.
4. Ask teachers and students in your school to vote for the home page they believe is the best business Web site design. When the voting is finished, tally the ballots and post the results so everyone knows which business received the most votes.

Group Activity 2

Following your teacher's instructions, form teams to complete the following activity.

With your teammates, identify a business in your community that uses e-commerce. The business can be a dot-com business or a bricks-and-mortar business. Arrange an interview with the owner or manager of the business and ask the following questions.

1. Why did you decide to use e-commerce in your business?

2. What steps did you follow to begin the business?

3. What were the most important resources you used to learn about e-commerce and to develop the e-commerce business?

4. What percentage of your business comes from e-commerce? Is the percentage increasing, decreasing, or staying about the same? Are the customers who use e-commerce different from those who do not?

5. What are the most positive and the most negative aspects of operating an e-commerce business? What improvements, if any, do you plan to make in your e-commerce business?

When your team has completed the interview, prepare a written report of what you learned to share and discuss with the other teams. When all teams have completed their reports, join in a class discussion to determine what was similar and different among the e-commerce businesses.

<table>
<tr><td rowspan="3">Chapter 10

Organizational Communications</td><td rowspan="3">Name _______________

Date _______________</td><td colspan="5" align="center">Scoring Record</td></tr>
<tr><td></td><td>Part A</td><td>Part B</td><td>Part C</td><td>Total</td></tr>
<tr><td>Perfect score</td><td>20</td><td>10</td><td>5</td><td>35</td></tr>
<tr><td colspan="2"></td><td>My score</td><td></td><td></td><td></td><td></td></tr>
</table>

Study Guide

Part A—*Directions:* Indicate your answer to each of the following questions by circling either yes or no in the Answers column.

		Answers	For Scoring
1.	Is "communication" defined as "the sending of information"?	yes no	1. _______
2.	Does the receiver of communication have a responsibility to try to understand the message as the sender intended?	yes no	2. _______
3.	Is a distraction created when two students whisper during a class presentation?	yes no	3. _______
4.	Are messages usually distorted unconsciously?	yes no	4. _______
5.	Is it possible for outsiders to access a company's e-mail messages?	yes no	5. _______
6.	Might abusive sexual language lead to a lawsuit by offended employees?	yes no	6. _______
7.	Is information overload a rare complaint of employees?	yes no	7. _______
8.	Is spam unsolicited advertising that finds its way into e-mail boxes?	yes no	8. _______
9.	Do many emoticons make a message seem professional?	yes no	9. _______
10.	Is avoiding eye contact considered a form of body language?	yes no	10. _______
11.	Do non-verbal messages convey as much meaning as do verbal messages?	yes no	11. _______
12.	Are distrust and secrecy apt to be found in open cultures?	yes no	12. _______
13.	Do employees often fear revealing negative information and avoid making honest criticisms in closed cultures?	yes no	13. _______
14.	Should managers usually try to block informal communication channels in a business?	yes no	14. _______
15.	Are grapevine messages usually accurate?	yes no	15. _______
16.	Is time lost attending meetings considered a major disadvantage of meetings?	yes no	16. _______
17.	Are wild and imaginative ideas encouraged during brainstorming sessions?	yes no	17. _______
18.	Does a win/lose strategy to resolve a conflict occur when everyone involved in a conflict agrees to a mutually acceptable solution?	yes no	18. _______
19.	Does how close a person stands when talking to someone else differ from one country to another?	yes no	19. _______
20.	Is the written communication channel best when managers want to communicate information about a new policy?	yes no	20. _______

Part B—*Directions:* For each of the following statements, select the word, or group of words, that best completes the statement. In the Answers column, write the letter corresponding to the answer selected.

		Answers	For Scoring

1. Which is NOT a form of communication feedback? (a) returning a questionnaire, (b) restating the sender's message in your own words, (c) asking questions to clarify a point, (d) assuming a message is understood. .... ________ 1.________
2. Which statement is *true* about distortions? (a) Self-enhancement is not a form of distortion. (b) Self-protection is not a form of distortion. (c) Giving an employee a deserved poor rating is not a form of distortion. (d) An exaggeration about one's personal performance is not a form of distortion. .... ________ 2.________
3. Carelessly prepared messages reflect (a) neutrally on the writer only, (b) neutrally on the organization only, (c) negatively on the writer and on the organization, (d) negatively on the writer only. .... ________ 3.________
4. When creativity and problem solving are encouraged at all levels and trust and confidence exist to a high degree in an organization, what type of communication system exists? (a) open, (b) upward, (c) downward, (d) closed. .... ________ 4.________
5. How does the NGT differ from a regular meeting of workers involved in solving a problem? (a) The NGT requires everyone to agree to the solution. (b) The NGT requires open voting. (c) The NGT requires all members to offer solutions. (d) The NGT forces the manager to select the solution. .... ________ 5.________
6. Which statement is *false* about conflicts? (a) Conflicts that are not resolved often result in long-term problems. (b) Conflicts sometimes are an obstacle to job performance. (c) Conflicts do not lead to healthy discussions. (d) Conflicts may occur between groups. .... ________ 6.________
7. When conflicts are relatively unimportant, which strategy should managers use? (a) avoidance, (b) compromise, (c) win-lose, (d) interference. .... ________ 7.________
8. What has the typical international business done to help prepare managers who are about to be transferred to foreign countries? (a) Teach the manager how to teach the workers in the new country to speak English. (b) Encourage the manager to make social contacts with English-speaking people in the new country. (c) Provide intensive training in the culture and language of the new country. (d) Provide a dictionary for the language of the new country. .... ________ 8.________
9. Which of the ten rules of good listening is the one on which all others depend? (a) Ask questions. (b) Hold your temper. (c) Listen to understand, not to oppose. (d) Stop talking. .... ________ 9.________
10. The best way to deliver a compliment to an employee for excellent work is (a) orally to personalize it, (b) in writing in order to record it, (c) both orally and in writing, (d) orally in a private meeting. .... ________ 10.________

Part C—*Directions:* In the Answers column, write the letter of the word or expression in Column I that most closely matches each statement in Column II.

Column I	Column II	Answers	For Scoring
A. Brainstorming	1. Sharing ideas, beliefs, and opinions.	________	1.________
B. Closed culture	2. Someone slams a door.	________	2.________
C. Communication	3. How people consciously or unconsciously change messages.	________	3.________
D. Conflict			
E. Culture	4. A discussion technique that stimulates ideas.	________	4.________
F. Distortion	5. Develops when interfering with the achievement of another person's goals.	________	5.________
G. Distraction			
H. Grapevine			

     Name _______________________________

Directions: Study each controversial issue carefully. Follow the advice of your teacher before listing in the columns provided reasons why people might answer Yes or No. Your teacher may want you to work with a classmate, talk with others in your community to gather information, or use the library or Internet to gather facts.

10-1. Do employers have the right to examine all e-mail messages before, during, and after working hours from business computers and to punish workers who use business computers for non-business purposes?

Reasons for "Yes"	Reasons for "No"

10-2. Should most meetings be limited to 30 minutes because so much valuable work time is lost talking about trivial business and non-business matters?

Reasons for "Yes"	Reasons for "No"

PROBLEMS

10-A. Check whether each of the following situations describing a barrier to communication is a distraction or a distortion.

		Distraction	Distortion
1.	During a meeting, a worker throws a wad of paper into a wastebasket located across the room.	____	____
2.	A lawyer's beeper beeps during a conversation with a client.	____	____
3.	When the receptionist told her manager he had a call, she neglected to say that the call was from the doctor who had just completed major surgery on the manager's wife.	____	____
4.	A client's name was misspelled on an otherwise well-written message.	____	____
5.	Telephone calls constantly interrupted the manager, who was composing an important report.	____	____
6.	A supervisor had a serious problem with an employee. When reporting to the manager, the supervisor merely said, "One of my employees has a small problem, but I'm sure it can be worked out."	____	____
7.	"Skip the minor details, Cindy. What are the important points?"	____	____
8.	"At today's meeting, please don't mention that some of the gang was smoking again, because written warnings or pink slips will be issued. Instead, let's ask for a discussion of the importance of not smoking in the plant."	____	____

10-B. For each of the following communication situations, identify (a) the sender, (b) the receiver, and (c) the message channel.

1. A customer calls the service manager of an auto-repair shop to make an appointment to have her car repaired.

    a. sender _______________________________________

    b. receiver _______________________________________

    c. message channel _______________________________________

2. A sales manager sends an e-mail message to the head of the accounting department, requesting a report on customers who have not paid their balances owed.

    a. sender _______________________________________

    b. receiver _______________________________________

    c. message channel _______________________________________

3. While they are working, Jack tells Colleen about a rumor that some other employees might get an increase in pay next month.

    a. sender _______________________________________

    b. receiver _______________________________________

    c. message channel _______________________________________

4. The branch manager of the Redlands National Bank sends Harvey Kwolek a computerized form letter to inform him that his checking account is overdrawn.

    a. sender _______________________________________

    b. receiver _______________________________________

    c. message channel _______________________________________

10-C. On the line to the right of each listed "feeling" that people might express in e-mail messages, hand print the keyboard strokes that best represent the feeling. If you are not aware of an emoticon to express the feeling, create one.

1. Happiness ___________________________

2. Sadness ___________________________

3. Person is tongue-tied ___________________________

4. Wink ___________________________

5. Just kidding ___________________________

6. Someone wearing a walkman ___________________________

7. Someone wearing glasses ___________________________

8. Create one of your own ___________________________

10-D. By checking the appropriate column, indicate whether the nonverbal message confirms or contradicts the verbal message.

	Verbal Message	**Nonverbal Message**	**Confirms**	**Contradicts**
1.	"Please sit and listen, students."	Snaps fingers.	_____	_____
2.	"I'll wait patiently for another five minutes."	Taps fingers on the desk.	_____	_____
3.	"Sure. I'll be happy to work on that project."	Turns eyes toward window and drops voice.	_____	_____
4.	"I'm thinking... I'm thinking."	Looks downward and places finger over lips.	_____	_____
5.	"I'm interested in your ideas."	Leans toward person with steady eye contact.	_____	_____

10-E. Place a check mark in one of the two columns on the right for each item below that describes a characteristic within an organization.

		Corporate Culture	
		Open	Closed
1.	Employees call their bosses by their first names and eat in the same cafeteria.	_____	_____
2.	Employees may send their complaints using e-mail directly to upper-level managers, who respond quickly.	_____	_____
3.	All contact about business matters must be done through formal appointments, at meetings, or by memos.	_____	_____
4.	Informal communication methods are discouraged, and most messages flow downward.	_____	_____
5.	Self-directed work teams were introduced but failed because most managers would not surrender authority.	_____	_____

10-F. How do you handle conflict situations? Place a "1" in the column that represents your preferred strategy and a "2" in the column that represents your second-choice strategy. Discuss answers with your classmates to compare similarities and differences.

Conflict Situations	*Strategies*		
	Avoid	Compromise	Win/Lose
1. An office mate who is a good friend wants to take her daily mid-morning break with you at 10:00 a.m., but another friend definitely prefers 10:30.	____	____	____
2. Two other managers cannot agree on what amount should be budgeted for hiring a part-time worker who will help all three of you. They turn to you for support.	____	____	____
3. Two co-workers are moving with you to a new office area. Both want the larger desk that overlooks a courtyard. Although you work well with one co-worker, you do not get along with the other. However, you also want the desk that overlooks the courtyard.	____	____	____
4. Your sales manager promised an added cash award to the person with the highest weekly sales. You and five other salespeople want to win the award.	____	____	____
5. A newly hired worker was just promoted. Because you had worked longer and harder, you complained bitterly to your supervisor and accused him of showing favoritism. You stormed out of the office and now must decide what to do.	____	____	____

10-G. The results of a survey of 675 workers in a recent year produced the following answers to this question: "How would you rate your manager's willingness to listen to new ideas and suggestions for improvement?" The responses appear below, followed by questions to be answered.

Very willing 38%
Somewhat willing 44%
Not willing at all 15%
Don't know or no answer 3%

1. How many workers responded to each choice? _______________________________________

____

2. How many of the workers believed their managers were willing to listen to their ideas?

____

3. Based on the answers to the question, does it appear that managers generally have open-door policies and encourage employees to talk with them?

____

____

4. Does the study show that most managers support and practice an open culture?

____

5. What advice would you give the heads of the firms for which the employees work?

____

____

____

____

10-H. A new president for a business that has problems just hired you as its communications expert. As your first task, the president wants to know how you would handle the following situations, which have occurred regularly over the past several months. Provide two suggestions for each situation.

1. "Whenever a problem arises, everyone has a solution, but no one does anything because everyone talks and

    no one listens."

    a. ________________________________

    b. ________________________________

2. "I never know whether to chew someone out on the phone, in person, or by memo. Of course, the same

    question applies to praising a good worker or informing workers of new policies."

    a. ________________________________

    b. ________________________________

    ____

    ____

3. "My managers seem great at communicating down to others, but not enough information flows upward."

    a. ________________________________

    b. ________________________________

4. "Our workers don't talk to their managers enough. They do their jobs, but often there are errors because

    they don't understand the instructions. Not even the managers talk to one another enough."

    a. ________________________________

    b. ________________________________

10-I. Read each of the communications situations described below. For each situation, indicate whether oral or written communications will be more effective by checking the appropriate column.

Situation	Type of Communication Written	Oral
1. A manager wants to tell a few employees how to use a new cash register.	____	____
2. An employee wants to tell the company president about a more efficient way to unload merchandise from trucks.	____	____
3. A committee chairperson wants to describe a new assignment to committee members.	____	____
4. A sales manager needs to give all salespeople a new set of list prices for products.	____	____
5. A worker wants to tell another worker her opinion of the new manager.	____	____
6. The president of a corporation wants to summarize the year's activities of the company for the stockholders.	____	____
7. A group leader wants the group to determine several ways to solve a problem.	____	____
8. A large company wants all employees to know about several recent promotions.	____	____

SMALL GROUP ACTIVITIES

Group Activity 1

Background

Good writers and speakers, especially in business, are careful about the words they select when writing memos, e-mail messages, letters, advertisements, and press releases for newspapers. The chairperson of a meeting or a public speaker must be equally careful in selecting words that match the audience's backgrounds. Many words such as "cat" are neutral, but people often assign emotional feelings to neutral words. To one person a cat is one's best friend, and to another, a selfish, independent creature. One emotional reaction is positive while the other is negative.

Good writers must consider their readers thoughtfully before picking key words for employees, customers, and others. Generally, writers should select words that the typical reader will see positively, not negatively. That is why the former Complaint Department in stores is now typically named the Service Department. Similarly, "physically handicapped" people are now referred to as "physically challenged." Do you see the difference? Avoid words that contain an undesirable bias, because you want the reader or listener to feel respected, not degraded.

Directions

Your instructor will place you into groups of three to five people. In the diagram below, each group member is to study the neutral nouns in the first column and then to jot on a small slip of paper what emotions or feelings the word gives to him or her. Two examples are provided. Then each student is to reveal his or her written feelings by a word or phrase. Group members should discuss each term and their collective feelings about it. Determine whether each term is more positive or negative and why it is. Record the feelings of others in the second and third columns as well as your own.

Neutral (Noun)	Positive	Negative
Retiree	Friend	Complainer
Bank	Savings	Rich
Work		
Group Meetings		
Corporation		
Entrepreneur		
Credit		
Economics		
Union		
BMW		

The group should now discuss how this exercise could provide them with insights about how to compose business messages orally or in writing. Be prepared to report those ideas to the class when called upon to do so.

Group Activity 2

Effective managers in firms with open cultures often involve their workers in solving problems. Different techniques such as brainstorming and the nominal group techniques (NGT) often prove useful for tough problems. For this group activity, the class will be divided in half to form Team A and Team B. Each team will address one of two serious problems that face those who are in charge of the school's largest and newest computer lab. Your instructor will provide both teams with general instructions. Review the steps in Figure 10-6 for using the NGT. Next are the problems to be solved.

Team A's Problem: The first problem to be solved is to safeguard the school's newest instructional computer lab from thieves. Strangers seem to enter unseen and take computer-related equipment because of lax security. Some teachers believe thefts occur mostly during the breaks between classes and when the lab is left open for students to use to do homework during the school day. This security problem needs to be solved soon.

Team B's Problem: The second problem has gotten worse with each passing week. Hackers have been breaking into the system on a fairly regular basis. Virus scares are frequent, and sometimes the system is down for days, upsetting students and instructors. The lab aide has had to work overtime on a somewhat regular basis. Both problems reduce the effectiveness of instruction and are costing taxpayers money.

Your instructor will provide all team members with any special instructions. Each team is expected to generate many ideas for solving their problem. From the list of possible solutions, the three most effective and practical ones will be presented to the instructor and class. The entire class can then discuss and select the one or two best suggestions for solving each problem.

<table>
<tr><td rowspan="3">Chapter 11

Management Functions and Decision Making</td><td rowspan="3">Name ______________

Date ______________</td><td colspan="5" align="center">Scoring Record</td></tr>
<tr><td></td><td>Part A</td><td>Part B</td><td>Part C</td><td>Total</td></tr>
<tr><td>Perfect score</td><td>25</td><td>12</td><td>5</td><td>42</td></tr>
<tr><td colspan="2">My score</td><td></td><td></td><td></td><td></td></tr>
</table>

Study Guide

Part A—*Directions:* Indicate your answer to each of the following questions by circling either yes or no in the Answers column.

		Answers	For Scoring
1.	Will most people who want to become managers start their management careers as supervisors?	yes no	1. ______
2.	Are managers responsible for the success or failure of a company?	yes no	2. ______
3.	Do all managers perform certain activities no matter what the type or size of the company or in what part of the business they work?	yes no	3. ______
4.	Is the primary work of all managers grouped within the six functions: planning, organizing, controlling, implementing, decision making, and supervising?	yes no	4. ______
5.	Do many employees of a business complete management?	yes no	5. ______
6.	Would an experienced employee who is given the responsibility to be the leader of a group project be classified as a manager?	yes no	6. ______
7.	In order to be a manager, does a person have to complete all of the management functions and have authority over other jobs and people?	yes no	7. ______
8.	Do most supervisors spend all of their time on management activities?	yes no	8. ______
9.	Do a manager's responsibilities remain the same after he or she is promoted in the organization?	yes no	9. ______
10.	Are most supervisors promoted into management in the same area in which they have worked?	yes no	10. ______
11.	Are supervisors responsible for implementing the plans of executives by getting employees to perform effectively on a day-to-day basis?	yes no	11. ______
12.	Are employee performance reviews a typical supervisory responsibility?	yes no	12. ______
13.	Do most employees prefer to work for managers who are interested in them?	yes no	13. ______
14.	Can a supervisor contribute to the profitability of the company by controlling costs in the area where he or she works?	yes no	14. ______
15.	Is a work schedule an important tool for supervisors to use in daily planning?	yes no	15. ______
16.	Is much of the communication between supervisors and their employees done orally?	yes no	16. ______
17.	Should most supervisors spend more time on non-managerial activities and less time on management functions?	yes no	17. ______
18.	Does every company, whether it is small or large, need a management information system as an important management tool?	yes no	18. ______
19.	When managers use a management information system, do they spend more time on controlling activities?	yes no	19. ______
20.	Do even small companies usually have research departments?	yes no	20. ______
21.	Do business problems generally have only one solution?	yes no	21. ______
22.	Do the terms "problem" and "symptom" mean essentially the same thing?	yes no	22. ______
23.	Are customers a potential source of possible solutions to business problems?	yes no	23. ______
24.	Are studying and evaluating the results of solutions to problems a part of the planning function for managers?	yes no	24. ______
25.	Once a solution to a problem is implemented in a company, should a manager avoid changing the solution even if evidence suggests it is not working well?	yes no	25. ______

Part B—*Directions:* For each of the following statements, select the word, or group of words, that best completes the statement. In the Answers column, write the letter corresponding to the answer selected.

		Answers	For Scoring
1.	Employees will be most successful when they move into a management position if (a) they have worked for a poor supervisor so they know what not to do, (b) they begin work as a supervisor before receiving training, (c) they have the chance to try supervision before making a final decision, (d) all of the responses.	_______	1._______
2.	Which of the following is most likely to perform all of the management functions? (a) a small business owner, (b) the top executive of a multinational corporation, (c) a middle manager, (d) all of the responses.	_______	2._______
3.	A top-level manager who spends most of his or her time on management functions is (a) an executive, (b) a mid-manager, (c) a supervisor, (d) a team leader.	_______	3._______
4.	The type of manager who works most directly with employees on a daily basis is (a) an executive, (b) a mid-manager, (c) a supervisor, (d) none of the responses.	_______	4._______
5.	Which of the following is NOT one of the common responsibilities of supervisors? (a) communicating goals and directions, (b) motivating employees to work effectively, (c) keeping management informed of employee ideas and concerns, (d) developing long-range plans for the organization.	_______	5._______
6.	Which of the following activities of supervisors relates most directly to quality control? (a) developing work schedules, (b) developing and checking standards, (c) using effective listening skills, (d) setting priorities so that the most important work gets done.	_______	6._______
7.	The effectiveness of a supervisor's job is determined by which factor? (a) the quality of the work of the supervised employees, (b) the efficient use of the company's resources, (c) the satisfaction of the supervisor's employees, (d) all of the responses.	_______	7._______
8.	To manage time efficiently, supervisors must be able to (a) determine the work to be done, (b) set priorities for the most important work, (c) ensure that the work is completed properly and on time, (d) all of the responses.	_______	8._______
9.	A difficult situation requiring a solution is (a) a problem, (b) a symptom, (c) a standard, (d) an alternative.	_______	9._______
10.	Which of the following steps in problem solving are in the correct order? (a) analyze solutions, identify the problem; (b) determine possible solutions, identify the problem; (c) analyze solutions, select the best solution; (d) all of the responses.	_______	10._______
11.	Which of the following would NOT be appropriate in selecting the solution to be implemented to solve an important problem? (a) take time rather than make a quick decision, (b) involve others to help with the decision, (c) select the least expensive solution, (d) all of the responses.	_______	11._______
12.	Analyzing the solutions involves (a) brainstorming ideas, (b) listing advantages and disadvantages, (c) determining symptoms, (d) identifying the problem.	_______	12._______

Part C—*Directions:* In the Answers column, write the letter of the word or expression in Column I that most closely matches each statement in Column II.

Column I	Column II	Answers	For Scoring
A. Planning	1. Accomplishing the goals of an organization through the effective use of people and other resources.	_______	1._______
B. Organizing	2. Deciding how plans can most effectively be accomplished and arranging resources to complete work.	_______	2._______
C. Implementing	3. Evaluating results to determine if the company's objectives have been accomplished as planned.	_______	3._______
D. Controlling	4. Analyzing information and making decisions about what needs to be done.	_______	4._______
E. Management	5. Carrying out the plans and helping employees to work effectively.	_______	5._______

Directions: Study each controversial issue carefully. Follow the advice of your teacher before listing in the columns provided reasons why people might answer Yes or No. Your teacher may want you to work with a classmate, talk with others in your community to gather information, or use the library or Internet to gather facts.

11-1. Since supervisors are responsible for the day-to-day operations of a business, are they more important to the success of the business than executives who are responsible for long-range planning and direction of the business?

Reasons for "Yes"	Reasons for "No"

11-2. Should supervisors be selected from among the employees who are the top performers in their areas, or should they be selected from those who have the ability to work well with and motivate other employees?

Reasons for "Yes"	Reasons for "No"

PROBLEMS

11-A. All managers perform four functions: planning, organizing, implementing, and controlling. While each manager completes all functions, managers at different levels in a business spend more time on some functions than on others. One company collected information on the average number of hours spent by executives, mid-managers, and supervisors each week completing each of the functions. The results were:

	Planning	Organizing	Implementing	Controlling
Executives	24	15	12	8
Mid-managers	17	15	19	14
Supervisors	6	10	16	12

Complete the following figure by shading in the appropriate sections representing the percentage of work time spent by each group of managers during the week.

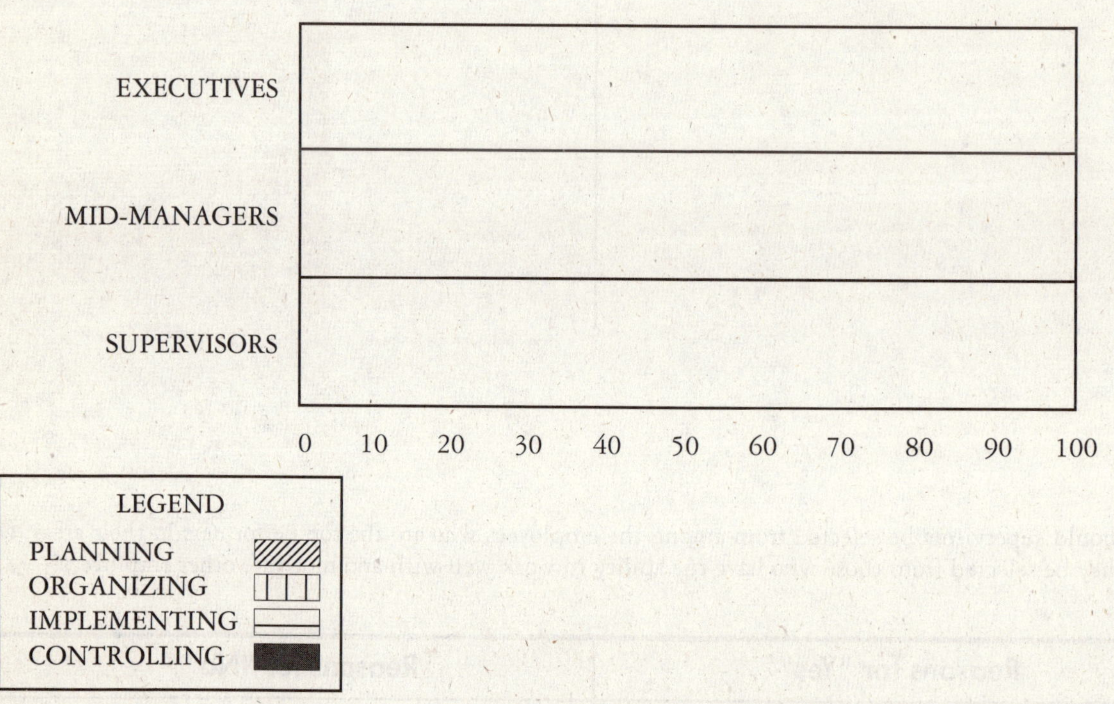

11-B. For each of the following management activities, identify which of the four management functions is being completed. Place the letter of the correct function in the blank beside the item number:

P = Planning
O = Organizing
I = Implementing
C = Controlling

_____ 1. Determining the types of raw materials to use in order to develop a high-quality product.

_____ 2. Completing an employee performance appraisal.

_____ 3. Dividing a large sales territory into two smaller territories and assigning managers and salespeople to the territory.

_____ 4. Deciding if a new product should be added after reviewing test-market results.

_____ 5. Discussing a problem with two employees to encourage them to work more closely together rather than continuing to have conflicts.

_____ 6. Reviewing the financial statements for the past six months.

_____ 7. Deciding to hire an advertising agency to promote a new product because the promotion manager is currently overworked.

_____ 8. Conducting a department meeting.

_____ 9. Determining salary increases based on annual performance evaluations.

_____10. Deciding whether to sell stock in the company or borrow money in order to finance a new building.

11-C. You have learned that while supervisors from various companies have many differences in their jobs, they still have a common set of responsibilities. Those common responsibilities are listed in the left column of the following chart. Locate a newspaper that has a large section of classified advertisements for employment or an Internet site that lists employment opportunities. Identify several job announcements for supervisors. Use those advertisements to complete the remaining columns of the chart. For each of the responsibilities listed, (1) identify a part of the job description from one of the advertisements that relates to that responsibility and copy the statement into the second column; (2) copy the job title for that position in the third column; (3) write the name of the company offering the position in the fourth column; and (4) identify the type of business (manufacturer, retailer, etc.) in the last column. Try to identify a different job and company for each of the supervisor responsibilities.

Supervisor Responsibility	Job Description	Job Title	Company	Type of Business
Communicate goals and directions				
Keep management informed				
Evaluate and improve employee performance				
Motivate employees				
Use resources efficiently				

11-D. As a manager of a printing department, you are responsible for scheduling the time of three employees. Each employee works from 9 a.m. until 5 p.m., with lunch from 12:00 until 1:00. You have the following jobs that can be assigned to your employees. All jobs must be assigned.

Job 1	2 hours to complete	must be completed today
Job 2	3 1/2 hours to complete	can be completed tomorrow
Job 3	5 1/2 hours to complete	must be completed today
Job 4	1 1/2 hours to complete	must be completed today
Job 5	3 hours to complete	can be completed tomorrow; cannot be divided
Job 6	4 hours to complete	must be completed today
Job 7	3 hours to complete	must be completed today
Job 8	2 1/2 hours to complete	must be completed today
Job 9	4 hours to complete	can be completed tomorrow
Job 10	2 hours to complete	can be completed tomorrow; cannot be divided

Using the following form, assign the jobs to your three employees. You must make certain that jobs 1, 3, 4, 6, 7, and 8 are done today. Employees should be busy all day, but they cannot begin a job that cannot be completed before 5 p.m. if it is noted that the job cannot be divided.

Time	Day 1			Day 2		
	Employee 1	Employee 2	Employee 3	Employee 1	Employee 2	Employee 3
9:00						
10:00						
11:00						
12:00						
1:00						
2:00						
3:00						
4:00						
5:00						

1. How many hours are your employees available to work during the two-day period?

2. How many hours of jobs did you schedule?

3. Based on this information, what problems do you have within your department?

4. Using the decision-making process, define the problem and brainstorm some possible solutions.

11-E. You are the manager of a small gift shop located in a mall. Your store hours are 10:00 a.m. until 9:00 p.m. You typically work during the day with two or three other employees and have a small part-time staff to work the evening hours unsupervised. You receive a monthly projected sales report based on the previous year's sales volume and the season of the year. In reviewing these figures, you have noticed a consistent decline in your sales volume for the last three months. Based on this information, answer the following questions.

1. Is this a symptom or a problem? If this is a symptom, identify at least three possible problems that might be the cause of the symptom.

   ____

   ____

   ____

   ____

2. From your list of possible problems, select one and determine the possible solutions, analyze the solutions, and select the best solution.

   ____

   ____

   ____

3. Establish a method to monitor the solution to determine whether or not you have solved the problem.

   ____

   ____

   ____

   ____

SMALL GROUP ACTIVITIES

General Directions

Small groups of three or four students each should be created. Each group should take one of the following problems, or the group can select the problem on which the members want to work. Groups should have about 10-15 minutes to discuss the issues and develop answers. When they have completed the activity, the groups should report their answers and record them on the board, an overhead transparency, or a computer with projection capabilities.

Group Activity 1

You are the manager of a kitchen appliance store. For each of the following categories [(1) customer needs, (2) competition, and (3) the economy], identify the types of information you need in order to make management decisions about your appliance business. Then develop a procedure for collecting the needed information.

Customer Needs –

Competition –

Economy –

Group Activity 2

You are interested in creating and managing a dot-com (Internet) company that allows people to list and resell used music CDs and tapes at discounted prices. You will make a profit by charging a fee to the people who list their CDs and tapes for resale. Using the four management functions of planning, organizing, implementing, and controlling, list several activities you will need to do under each function.

Planning –

Organizing –

Implementing –

Controlling –

Group Activity 3

Imagine you are the principal of your school. A principal is a manager, just like the manager of a business. As your school's principal, list the types of activities you would need to perform under each management function.

Planning –

Organizing –

Implementing –

Controlling –

<table>
<tr><td rowspan="3">Chapter 12

The Manager as Leader</td><td rowspan="3">Name _______________

Date _______________</td><td colspan="5" align="center">Scoring Record</td></tr>
<tr><td></td><td>Part A</td><td>Part B</td><td>Part C</td><td>Total</td></tr>
<tr><td>Perfect score</td><td>20</td><td>10</td><td>5</td><td>35</td></tr>
<tr><td colspan="2"></td><td>My score</td><td></td><td></td><td></td><td></td></tr>
</table>

Study Guide

Part A—*Directions:* Indicate your answer to each of the following questions by circling either yes or no in the Answers column.

		Answers	For Scoring
1.	Do the people who are responsible for an organization need to have leadership skills in order for the organization to be effective?	yes no	1. ______
2.	Do managers today have total authority over the employees in a business?	yes no	2. ______
3.	Does human relations refer to how well people get along together?	yes no	3. ______
4.	Can supervisors get by without leadership skills since they are at the lowest level of management?	yes no	4. ______
5.	Is dependability an important leadership characteristic?	yes no	5. ______
6.	Do effective leaders encourage others to share their ideas, experiences, and opinions?	yes no	6. ______
7.	If a manager is able to get others to do what he or she wants, is that manager an effective leader?	yes no	7. ______
8.	Is position power based on the ability to control resources, rewards, and punishments?	yes no	8. ______
9.	Can a person have power because others identify with and want to be accepted by him or her?	yes no	9. ______
10.	Are managers the only people who have power in an organization?	yes no	10. ______
11.	Do expert and identity power come from a manager's position in the company?	yes no	11. ______
12.	Are human relations skills considered to be as important to the success of a business as the ability to make decisions or operate a complicated piece of equipment?	yes no	12. ______
13.	Should managers treat all employees in the same way?	yes no	13. ______
14.	Should managers attempt to match job tasks with the needs and interests of employees?	yes no	14. ______
15.	Have studies found that, in general, all employees will not complete work well unless they are closely managed?	yes no	15. ______
16.	Is an autocratic style of leadership most effective when efficiency is important?	yes no	16. ______
17.	Will managers who use a democratic style of leadership generally take more time to make a decision than if another style is used?	yes no	17. ______
18.	Will the open style of leadership work best with inexperienced employees?	yes no	18. ______
19.	Do most management training programs prepare managers to deal with difficult personal problems of their employees?	yes no	19. ______
20.	Do managers who involve employees in developing rules and procedures usually find greater support for those rules and fewer problems when penalties need to be applied for rules violations?	yes no	20. ______

Part B—*Directions:* For each of the following statements, select the word, or group of words, that best completes the statement. In the Answers column, write the letter corresponding to the answer selected.

		Answers	For Scoring
1.	The ability to influence individuals and groups to achieve organizational goals is (a) management, (b) human relations, (c) leadership, (d) none of the responses.	_______	1. _______
2.	When leaders have ambition and persistence in reaching goals, they are demonstrating (a) cooperation, (b) initiative, (c) objectivity, (d) stability.	_______	2. _______
3.	The ability to control behavior in an organization is known as (a) power, (b) leadership, (c) rewards, (d) cooperation.	_______	3. _______
4.	Expert power is given to people (a) who hold management positions in an organization, (b) who are considered the most knowledgeable, (c) with whom others identify, (d) all of the responses.	_______	4. _______
5.	The two types of power given to managers by their employees are (a) position and reward, (b) autocratic and democratic, (c) human relations and leadership, (d) expert and identity.	_______	5. _______
6.	Which of the following is NOT an important human relations skill needed by managers? (a) self-understanding, (b) communication, (c) developing job satisfaction, (d) judgment.	_______	6. _______
7.	Managers who are able to get people to work well together to accomplish the goals of the organization are using which human relations skill? (a) initiative, (b) team-building, (c) power, (d) authority.	_______	7. _______
8.	Managers who believe employees dislike work are more likely to (a) give employees more responsibility, (b) be effective leaders, (c) use closer supervision and control, (d) have little concern for the quality of employees' work.	_______	8. _______
9.	Which of the following is a leadership characteristic that employees prefer in their managers? (a) encourages employee participation and questions, (b) informs employees of information only when they need to know, (c) implements few changes, (d) keeps employee training to a minimum.	_______	9. _______
10.	If a business does not have a formal set of work rules, (a) a union will likely be organized, (b) employees will be highly motivated, (c) managers will receive greater respect from employees, (d) each manager should develop his or her own set of procedures and policies.	_______	10. _______

Part C—*Directions:* In the Answers column, write the letter of the word or expression in Column I that most closely matches each statement in Column II.

Column I	Column II	Answers	For Scoring
A. Open leader	1. Encourages workers to share in making decisions about work-related problems.	_______	1. _______
B. Democratic leader	2. The ability of an employee's boss to give directions and expect the employee to complete the work.	_______	2. _______
C. Autocratic leader			
D. Leadership	3. The ability to influence individuals and groups to achieve organizational goals.	_______	3. _______
E. Position power	4. Gives direct, clear, and precise orders with detailed instructions.	_______	4. _______
	5. Gives little or no direction to others.	_______	5. _______

Directions: Study each controversial issue carefully. Follow the advice of your teacher before listing in the columns provided reasons why people might answer Yes or No. Your teacher may want you to work with a classmate, talk with others in your community to gather information, or use the library or Internet to gather facts.

12-1. Do all managers in an organization need effective leadership skills in order for the organization to be successful?

Reasons for "Yes"	Reasons for "No"

12-2. Do you believe some people are "natural leaders"? That is, they do not need leadership training, while other people will never be leaders no matter how much training they receive.

Reasons for "Yes"	Reasons for "No"

PROBLEMS

12-A. Studies of leaders have found that most effective leaders share common personal characteristics. It is possible to determine if you have those characteristics and to develop a personal plan to improve those characteristics that are not as strong as you would like. You can evaluate your leadership characteristics by answering the following questions. Questions that you answer "always" or "usually" indicate areas where you already have developed leadership skills. The areas where you answer "sometimes" or "never" indicate traits you will need to improve if you are to become a more effective leader.

	Always	Usually	Sometimes	Never
1. Do you perform above average in your classes in school?	___	___	___	___
2. Do you enjoy making decisions?	___	___	___	___
3. Do your parents and friends trust your judgment?	___	___	___	___
4. Are you able to put your personal feelings aside when you have to make important decisions?	___	___	___	___
5. Do you take time to gather information before you draw conclusions?	___	___	___	___
6. Do you look forward to starting new tasks?	___	___	___	___
7. When you face a challenge, do you keep working until you find a solution?	___	___	___	___
8. Can people depend on you to do what you say you will do?	___	___	___	___
9. Are you involved in team sports and group activities?	___	___	___	___
10. Do you prefer working with others rather than alone?	___	___	___	___
11. Are you upset when you see others being dishonest?	___	___	___	___
12. Are you willing to say no to your friends when they ask you to do things you disagree with?	___	___	___	___
13. Do you prefer to find new ways to do routine activities rather than continuing to do them the same way?	___	___	___	___
14. When you have to do something you have never done before, do you believe you will be successful?	___	___	___	___
15. When you are in a difficult situation, do you remain calm?	___	___	___	___
16. Do you listen to the concerns and problems of your friends more often than you tell them about yourself?	___	___	___	___
17. When working in a group, do you encourage everyone to participate and contribute?	___	___	___	___
18. Do you have friends who have different backgrounds and interests than you?	___	___	___	___
19. Do you respect the feelings and beliefs of others, even if you do not agree with them?	___	___	___	___
20. When you are in situations where you don't know other people, do you take the initiative to get to know them?	___	___	___	___

12-B. For each of the following items, indicate whether the manager was using an autocratic, democratic, or open style of leadership by placing a check mark in the appropriate column.

	Autocratic	Democratic	Open
1. Each worker is allowed to decide how his or her job will be done.	___	___	___
2. An employee meeting is held each week to discuss problems.	___	___	___
3. The manager lets employees cooperatively decide when breaks should be scheduled.	___	___	___

	Autocratic	Democratic	Open
4. There are no work rules for the department.	____	____	____
5. Before changing an evaluation system, the manager explained to the employees why it was being changed.	____	____	____
6. The manager tells each new employee how the job should be done.	____	____	____
7. When two employees had an argument, the manager told them how to solve their problem.	____	____	____
8. The store owner lets department managers order any merchandise they choose.	____	____	____
9. The store owner sets all department budgets.	____	____	____
10. The manager conducts an employee brainstorming session to develop a new advertising slogan.	____	____	____

12-C. The marketing manager for a manufacturing firm has been given the task to select new automobiles for ten of the company's salespeople. The company has lease agreements with dealers representing three brands of automobiles. The manager knows that each salesperson has personal preferences about the brand, model, and options in an automobile. The company also will save money if all of the cars are leased from the same dealer and even more money if all cars are the same model with the same options.

For each of the three leadership styles, describe how the manager would make the decision on the automobiles to purchase. Then list one advantage and one disadvantage of the use of that leadership style in this situation.

Autocratic Style: ____

____

Advantage: ____

Disadvantage: ____

Democratic Style: ____

____

Advantage: ____

Disadvantage: ____

Open Style: ____

____

Advantage: ____

Disadvantage: ____

12-D. A recent survey of 150 employees with five or more years of experience asked the employees to identify the type of leadership style they preferred from their supervisors. The following results were obtained:

Autocratic—38 employees; Democratic—66 employees; Open—22 employees; a Combination of styles—24 employees.

1. In the space below, construct a pie chart showing the percentage of employees preferring each type of leadership style.

Employees' Preferred Leadership Styles

2. In the space below, identify the leadership style you would prefer from a supervisor and the reasons for your preference. ____

____

____

____

3. Why do you believe employees prefer very different leadership styles? How can a manager respond when his or her employees work best under different leadership styles? ___________________________

____

____

____

12-E. Work rules are developed to create and maintain an effective work environment and to help employees work efficiently. In the space below, write two work rules for you and the other students in your class. Also write a sentence that describes why you believe the rule would result in an effective work atmosphere in the class and would help students work more efficiently. After you finish writing your statements, the other students in the class will vote on each statement. The vote will determine whether they agree that each of your rules would help to maintain an effective and efficient working atmosphere.

Work Rule #1: ____

____

____

Justification: ____

____

____

Student Vote: Agree _______ Disagree _______

Work Rule #2: ____

____

____

Justification: ____

____

____

Student Vote: Agree _______ Disagree _______

SMALL GROUP ACTIVITIES

Group Activity 1

With instructions from your teacher, divide into small groups of four or five students. Review the list of leadership characteristics on page 300 of your text. Then, as a group, choose five people, either living or dead, who exhibited an excellent leadership style and give the reasons for your choice. Using an overhead transparency, chart paper and markers, or a computer with projection capabilities, prepare your answers for presentation to the class.

Group Activity 2

This group activity will take more than one class period and involves an interview with a businessperson during non-school time.

With instructions from your teacher, divide into small groups of four or five students. With your group, brainstorm a list of questions to ask a businessperson about management styles, leadership styles, employee management techniques, and employee work groups. Individually or in pairs, either locate a businessperson on your own or your teacher will give you a person to contact. Make an appointment and interview this person, using your questions as a basis for the interview. When you have completed the interviews, meet with your group and share your information. Your teacher might ask you to consolidate your information and prepare it in either written form or for presentation to the class.

<table>
<tr><td rowspan="2">Chapter 13

Planning and Organizing</td><td rowspan="2">Name _______________

Date _______________</td><td colspan="5">Scoring Record</td></tr>
<tr><td></td><td>Part A</td><td>Part B</td><td>Part C</td><td>Total</td></tr>
<tr><td>Perfect score</td><td>20</td><td>10</td><td>5</td><td>35</td></tr>
<tr><td>My score</td><td></td><td></td><td></td><td></td></tr>
</table>

Study Guide

Part A—*Directions:* Indicate your answer to each of the following questions by circling either yes or no in the Answers column.

		Answers	For Scoring
1.	Should a business plan include a detailed financial analysis showing the potential profitability of the firm?	yes no	1. _______
2.	Are all business managers involved in planning in some way?	yes no	2. _______
3.	Do plans serve as guides for decision making?	yes no	3. _______
4.	Does planning usually result in more communication and coordination problems in the business?	yes no	4. _______
5.	Is long-term planning that provides broad goals and directions for the entire business known as operational planning?	yes no	5. _______
6.	Is the development of a business plan an example of strategic planning?	yes no	6. _______
7.	Is external analysis the first step in strategic planning?	yes no	7. _______
8.	Are supervisors usually responsible for strategic planning?	yes no	8. _______
9.	Does operational planning include decisions about the resources that will be needed to get the work done in a specific area of the business?	yes no	9. _______
10.	Are goals statements of the results that a business expects to achieve?	yes no	10. _______
11.	Is it better for goals to be general rather than specific?	yes no	11. _______
12.	Does a schedule include both the identification of tasks to be completed and the time needed to complete each task?	yes no	12. _______
13.	Is a schedule a measure against which something is judged?	yes no	13. _______
14.	Is a policy more specific than a procedure?	yes no	14. _______
15.	Does an organizational chart explain the reporting relationships among the organization's personnel?	yes no	15. _______
16.	As a business grows, do the number of major divisions in the organization usually decrease?	yes no	16. _______
17.	Is authority the obligation to do an assigned task?	yes no	17. _______
18.	In an effective organization, do most employees have more than one supervisor from whom they receive job assignments?	yes no	18. _______
19.	In general, is the span of control larger at the lower levels of an organization than at the higher levels?	yes no	19. _______
20.	Is the most flexible type of organizational structure the matrix organization?	yes no	20. _______

—*Directions:* For each of the following statements, select the word, or group of words, that best completes the statement. In the Answers column, write the letter corresponding to the answer selected.

	Answers	For Scoring

1. Which of the following would NOT be a part of strategic planning? (a) mission statement, (b) goals, (c) strategies, (d) department work assignments. .... ______ 1. ______

2. To be effective, goals should be (a) general rather than specific, (b) slightly higher than can be realistically achieved, (c) independent from all other goals, (d) meaningful. .... ______ 2. ______

3. One type of financial planning tool is a (a) goal, (b) budget, (c) standard, (d) schedule. .... ______ 3. ______

4. Guidelines used in making decisions regarding specific recurring situations are known as (a) policies, (b) procedures, (c) standards, (d) goals. .... ______ 4. ______

5. The management function responsible for arranging resources and relationships between departments and employees and defining the responsibility each has for accomplishing the job is (a) planning, (b) organizing, (c) implementing, (d) controlling. .... ______ 5. ______

6. A visual device that shows the structure of an organization and the relationships among workers and divisions of work is (a) a schedule, (b) a strategic plan, (c) an organization chart, (d) an operational plan. .... ______ 6. ______

7. Companies that have started using work teams and that involve employees in planning and decision making have found that span of control (a) must be decreased, (b) can be increased, (c) is no longer needed, (d) is not affected. .... ______ 7. ______

8. The organization in which all authority and responsibility can be traced directly from the top executive to the lowest employee level in an organization is the (a) line organization, (b) line-and-staff organization, (c) matrix organization, (d) decentralized organization. .... ______ 8. ______

9. Specialists are available to give advice and assistance to managers in the (a) line organization, (b) line-and-staff organization, (c) matrix organization, (d) decentralized organization. .... ______ 9. ______

10. A few top managers do all major planning and decision making in a (a) line organization, (b) line-and-staff organization, (c) centralized organization, (d) decentralized organization. .... ______ 10. ______

Part C—*Directions:* Complete each sentence by filling in the missing word or words.

	For Scoring

1. ________________ to make decisions about work assignments is delegated from the __________ of the organization to the ____________ of the organization. .... 1. ______

2. Accountability is the obligation to accept responsibility for the ____________ of assigned tasks, including the ____________, ____________, and completion time. .... 2. ______

3. ____________ ____ ____________________ requires that no employee have more than one supervisor at a time. .... 3. ______

4. Span of control refers to the ____________ of employees who are directly ____________________ by one person. .... 4. ______

5. A project or matrix organization combines workers into temporary ________ ________ to complete a specific project, and a project ____________________ has the authority and responsibility for the project. .... 5. ______

Directions: Study each controversial issue carefully. Follow the advice of your teacher before listing in the columns provided reasons why people might answer Yes or No. Your teacher may want you to work with a classmate, talk with others in your community to gather information, or use the library or Internet to gather facts.

13-1. Do you believe that long-range plans should be developed in businesses where economic conditions and competition are changing very rapidly?

Reasons for "Yes"	Reasons for "No"

13-2. Do you believe most businesses would be more successful if they used a project or matrix organizational structure rather than a line or a line-and-staff organizational structure?

Reasons for "Yes"	Reasons for "No"

PROBLEMS

13-A. Classify each of the following activities of a business as either strategic planning or operational planning by placing a check mark in the appropriate column.

	Business Activity	Strategic Planning	Operational Planning
1.	A new warehouse will be built to serve the markets in the northeast section of the country.	_____	_____
2.	The advertising budget for the next three months will be increased by 2 percent to attract more customers into the store.	_____	_____
3.	The Cleveland facility will schedule a one-week shutdown in December to allow equipment repairs.	_____	_____
4.	An export office in Rome will be used to develop plans for European market development.	_____	_____
5.	A small business owner decides to expand into other states by selling franchises.	_____	_____
6.	Employees will be asked to work three hours of overtime each week to meet the increased summer demand.	_____	_____

13-B. Business goals must be specific and meaningful in order to be useful to managers and employers. Each of the following statements is very general, but can be used as a basis for developing a goal for the business. Rewrite each statement to make it an effective goal.

1. The men's shoe department needs an increased sales volume.

____

____

2. Too many radios produced on the third shift are defective and have to be discarded.

____

____

3. We've seen an increase in employee turnover since January.

____

____

4. We would like to increase the amount each customer spends when he or she shops in our Westgate store.

____

____

13-C. A well-developed procedure for completing a task can be an effective tool to help a new employee learn a job. However, it is not easy to develop a procedure that includes every necessary step. In the space below, write the steps of the procedure someone should follow to accurately write a check. To determine if the procedure works, have another student follow the steps exactly to fill out the blank check shown below. When the student is finished, evaluate the work to see if it has been done correctly.

____

____

____

____

____

____

N.E. Name
33 Your Street
Anytown, U.S. 11223

\# ________

____________ 20 ______ 72–7073/2739

PAY TO THE
ORDER OF ______________________________ $ ____________

______________________________ DOLLARS

FOR CLASSROOM USE ONLY

THE FIRST NATIONAL BANK
ANYTOWN, U.S. 11223

MEMO ______________________

|: 27390734 |:

13-D. Your school requires all students to complete 100 hours of community service in order to be eligible for graduation. As the president of a high school club, you have decided to begin a program after school to tutor reading and math at an area middle school to help your club members earn the necessary volunteer hours. You and the other club officers want to establish policies regarding this program before you take your suggestion to the middle school principal for approval. Write at least five policies regarding this new tutoring program. (*Suggestions: attendance, dress, conduct, transportation, hours, academic performance, recommendations.*)

____

____

____

____

____

____

13-E. The most common type of organization in a large business is line-and-staff. In such an organization, the staff person investigates problems and consults with and advises line administrators. The line administrators determine policies and procedures and give orders for carrying out their decisions.

The chart below describes ten positions within a company, whether they are line or staff positions, and their responsibilities. After reviewing the information, draw a line-and-staff organizational chart on the next page, showing the relationships between the ten positions.

	Position	Line or Staff	Responsibilities
1.	President	line	Directs the company
2.	Vice president of manufacturing	line	Reports to president
3.	Company attorney	staff	Reports to the president and advises the vice presidents of manufacturing and sales
4.	Chemist who tests raw materials purchased	staff	Reports to the vice president of manufacturing and advises the manufacturing and production managers
5.	District sales manager	line	Reports to vice president of sales
6.	Advertising specialist	staff	Reports to the vice president of sales and works with sales management
7.	Superintendent of manufacturing	line	Reports to vice president of manufacturing
8.	Supervisor of production	line	Reports to superintendent of manufacturing
9.	Vice president of sales	line	Reports to president
10.	Personnel manager	staff	Reports to the president and works with the vice presidents of manufacturing and sales

Line-and-Staff Organizational Chart

SMALL GROUP ACTIVITIES

You are a member of the Leadership Club, which has decided to hold a pre-prom fashion show during your school's lunch periods. Your club will collaborate with three major department stores in a nearby mall and two tuxedo rental stores. In addition, area florists and restaurants are interested in setting up booths during the same lunch periods to advertise their merchandise and services.

Group Activity 1

With instructions from your teacher, divide into groups of four or five students. In your group, develop a strategic plan for the fashion show, including goals and operational plans showing a timeline and identifying the people responsible for each activity.

Group Activity 2

Create an organizational chart for the pre-prom fashion show. You can choose a line, line-and-staff, matrix, or work-team structure to accomplish your goals. Develop a written justification for your choice of organization structure.

<table>
<tr><td rowspan="3">Chapter 14

Implementing and Controlling</td><td rowspan="3">Name ________________

Date ________________</td><td colspan="5" align="center">Scoring Record</td></tr>
<tr><td></td><td>Part A</td><td>Part B</td><td>Part C</td><td>Total</td></tr>
<tr><td>Perfect score</td><td>20</td><td>10</td><td>5</td><td>35</td></tr>
<tr><td colspan="2">My score</td><td></td><td></td><td></td><td></td></tr>
</table>

Study Guide

Part A—*Directions:* Indicate your answer to each of the following questions by circling either yes or no in the Answers column.

		Answers	For Scoring
1.	Are plans likely to be ineffective if they are not implemented well?	yes no	1. _______
2.	Does implementing involve guiding employee work toward achieving the company's goals?	yes no	2. _______
3.	Is any reward motivating?	yes no	3. _______
4.	Is employee motivation influenced by both internal and external factors?	yes no	4. _______
5.	Is there a positive relationship between an employee's need satisfaction and motivation?	yes no	5. _______
6.	Will each member of a work team usually be working to achieve different goals?	yes no	6. _______
7.	Is process improvement the efforts to increase the effectiveness and efficiency of specific business operations?	yes no	7. _______
8.	Will a group of employees usually have about the same level of motivation?	yes no	8. _______
9.	Is self-actualization the lowest level on Maslow's hierarchy of needs?	yes no	9. _______
10.	Is McClelland's achievement motivation theory based on a belief that people are influenced most strongly by a need for power, affiliation, or achievement?	yes no	10. _______
11.	Do the hygiene factors identified by Fredrick Herzberg motivate employees?	yes no	11. _______
12.	In Herzberg's theory of motivation, do the same factors provide both satisfaction and dissatisfaction for people?	yes no	12. _______
13.	Do people usually accept change easily?	yes no	13. _______
14.	Is it usually best for managers to say nothing to employees about possible changes until a final decision has been made?	yes no	14. _______
15.	To make changes effectively, should managers provide information and training to employees?	yes no	15. _______
16.	Does the controlling process include measuring performance?	yes no	16. _______
17.	Would the minimum number of units to be produced in a day be an example of a quantity standard?	yes no	17. _______
18.	Is increasing sales the only way a business can increase its profits?	yes no	18. _______
19.	Can a variance be positive or negative?	yes no	19. _______
20.	Should managers ever change the standard if a business is not meeting the standard that was set?	yes no	20. _______

	Answers	For Scoring

1. The set of factors that influence an individual's actions toward accomplishing a goal is (a) management, (b) effective communication, (c) control, (d) motivation. .... ______ 1. ______

2. A group of individuals who cooperate to achieve a common goal is (a) a supervisory group, (b) an employee group, (c) a work team, (d) a grapevine. .... ______ 2. ______

3. The motivation theory based on a progression through five categories of need was developed by (a) Herzberg, (b) Maslow, (c) McClelland, (d) Taylor. .... ______ 3. ______

4. According to McClelland, people who want to influence and control others have (a) an achievement need, (b) an affiliation need, (c) a power need, (d) all of the responses. .... ______ 4. ______

5. Motivators are to hygiene factors as (a) Herzberg is to Maslow, (b) basic needs are to affiliation needs, (c) recognition is to achievement, (d) recognition is to working conditions. .... ______ 5. ______

6. Which of the following is an important step in effective change? (a) Move rapidly to implement the change. (b) Delay communications about the change until decisions have been made. (c) Involve the people affected in making decisions about the change. (d) Avoid offering too much support as people adjust to the change. .... ______ 6. ______

7. Which of the following is NOT a part of the controlling process? (a) establishing standards, (b) motivating employees, (c) measuring and comparing performance, (d) taking corrective action. .... ______ 7. ______

8. The value of a variance report to a manager is that (a) standards not being met are identified, (b) the amount of difference between a standard and actual performance can be determined, (c) it helps managers identify problems quickly, (d) all of the responses. .... ______ 8. ______

9. A just-in-time control system would be most useful for managing (a) inventory, (b) credit, (c) theft, (d) none of the responses. .... ______ 9. ______

10. On average, the percentage of total sales lost each year by retailers to theft from customers and employees is (a) almost nothing, (b) 1-2%, (c) 6%, (d) 15%. ... ______ 10. ______

Column I	Column II	Answers	For Scoring
A. Implementing	1. Determining if goals are being met and the actions needed if they are not.	______	1. ______
B. Controlling			
C. Herzberg	2. Two-factor theory of motivation.	______	2. ______
D. McClelland	3. People's behavior is most strongly influenced by one of three needs: power, affiliation, or achievement.	______	3. ______
E. Maslow			
	4. Carrying out plans and helping employees to work effectively.	______	4. ______
	5. People are motivated by five levels of needs, beginning with physiological needs.	______	5. ______

Directions: Study each controversial issue carefully. Follow the advice of your teacher before listing in the columns provided reasons why people might answer Yes or No. Your teacher may want you to work with a classmate, talk with others in your community to gather information, or use the library or Internet to gather facts.

14-1. Even if a business is operating effectively and profitably, should the company's managers be planning for and implementing changes?

Reasons for "Yes"	Reasons for "No"

14-2. Do you agree with Herzberg's theory of motivation that the absence of good pay, benefits, and working conditions can dissatisfy employees, but the presence of these factors cannot satisfy them?

Reasons for "Yes"	Reasons for "No"

PROBLEMS

14-A. Effective teams can make the difference between success and failure in a business, an athletic event, a class project, a club, or other group. Using your own experience, identify one team or work group you have been a part of that you considered to be effective and one that you considered to be ineffective. Complete the following chart describing the characteristics of the team. Then answer the questions that follow the chart.

	Effective Team	Ineffective Team
Characteristics		
Description of the team		
Purpose of the team		
Did team members support the team's purpose?		
Did each member understand his/her responsibilities?		
Were all members committed to the group?		
Were the activities to be completed clear?		
Did members have the needed skills for success?		
Did team members communicate effectively?		
Did the team members work to solve problems?		

1. Did the characteristics of the team appear to affect whether the group was successful or not?

   ____

2. Which of the characteristics seemed to be most important to the group success?

   ____

3. Which of the characteristics seemed to contribute to group problems?

   ____

4. If you were helping to organize a new group or team, what would you do to try to make it more effective in achieving its goals? ____

14-B. Each of the following statements describes a principle of motivation. Read each statement and then select the theory that includes the principle by placing a check mark in the appropriate column.

Principle of Motivation	Maslow	Herzberg	McClelland
1. People must satisfy their security needs before social needs motivate their behavior.	____	____	____
2. The highest level of need is self-actualization.	____	____	____
3. Managers working with individuals with a high achievement need should provide opportunities for them to make decisions and control their own work.	____	____	____
4. Two distinct factors contribute to employee satisfaction or dissatisfaction.	____	____	____
5. A person with a power need wants to control and influence people.	____	____	____
6. Until physiological needs are satisfied, people will be concerned about little else.	____	____	____
7. Pay increases will prevent employees from being dissatisfied but will not motivate them to better performance.	____	____	____
8. One group of workers will take personal responsibility for their work, while another group will be more concerned about getting along.	____	____	____
9. Great motivators are challenging work, recognition, and personal development.	____	____	____

14-C. Hasme Manufacturing, Inc., produces small components for computer systems. Quality control is very important, so each product is carefully tested when it is completed. If the product does not meet quality standards, it is rejected and returned for improvement. Management is also concerned that quantity standards are maintained so that orders are filled on schedule.

Jan Rankin, vice president of manufacturing, has collected information on production levels for four weeks. The production for each day of the week was totaled during the four-week period. The chart below shows the total number of items produced and the total number rejected for each day of the week for four weeks.

	Monday	Tuesday	Wednesday	Thursday	Friday
Total Parts Produced	1,480	1,500	1,520	1,550	1,460
Total Parts Rejected	172	140	125	111	169

1. On which day of the week were the most acceptable components produced? _______________________

2. On which day were the fewest acceptable components produced? _______________________

3. How many parts were produced on an average workday at the Hasme Company? _______________________

4. How many parts were rejected on an average workday? _______________________

5. Using the information in the chart above, construct a bar graph on the form on the next page. The graph should show the percentage of component parts rejected for each day of the week.

14-D. The following chart shows the projected and actual sales for several models of televisions in an appliance store. Complete the chart by calculating the amount the actual sales varied from the budgeted amounts. Next, calculate the percentage of variance from projected sales for each item. Finally, determine the total variance between projected and actual sales and the percentage of variance between planned and actual sales.

Model No.	Projected Sales	Actual Sales	Variance	Percentage Variance
XTL-13	$ 11,325	$ 13,250	_______	_______
ZT-13	11,985	9,995	_______	_______
XTL-15	12,840	10,620	_______	_______
ZT-15	13,825	15,385	_______	_______
MG-19	11,540	11,540	_______	_______
RC-19	12,650	9,985	_______	_______
MG-25	19,020	21,855	_______	_______
RC-25	20,330	20,960	_______	_______
MB-45	13,790	15,015	_______	_______
Totals	_______	_______	_______	_______

14-E. A company that manufactures bicycles received an order from a national sporting-goods chain. The order was for 150 bicycles that must be manufactured in 30 days. After 10 days, 45 bicycles had been produced. The manager scheduled the employees to work overtime for two Saturdays. At the end of 20 days, 110 bicycles were completed.

1. Write a standard for daily bicycle production that the company must meet in order to complete the order in the required 30 days. ____

2. At the end of the first 10 days, what was the total variance from the number of bicycles that should have been completed? ____

3. What was the variance from the daily standard at the end of the first ten days? _______________________
____
____

4. What was the corrective action taken by the manager? ____
____

5. At the end of 20 days, what was the total variance from the number of bicycles that should have been completed? ____
____

6. Write a standard for the daily production of bicycles for the last 10 days in order to complete the contract on schedule. ____
____

7. What should the manager do if the production level exceeds the standard during the first two of the remaining production days? ____
____
____
____

SMALL GROUP ACTIVITIES

Group Activity 1

With instructions from your teacher, divide into groups of four or five students. In your group, read the following scenario and answer the questions.

As the owner/manager of a medium-sized wholesale florist shop, you have many dedicated employees who have been with your company for years. Your shop has been in business since the 1960s, and the records of your operations—including purchasing, accounting, shipping, and receiving—are maintained manually. You have contracted with a computer software company to develop a computerized system for your entire operation. The system is now ready to be implemented. You are sure that many of your employees will resist the change.

Using what you have learned about managing change, make recommendations to the owner/manager regarding the change to the new computerized system.

Group Activity 2

With instructions from your teacher, divide into groups of four or five students. In your group, read the following scenario.

Raoul Estevez, the manager of The Corner Eatery, a medium-sized family restaurant, has been recently experiencing declining sales and customer complaints about poor service. In addition, his wait staff has been complaining about reduced tips, and several have indicated they are considering looking for new jobs at other restaurants. Mr. Estevez is considering raising prices to counteract the declining sales but does not know what to do about the poor-service complaints. In the past, his management style was to publicly reprimand employees to motivate them when he saw a performance problem.

Your group represents a management consulting firm. Mr. Estevez has decided to ask your firm to make recommendations to correct the problems in his restaurant. Drawing on information from the chapter regarding implementing and controlling, policy change, motivating employees, and setting standards, develop a plan for Mr. Estevez to correct the problems he is experiencing in his restaurant.

<table>
<tr><td rowspan="2">Chapter 15

Financial Records in a Business</td><td rowspan="2">Name _______________

Date _______________</td><td colspan="4" align="center">Scoring Record</td></tr>
<tr><td></td><td align="center">Part A</td><td align="center">Part B</td><td align="center">Total</td></tr>
<tr><td></td><td></td><td>Perfect score</td><td align="center">20</td><td align="center">15</td><td align="center">35</td></tr>
<tr><td></td><td></td><td>My score</td><td></td><td></td><td></td></tr>
</table>

Study Guide

Part A—*Directions:* Indicate your answer to each of the following questions by circling either yes or no in the Answers column.

		Answers	For Scoring
1.	Are accounting records summaries of a business's financial activities?	yes no	1. _______
2.	Can small firms get most of the financial information they need from their cash register tapes?	yes no	2. _______
3.	Can one software program handle deposits, checkbook payments, purchase orders, and payroll?	yes no	3. _______
4.	Do most large businesses put one person in charge of all financial records?	yes no	4. _______
5.	Is outsourcing usually more expensive than hiring someone into the business who has the needed expertise?	yes no	5. _______
6.	Do data processing centers prepare bills for other businesses?	yes no	6. _______
7.	Can a point-of-sale terminal calculate when a store needs to reorder merchandise?	yes no	7. _______
8.	Is a petty cash fund used for small emergency payments?	yes no	8. _______
9.	If the checkbook balance and the bank statement balance do not agree, is it necessary to determine the reason for the difference?	yes no	9. _______
10.	Do accounts receivable records show the money that businesses owe and payments they make to purchase supplies and merchandise on credit?	yes no	10. _______
11.	Are tools and computers used in a business's operations examples of assets?	yes no	11. _______
12.	Are fixed assets known as plant assets that last a short time?	yes no	12. _______
13.	Is obsolescence the increase in value of an asset as it appreciates over time?	yes no	13. _______
14.	Is asset book value calculated by subtracting depreciation from the original cost of the asset?	yes no	14. _______
15.	Does the federal income tax law require every business to keep satisfactory records of income and expenses?	yes no	15. _______
16.	Is an employer required to keep complete payroll records that show the hours worked, regular wages paid, overtime wages, and all types of deductions from wages for each employee?	yes no	16. _______
17.	Should critical records such as leases and contracts be placed in safe deposit boxes?	yes no	17. _______
18.	Do companies protect records by using off-site computers for storage?	yes no	18. _______
19.	Are budgets based on actual costs rather than on projections?	yes no	19. _______
20.	Is it likely that sales will always be in direct proportion to the amount spent on advertising?	yes no	20. _______

	Answers	For Scoring

1. Which statement is *false* about accounting records? (a) Accounting records should not identify expenses owed to others. (b) Accounting records should identify the source of receipts and the kinds of assets. (c) Accounting records should identify expenses owed to others as well as the amounts paid to others. (d) Accounting records should identify the value of assets in addition to the kinds of assets. .... _______ 1._______

2. Data processing service centers can (a) collect data, (b) decide on the right inventory size, (c) prepare payroll records and sign checks, (d) prepare bills, track inventory, and prepare records and checks. .... _______ 2._______

3. Scanners electronically read product codes stamped on merchandise when using (a) petty cash vouchers, (b) audit strips, (c) point-of-sale terminals, (d) daily balance forms. .... _______ 3._______

4. When a cash register is used and there is no special petty cash fund, the usual practice is to (a) take cash from the register and take a petty cash voucher from the fund, (b) take cash from the register and replace it with a petty cash voucher, (c) write an IOU note rather than take cash from the register, (d) write a check and take cash from the register. .... _______ 4._______

5. What type of record shows what each customer owes and pays? (a) accounts receivable record, (b) accounts payable record, (c) charge ticket record, (d) daily balance record. .... _______ 5._______

6. What type of record shows money owed and payments made by a business? (a) accounts receivable, (b) accounts payable, (c) charge ticket record, (d) daily record. _______ 6._______

7. Because of depreciation, (a) the company's equipment will be worth more next year than it is today, (b) the company's equipment will be worth less next year than it is today, (c) the company must buy more equipment than it needs, (d) the company must buy less equipment than it needs. .... _______ 7._______

8. Which fixed asset is NOT likely to lose its value over time? (a) land, (b) equipment, (c) buildings, (d) a newly purchased delivery van. .... _______ 8._______

9. Which statement is *false* about fixed assets? (a) Fixed assets last a long time. (b) Fixed assets tend to lose their value over time. (c) Fixed assets are recorded on the books at the time they are sold. (d) Fixed assets become part of the property owned by the business. .... _______ 9._______

10. Say that a DVD becomes inadequate because a better type of DVD comes on the market. What term describes this example? (a) asset book value, (b) depreciation, (c) replacement value, (d) obsolescence. .... _______ 10._______

11. What type of information is NOT provided in a detailed special record for fixed assets? (a) asset description, (b) asset cost, (c) depreciation expense, (d) obsolescence value. .... _______ 11._______

12. A study conducted by the U.S. Department of Commerce revealed that stores that are most successful do all of the following *except* (a) take inventory once a year, (b) have their accounts audited regularly by an experienced accountant, (c) operate under a financial budget, (d) keep recommended accounting records. . _______ 12._______

13. What is the time period that a budget usually covers? (a) one year, (b) three years, (c) five years, (d) ten years. .... _______ 13._______

14. A sales budget is (a) a report of the actual sales for the last year, (b) a report of stock on hand that is ready to be sold, (c) an estimate of the sales for the next month or year, (d) a report of the actual sales of each salesperson. .... _______ 14._______

15. A plan showing projected sales, costs, expenses and profits for a future period is (a) a purchasing budget, (b) an income statement budget, (c) a sales budget, (d) an inventory budget. .... _______ 15._______

Directions: Study each controversial issue carefully. Follow the advice of your teacher before listing in the columns provided reasons why people might answer Yes or No. Your teacher may want you to work with a classmate, talk with others in your community to gather information, or use the library or Internet to gather facts.

15-1. Because small cash overages and shortages are common when cashiers check their cash drawers at the end of the day, should those amounting to less than a dollar be ignored?

Reasons for "Yes"	Reasons for "No"

15-2. Should budgets be given limited attention in business because they take much valuable time to prepare, are rarely accurate, and are seldom followed carefully?

Reasons for "Yes"	Reasons for "No"

PROBLEMS

15-A. Visitors from another country received the cash register receipt shown below after making a purchase in your store. They were confused about what they saw and came to you. As store manager, answer the questions that follow:

1. What is REG #2 MELISSA?

   ____

   ____

2. What does 19:43 mean?

   ____

   ____

   ____

3. What is 1@135271?

   ____

   ____

   ____

4. What is CASH Tendered?

   ____

   ____

   ____

5. What is the tax rate?

   ____

   ____

   ____

```
      STRAUSS
     Store # 45
     08/10/20--
   REG# 2  MELISSA
        19:43
-------------------
TR # 16224
SALE

1@135271        1.06
Subtotal  =     1.06
Tax       =     0.07
Total     =     1.13

CASH
Tendered  =     2.03
Change    =     0.90

-------------------
   THANK YOU
```

15-B. London's Market is a small grocery store where you are employed. For each business practice, indicate by a check mark in the columns at the right whether they are good or bad practices for the safe handling of cash.

	Good	Bad
1. The daily change fund is placed in each cash register at the end of each day.	____	____
2. Clerks use change from the cash registers to buy soft drinks from the vending machine.	____	____
3. Deposits are made daily in a nearby bank within an hour after the clerks check their cash drawers.	____	____
4. The payroll clerk pays cashiers weekly by check but the bookkeeper immediately cashes their checks for them.	____	____
5. The bookkeeper also serves as a cashier during busy hours.	____	____

15-C. Using the information below, complete the purchase order form provided for Crafts, Inc. You are to order the following items from Xerbic Supplies, 4582 N. Cromwell Place, Seattle, Washington, 38132, to be shipped by truck to your address as soon as possible under the usual conditions (F.O.B. Destination, N/30):

5	#87-C-42 Binders	$19.95 each
15	#84-A-73 Memo pad holders	$7.95 each
8	#86-C-10 Posting trays	$26.95 each
1	#83-B-18 Checkwriter	$149.50 each

CRAFTS Inc.
29 Lambert St.
Seattle, WA 38129
Ph. 206-555-8372

PURCHASE ORDER

No.   3258

Show the Purchase Order Number on all correspondence, invoices, shipping papers, and packages.

TO

DATE

SHIP TO

REQUISITIONED BY	WHEN SHIP	SHIP VIA	F.O.B. POINT	TERMS

QTY. ORDERED	QTY. RECEIVED	STOCK NO./DESCRIPTION	UNIT PRICE	TOTAL

1. Please send ___ copies of your invoice.
2. Order is to be entered in accordance with prices, delivery, and specifications shown above.
3. Notify us immediately if you are unable to ship as specified.

Authorized By: ___________________________________

15-D. Businesses must maintain many different records. Below are listed some of those records and the average time such records are kept by many firms. Study the information and answer the following questions:

Years Retained

Business Record	0	2	4	6	8	10	Permanently
Daily time reports							
Accounts receivable records							
Cash books							
Tax returns							
Correspondence (letters)							
Quality control reports							
Sales invoices							

1. Which type of business record is kept the shortest time? ___________________________

2. Which two records are kept indefinitely? ___________________________

3. Name three types of records that are retained for five years only. ___________________________

4. What problems might a business face when many records are maintained for long periods of time? ___________________________

15-E. Brian Douglas is the manager of the vending machines in a new shopping mall. These machines operate when customers insert coins. Each day he is responsible for removing coins from the machines and counting the total cash. Determine the amount of cash taken in today from the number of coins removed from the machines.

Nickels	708	$__________
Dimes	1,140	$__________
Quarters	3,027	$__________
Half-dollars	42	$__________
TOTAL		$__________

15-F. From the following data, prepare an estimate of cash needs on the form provided for the month of May: expected sales in May, $45,000; expected collections from customers, $39,000; beginning cash balance, $8,250; ending cash balance desired, $6,000; estimated payments—accounts to be paid, $30,600; salaries and wages, $11,000; other operating expenses, $4,000; purchase of display cases, $2,400.

<table>
<tr><td colspan="3" align="center">Estimate of Cash Needs, Month of May, 20- -</td></tr>
<tr><td>Beginning cash balance</td><td>1</td><td>$__________</td></tr>
<tr><td>Collections from customers</td><td>2</td><td>__________</td></tr>
<tr><td>   Total cash available</td><td>3</td><td>$__________</td></tr>
<tr><td>Payments:</td><td></td><td></td></tr>
<tr><td>   Accounts to be paid</td><td>4</td><td>$__________</td></tr>
<tr><td>   Salaries and wages</td><td>5</td><td>__________</td></tr>
<tr><td>   Other operating expenses</td><td>6</td><td>__________</td></tr>
<tr><td>   Purchase of fixed assets</td><td>7</td><td>__________</td></tr>
<tr><td>   Total payments</td><td>8</td><td>$__________</td></tr>
<tr><td>Expected cash shortage</td><td>9</td><td>$__________</td></tr>
<tr><td>Bank loans needed</td><td>10</td><td>$__________</td></tr>
<tr><td>Desired ending cash balance</td><td>11</td><td>$__________</td></tr>
</table>

15-G. Most businesses, especially retail stores, use a cash register or point-of-sale terminal. When one is used, it is desirable to prepare daily proof of cash. For this purpose, a form such as the one on the next page may be used.

Using the following data, fill out the form on the next page for the current date: change fund at the beginning of the day, $160.00; cash sales for the day, $1,440.00; money taken from the register and deposited in the bank, $1,280.00; total cash paid out during the day for miscellaneous items, $59.60; actual cash on hand at the end of the day, $259.60.

Daily Proof of Cash

Date ________________________________

1. Change fund .... $__________

2. Cash received (as shown by cash register reading) .... $__________

3. Cash paid out .... $__________

4. Net receipts for the day (Item 2 minus Item 3) .... $__________

5. Total (Item 1 plus Item 4) .... $__________

6. Deposited in the bank .... $__________

7. Cash that should be on hand (Item 5 minus Item 6) .... $__________

8. Actual cash on hand .... $__________

9. Cash:

   (a) Shortage .... $__________

   (b) Overage .... $__________

15-H. In the previous problem, why might the actual cash on hand not agree with the cash that should be on hand according to the daily proof of cash? ____

____

____

15-I. A manufacturing firm has four new pieces of equipment. Determine the depreciation expense for the first year of use from the following information:

Equipment	Price	Expected Life	Final Trade-In Value	First Year's Depreciation
A	$160,000	36 Months	$10,000	__________
B	$ 88,400	60 Months	-0-	__________
C	$754,000	54 Months	$14,000	__________
D	$ 930	30 Months	$ 100	__________

15-J. Fill in the following expense report for a business. Then answer the following questions:

	Budgeted Amount	Actual Amount	Difference
Production costs	$370,000	$287,000	__________
Salaries	150,000	185,000	__________
Depreciation	30,000	30,000	__________
Electricity	5,000	6,500	__________
Supplies	4,000	2,600	__________
Total Expenses	__________	__________	__________

1. Do you feel the manager did an effective job in preparing the total budgeted amount?

Yes________   No________

2. What are possible reasons that the budgeted amount for production costs is so much greater than the actual

amount? ____

____

____

3. What are possible reasons why the actual amount for salaries is so much greater than the budgeted amount?

____

____

4. Why might it be wise for the manager to prepare three different budget estimates? ____________________

____

____

SMALL GROUP ACTIVITIES

Group Activity 1

Your teacher will put students into groups of two or three. Each group is to select a grocery or fast-food store *and* a non-food retail store. Because no two groups should go to the same stores, follow the teacher's requirement for avoiding this. Then obtain approval from the store manager for conducting an interview and establish an interview date. Before holding your interview, however, be sure to study the store and observe how it operates.

Once your group has selected the stores and set the interview date, study the questions listed below and prepare additional questions to ask the store manager or the person in charge of store records and financial matters. Of course, responses from the person you interview may prompt team members to ask additional questions:

1. What qualifications do you require for someone to be hired by the store for bookkeeping or accounting jobs?
2. Does the business use a manual paper-and-pencil record keeping system or an electronic system, such as QuickBooks?
3. Does the company use a petty cash system? If yes, who is in charge?
4. Is the petty cash system used when something small in value is needed quickly, such as when you run out of rubber bands or paper clips? If yes, are forms used?
5. How is the cash used in the business protected against the possibility of theft?
6. What are the requirements for becoming a cashier?
7. What are the daily established cash register procedures for clerks when they start and end work?
8. What procedure is used to obtain cash needed each day for the registers and to end the day?
9. How much and what kind of training is provided new employees who must handle money?
10. How do you find qualified people to work in your store?

The team should now summarize what it has gained from the interviews and answer these questions:

1. How do the two stores differ on each of the questions asked?
2. In what ways are the two stores the same?
3. Did you detect any practices that might not seem adequate to protect the store's cash?
4. What did you learn that was not provided in the text chapter or was different from the textbook?

As specified by your instructor, summarize what you have learned and prepare either a written or oral report for the class. Also, send the people you interviewed a "thank you" note.

Group Activity 2

With assistance from your instructor, form a team of three to five students to either (a) prepare a budget, (b) work with an existing group to develop or revise a budget, or (c) form a group interested in budgeting the start of *one* member's own business. The following types of organizations would be possibilities for choices (a) and (b): an organization at your school, Boy Scouts or Girl Scouts, a civic organization, or a church, synagogue, or other type of religious group. Nearly any legal organization that receives and spends money might be appropriate. However, obtain approval from your teacher. Be sure to get information and assistance from the person or group in charge of budgetary matters in the organization.

Follow the general information in your textbook for creating one of these types of budgets: sales, product, cash, merchandise, advertising, cash, capital, or income statement. The time period could be any length of time up to a year. You may also wish to find other information from your library or the Internet. Place your budget in table form and show what the budget might be under average conditions for an existing business or organization. Show appropriate details; see examples in the chapter. An example of the items that would appear in an income statement budget may be found for the Crown Corporation in the next chapter.

Once the team has prepared its budget, present it to the class and explain how you arrived at your numbers. Also discuss the problems the group had in arriving at the projected numbers. What advice would your group give about budget preparation to people planning to start their own businesses?

<table>
<tr><td rowspan="3">Chapter 16

Financial Analysis of a Business</td><td>Name _______________</td><td colspan="4" align="center">Scoring Record</td></tr>
<tr><td rowspan="2">Date _______________</td><td></td><td>Part A</td><td>Part B</td><td>Total</td></tr>
<tr><td>Perfect score</td><td>20</td><td>15</td><td>35</td></tr>
<tr><td></td><td></td><td>My score</td><td></td><td></td><td></td></tr>
</table>

Study Guide

Part A—*Directions:* Indicate your answer to each of the following questions by circling either yes or no in the Answers column.

		Answers	For Scoring
1.	Is the amount of money a business earns one way to judge its success?	yes no	1. _______
2.	Are financial statements reports that summarize financial data over a period of time, such as a month, three months, or a year?	yes no	2. _______
3.	Are assets and capital the only categories listed on the balance sheet?	yes no	3. _______
4.	To determine the amount of capital in a business, should you subtract the liabilities from the assets?	yes no	4. _______
5.	Is the basic accounting equation represented on the balance sheet as Assets = Liabilities + Capital?	yes no	5. _______
6.	Does the heading of a balance sheet include the name of the person or business, the title "Balance Sheet," and the date?	yes no	6. _______
7.	Can the financial position of a business on a given date be determined from the balance sheet?	yes no	7. _______
8.	Is the merchandise inventory the value of goods purchased to sell to customers at a profit?	yes no	8. _______
9.	If a business purchased merchandise on credit, would the purchase be listed in the business's records under accounts receivable?	yes no	9. _______
10.	Can a business determine whether it can pay all its debts on a given date from looking at the income statement?	yes no	10. _______
11.	When the amount of capital increases, must liabilities also increase?	yes no	11. _______
12.	Is another name for a balance sheet a profit and loss statement?	yes no	12. _______
13.	Does the difference between total revenue and total expenses show the profit or loss of a business?	yes no	13. _______
14.	Will the net result of the income statement appear on the balance sheet?	yes no	14. _______
15.	Can a business budget future expenditures by doing an item-by-item analysis of the income statement?	yes no	15. _______
16.	Does money usually flow into and out of a business at the same rate?	yes no	16. _______
17.	Is the amount of working capital one possible indicator that a business can pay its long-term debts?	yes no	17. _______
18.	Would a business with very little working capital find it easy to borrow money?	yes no	18. _______
19.	Can a financial ratio show whether the average monthly inventory might be too large or too small?	yes no	19. _______
20.	Is a consultant an expert whom companies hire to help them solve problems?	yes no	20. _______

Part B—*Directions:* For each of the following statements, select the word, or group of words, that best completes the statement. In the Answers column, write the letter corresponding to the answer selected.

Answers   For Scoring

1. Because business success is judged in dollar terms, every business must do all of the following *except* (a) keep thorough and accurate records, (b) prepare financial reports on a regular basis, (c) interpret the financial information from the reports, (d) make decisions that affect past financial results. .... _______ 1. _______

2. Which financial reports do businesses use most? (a) income statement and statement of operations, (b) balance sheet and statement of financial position, (c) advertising statement and capital statement, (d) balance sheet and income statement. .... _______ 2. _______

3. What information is found on a balance sheet? (a) assets; (b) assets and liabilities; (c) assets, liabilities, and capital; (d) assets, liabilities, capital, and income. _______ 3. _______

4. On which financial record does a business list the building in which it does business? (a) balance sheet, (b) asset statement, (c) income statement, (d) capital statement. .... _______ 4. _______

5. After subtracting the liabilities from the assets, a business can determine (a) how much it owns, (b) how much it owes, (c) how much it is worth, (d) how much its expenses total. .... _______ 5. _______

6. How much are the liabilities for a local business if its assets are $750,000 and its capital is $500,000? (a) $250,000, (b) $500,000, (c) $750,000, (d) $1,250,000. .... _______ 6. _______

7. The balance sheet reveals the basic financial position of a business (a) on a given date, (b) for a month, (c) for a year, (d) for whatever time period is specified. ... _______ 7. _______

8. If a company just shipped 20 computers to your school, the school should record the value of the computers on its balance sheet under (a) expenses, (b) assets, (c) liabilities, (d) capital. .... _______ 8. _______

9. Which of the following is a liability to you? (a) the amount a friend owes you, (b) the amount you owe a friend, (c) the VCR you just purchased, (d) the billfold you recently lost. .... _______ 9. _______

10. Another name for an income statement is (a) net worth, (b) profit and loss statement (c) owner's equity, (d) statement of financial position. .... _______ 10. _______

11. A business can use an income statement to determine its (a) accounts payable, (b) assets, (c) operating expenses, (d) capital. .... _______ 11. _______

12. The three major parts of an income statement are (a) revenue, expenses, and profit or loss; (b) cash, expenses, and profit or loss; (c) sales, liabilities, and profit or loss; (d) capital, expenses, and profit or loss. .... _______ 12. _______

13. The difference between current assets and current liabilities is (a) profit, (b) working capital, (c) net worth, (d) loss. .... _______ 13. _______

14. To calculate return on sales, divide (a) net profit by sales revenue, (b) sales revenue by net profit, (c) net profit by total assets, (d) total assets by net profit. _______ 14. _______

15. An agency of the federal government that can assist small firms in getting loans under special conditions is the (a) Federal Trade Commission, (b) First National Association, (c) Retired Executives Administration, (d) Small Business Administration. .... _______ 15. _______

Directions: Study each controversial issue carefully. Follow the advice of your teacher before listing in the columns provided reasons why people might answer Yes or No. Your teacher may want you to work with a classmate, talk with others in your community to gather information, or use the library or Internet to gather facts.

16-1. Should each profit-making organization, whether large or small, be required yearly to hire a CPA to approve the financial records of the business?

Reasons for "Yes"	Reasons for "No"

16-2. If you were to loan money to a small business owner, would it be more important to know the company's return on sales rather than the current ratio?

Reasons for "Yes"	Reasons for "No"

PROBLEMS

16-A. Write in the correct accounting name for each item described below.

1. Goods that a store has purchased for sale to customers. _______________________________

2. Another name for an income statement. _______________________________

3. The movement of cash into and out of a business. _______________________________

4. A licensed accountant hired to approve the yearly financial records of a corporation.

____

16-B. Place a check mark in the appropriate column indicating in which financial statement you would find the following information:

	Balance Sheet	Income Statement
1. Total owed other businesses	____	____
2. Value of the land and buildings	____	____
3. Amount customers owe us	____	____
4. Gross profit	____	____
5. Depreciation expense	____	____
6. Cost of goods sold	____	____
7. Total liabilities	____	____
8. Net profit before taxes	____	____

16-C. On the form below, prepare this year's December 31 income statement for a business. Data needed: income from sales, $1,027,800; income from renting equipment to customers, $47,000. Cost of goods sold is $537,400. Expenses include salaries and wages, $145,000; rental of facilities, $170,600; depreciation of equipment, $3,000; electricity, $2,900; supplies, $1,850; and other expenses, $700.

CASWELL AND HOWELL

____

____

Revenue

_______________________ $ _______

_______________________ _______

Total Revenue _______

Cost of Goods Sold _______

Gross Profit $ _______

Operating Expenses

_______________________ $ _______

_______________________ _______

_______________________ _______

_______________________ _______

_______________________ _______

_______________________ _______

Total Operating Expenses _______

Net Profit (before taxes) $ _______

16-D. One way that managers decide what to change in operating the business is to compare financial statements from the same time period in previous years. Below is an income statement for a six-month period. It includes the percent of sales for each item. From the following data for the same six-month period in the following year, fill in the amounts and compute the sales percent for each item. Then answer the questions given below the comparative income statement.

Sales, $400,000; Cost of goods sold, $296,000; Wages, $68,000; Rent, $9,600; Advertising, $5,760; Utilities, $3,200; Insurance, $1,200; Depreciation, $800; Repairs, $1,240; Supplies, $960; Interest, $480; Miscellaneous expense, $2,000.

<table>
<tr><td colspan="5" align="center">WILMA T. KELLER
Comparative Income Statement</td></tr>
<tr><td></td><td colspan="2" align="center">July 1, 20-- to
December 31, 20--</td><td colspan="2" align="center">July 1, 20-- to
December 31, 20--</td></tr>
<tr><td>Sales</td><td>320,000</td><td>100.00%</td><td></td><td></td></tr>
<tr><td>Cost of goods sold</td><td>240,000</td><td>75.00%</td><td></td><td></td></tr>
<tr><td>Gross profit on sales</td><td>80,000</td><td>25.00%</td><td></td><td></td></tr>
<tr><td>Operating expenses:</td><td></td><td></td><td></td><td></td></tr>
<tr><td>   Wages</td><td>48,000</td><td>15.00%</td><td></td><td></td></tr>
<tr><td>   Rent</td><td>9,600</td><td>3.00%</td><td></td><td></td></tr>
<tr><td>   Advertising</td><td>3,200</td><td>1.00%</td><td></td><td></td></tr>
<tr><td>   Utilities</td><td>3,040</td><td>.95%</td><td></td><td></td></tr>
<tr><td>   Insurance</td><td>960</td><td>.30%</td><td></td><td></td></tr>
<tr><td>   Depreciation of equipment</td><td>800</td><td>.25%</td><td></td><td></td></tr>
<tr><td>   Repairs and maintenance</td><td>640</td><td>.20%</td><td></td><td></td></tr>
<tr><td>   Supplies</td><td>704</td><td>.22%</td><td></td><td></td></tr>
<tr><td>   Interest</td><td>480</td><td>.15%</td><td></td><td></td></tr>
<tr><td>   Miscellaneous</td><td>1,280</td><td>.40%</td><td></td><td></td></tr>
<tr><td>   Total operating expenses</td><td>68,704</td><td>21.47%</td><td></td><td></td></tr>
<tr><td>Net profit</td><td>11,296</td><td>3.53%</td><td></td><td></td></tr>
</table>

1. Total sales were what percent higher for the second six-month period than for the first? ___________________

2. The net profit as a percent of sales was higher in which six-month period? _______________________________

3. What might have been the reason that the rent expense was the same amount for each of the two six-month

   periods? ____

   ____

4. What is a possible reason for the increase in wages paid during the second six-month period?

   ____

5. Suggest a reason for the sales increase during the second six-month period. _______________________________

   ____

16-E. From the information provided, prepare a balance sheet using the form that follows. Data needed: Cash on hand, $48,500; customers owe the business, $16,400; goods bought and ready to be sold, $97,000; equipment, $100,000; buildings and land, $620,000; money owed other businesses, $64,300; and money owed on buildings and land, $208,000.

The Owl Outlet

Assets			Liabilities & Capital		
___________	$ _______		Liabilities:		
___________	_______		___________		
___________	_______		___________	$	_______
___________	_______		___________		_______
___________	_______		Total Liabilities	$	_______
___________	_______		Capital:		
			___________	$	_______
Total Assets	$ _______		Total Liabilities and Capital	$	_______

16-F. Complete the balance sheet for the Cracker Crumb Company for December 31 of the current year. The missing information consists of merchandise inventory, $70,000, and accounts payable, $43,000.

____

____

____

Assets		Liabilities & Capital	
Current Assets:		**Current Liabilities:**	
Cash	$ 50,000	Accounts Payable	$_______
Accounts Receivable	30,000	Notes Payable	20,000
Merch. Inventory	$_______	Total Liabilities	$_______
Total Current Assets	$_______	Capital:	
Fixed Assets:		Stockholders' Net Worth	$ 287,000
Equipment	$120,000		
Land	80,000		
Total Fixed Assets	$_______		
Total Assets	$_______	Total Liabilities and Capital	$_______

16-G. Answer the following questions based on the balance sheet for the Cracker Crumb Company completed in problem 16-F.

1. Complete the basic accounting formula for the company.

Assets	=	*Liabilities*	+	*Capital*
______________	=	______________	+	______________

2. How much working capital does the company have? ____

3. What is the current ratio? ____

4. Is the company in a good financial position for paying its current liabilities? _______________________

   Reason for your answer: ____

   ____

5. If the net profit for this company is $28,700, what is the

   a. Return on Owners' Equity (Capital): ____

   b. Return on Investment: ____

16-H. Record the name of the ratio a manager should use if the following information were desired, and then calculate the ratio using the data below.

Cost of goods sold	$330,000
Current assets	72,000
Net profit	60,000
Average mdse. inven.	48,000
Current liabilities	24,000
Owners' equity	300,000
Total assets	402,000

1. The owners want to know if they are making a fair return on their investment.

   a. Name of ratio: ____

   b. Ratio calculation: ____

2. The new purchasing manager would like to know how often, on average, the inventory is replaced yearly.

   a. Name of ratio: ____

   b. Ratio calculation: ____

3. Someone who is thinking of investing money in the company wants to know what the return on the investment is for the current owners and to those to whom money is owed.

   a. Name of ratio: ____

   b. Ratio calculation: ____

4. A bank that is planning to lend the business money wants to know whether the business can meet its current debts without much difficulty.

   a. Name of ratio: ____

   b. Ratio calculation: ____

SMALL GROUP ACTIVITIES

Group Activity 1

Your instructor will break the class into three groups. Each group is to discuss and agree upon the type of accountant that they would like to select to speak to your class. The type of accountant will depend upon the preferences of your group. Choose an accountant who works for a small company, a medium-sized company, a large corporation, a government office, or a public accounting firm. Each group should select a type of accountant that is different from the selections of other groups.

Once you have decided upon the type of accountant, use your library, school counselor, the Internet, or accountant friends to learn more about what accountants do in their jobs. What tasks do they perform and how often do they perform them? Now find an accountant who falls into your category and ask if he or she would be willing to speak to the class. Your instructor will help you select the date.

Your group's next task is to prepare a thorough list of questions to ask your speaker. The most important questions should be given to the speaker in advance. Less important questions can be asked in class. Two questions you might want to ask are: What is required to become an accountant? What might the career be like in the years ahead? You might also want to ask questions based on the chapter, such as how they use ratios in their work to help managers run their organizations well.

Be sure to send a "thank you" note to your speaker within a few days after the presentation.

Group Activity 2

Your teacher will place you into three-person teams of accountants, and the teams will engage in an accounting contest. Each team is to complete the steps that appear below:

Step 1: Each team must design a simple balance sheet. The balance sheet can look like the one in Figure 16-3, except those figures need to be changed. (Lined paper from your notebooks can be used to display your completed statements.) Create the financial statement in a way that gives the impression that the company is doing well but would not appear that way to any accountant or banker. Also prepare the ratios listed in Figure 16-8. The ratios might also be helpful in making your statement look misleading.

Step 2: When other groups have completed preparation of their financial statements, exchange your balance sheet with a team designated by your instructor. Your instructor will limit the answering time for the paired teams. When the time is up, the opposing team verifies whether the competing team's statement was properly prepared. If it did not follow the example in the text (Figure 16-3), the team creating the statement loses one point. If the competing team agrees that the statement does give the impression the firm is doing all right, the creating team gets one point. If the competing team finds a ratio that shows the company is not doing well, it gains a point for it plus an additional point for each additional ratio it properly identifies showing company weakness. The points gained or lost can be placed on the board or screen.

Step 3: The teams now prepare income statements for their company that may appear to look good to someone who is not an accountant, similar to what was done in Step 1. The same procedure of being paired with another team by your instructor and evaluating the other team's income statement should be followed as described in Step 2. Team scores should be calculated and posted. The one with the most points wins the income statement contest. These points can be added to the balance sheet points to determine the final winner.

Step 4: The competing teams now have both the income statement and the balance sheet of their opponents. Each team should calculate any remaining ratios shown in Figure 16-8. The teams can now make a final analysis of the competitor's firm and provide a report to the opposing team about the financial soundness of its company. What the company must do to improve itself should also be reported.

<table>
<tr><td rowspan="3">Chapter 17

Financing a Business</td><td rowspan="3">Name ___________________

Date ___________________</td><td colspan="5">Scoring Record</td></tr>
<tr><td></td><td>Part A</td><td>Part B</td><td>Part C</td><td>Total</td></tr>
<tr><td>Perfect score</td><td>20</td><td>10</td><td>5</td><td>35</td></tr>
<tr><td colspan="2">My score</td><td></td><td></td><td></td><td></td></tr>
</table>

Study Guide

Part A—*Directions:* Indicate your answer to each of the following questions by circling either yes or no in the Answers column.

		Answers	For Scoring
1.	If you take a partner into your business, is the partner's investment known as creditor capital?	yes no	1. _______
2.	Do businesses in financial difficulty often have trouble getting debt capital?	yes no	2. _______
3.	Does common stock represent a type of ownership that gives holders the right to share in the corporation's profits?	yes no	3. _______
4.	Do preferred stockholders usually have voting privileges at the stockholders' meetings?	yes no	4. _______
5.	When a corporation ceases operations, are preferred and common stockholders likely to get all their investment back from the sale of the assets?	yes no	5. _______
6.	Must the par value of a share of stock be $100?	yes no	6. _______
7.	If the par value of a share of stock is $100, can the market value be below $100?	yes no	7. _______
8.	When starting a business, is it usually desirable to issue only common stock?	yes no	8. _______
9.	Are the retained earnings part of the owner's equity?	yes no	9. _______
10.	Even when a business is not making a profit, should it plan to replace assets that decrease in value because of obsolescence?	yes no	10. _______
11.	Is a supplier who allows a business 60 days to pay for merchandise actually providing long-term capital?	yes no	11. _______
12.	If a business has an open line of credit, can it borrow an unlimited amount?	yes no	12. _______
13.	Can merchandise inventory be used as security for a loan?	yes no	13. _______
14.	Do sales finance companies buy installment sales contracts from businesses?	yes no	14. _______
15.	Can the maintenance of an asset be included in a leasing agreement?	yes no	15. _______
16.	Are bonds issued by the United States government classified as mortgage bonds?	yes no	16. _______
17.	If a company obtains capital by selling mortgage bonds, do bondholders usually have a lien on part of the company's assets?	yes no	17. _______
18.	Do those who provide short-term capital for a business usually have some control over the management of the business?	yes no	18. _______
19.	Does an investment bank make a profit by selling a corporation's bonds to the public for more than it pays to buy the bonds from the corporation?	yes no	19. _______
20.	If stockholders have stock rights options, can they buy new stock at a price below its market price?	yes no	20. _______

		Answers	For Scoring

1. Money invested in a business by its owner is called (a) retained earnings, (b) working capital, (c) equity capital, (d) creditor capital. .... ______ 1. ______
2. Retained earnings refer to (a) profits that owners do NOT save for use by the business, (b) profits that owners do NOT take out of the business, (c) money from the sale of bonds, (d) money from the sale of stock. .... ______ 2. ______
3. Preferred stockholders (a) are guaranteed dividends, (b) receive dividends before creditors, (c) typically have voting privileges in a business, (d) receive dividends before common stockholders. .... ______ 3. ______
4. Lane owns 50 shares of 7 percent preferred stock that has a par value of $100 a share. Last year he received no dividends. If profits are large enough this year, he should receive as dividends (a) $35, (b) $350, (c) $500, (d) $700. .... ______ 4. ______
5. What usually happens when a corporation ceases operations? (a) Assets that are sold usually raise enough cash to pay the company's debts. (b) Creditors are paid before preferred stockholders are paid. (c) Preferred stockholders are paid before creditors are paid. (d) Common stockholders are paid before creditors are paid. ... ______ 5. ______
6. "Plowing back earnings" means (a) distributing all profits earned as dividends to preferred stockholders, (b) distributing all profits earned as dividends to common stockholders, (c) reinvesting some of the profits in the business, (d) distributing all profits earned as dividends to all stockholders. .... ______ 6. ______
7. When a business replaces buildings or equipment or adds new facilities for expanding, (a) profits earned cannot be used for these purposes, (b) creditor capital cannot be used for these purposes, (c) profits can be withheld for these purposes, (d) owner capital cannot be used for these purposes. .... ______ 7. ______
8. An unconditional promise to pay a lender a certain sum of money at a particular time or on demand is called a (a) promissory note, (b) check, (c) factor, (d) warrant. ______ 8. ______
9. A contract that allows the use of an asset for a fee is a (a) mortgage, (b) factor, (c) warrant, (d) lease. .... ______ 9. ______
10. Which of the following statements is NOT true about bonds? (a) Bonds are long-term debts. (b) The borrowed amount is called the principal. (c) The issuer must pay the bondholder the amount borrowed at the maturity date. (d) Bonds represent a share in the ownership of the corporation. .... ______ 10. ______

Column I	Column II	Answers	For Scoring
A. Bond B. Common stock C. Debentures D. Factor E. Long-term capital F. Open line of credit G. Preferred stock H. Securities	1. Ownership that gives holders the right to share in the corporation's profits and to participate in managing the business by voting on basic issues.	______	1. ______
	2. Permits borrowing up to a specified amount for a specified period of time.	______	2. ______
	3. Specializes in lending money to businesses based on their accounts receivable.	______	3. ______
	4. A long-term written promise to pay a definite sum of money at a specified time.	______	4. ______
	5. Bonds that are not secured by assets but are based on the faith and credit of the corporation that issues them.	______	5. ______

          Name ______________________________

Directions: Study each controversial issue carefully. Follow the advice of your teacher before listing in the columns provided reasons why people might answer Yes or No. Your teacher may want you to work with a classmate, talk with others in your community to gather information, or use the library or Internet to gather facts.

17-1. Would an investment in debenture bonds in a financially strong company be better than an investment in mortgage bonds in a financially weak company?

Reasons for "Yes"	Reasons for "No"

17-2. Would stockholders in a strong, growing company prefer to raise additional capital by selling bonds rather than by selling common stock?

Reasons for "Yes"	Reasons for "No"

PROBLEMS

17-A. Use a check mark to indicate whether the sources of capital listed below are equity (owned) or debt (borrowed) capital.

Sources of Capital	Equity Capital	Debt Capital
1. Debentures	_____	_____
2. Common stock shares	_____	_____
3. Personal savings invested	_____	_____
4. A short-term loan	_____	_____
5. Preferred stock shares	_____	_____
6. A $5,000 line of credit	_____	_____
7. A mortgage bond for purchase of land	_____	_____

17-B. Use the data that follows to answer the questions below. Assets, $2,900,000; Liabilities, $1,400,000; Common Stock (5,000 shares), $1,000,000; Retained Earnings, $500,000; Total Capital, $1,500,000. A share of stock is selling for $225 at stock brokerage houses.

1. What is the book value of a share of stock? $_______________

2. What is the market value of a share of stock? $_______________

3. What is the amount of the equity capital? $_______________

4. Would a bank be willing to loan money to this business? Yes______   No______

Explain: ____

____

5. What is the source of retained earnings? _______________________________________

____

____

17-C. Below is a promissory note. After studying it, answer the questions that follow.

<table>
<tr><td>DUE <u>Sept. 15, 20--</u></td><td>NO. <u>1028</u></td></tr>
<tr><td colspan="2">$ <u>7,500</u>   <u>BALTIMORE, MD., June 15, 20--</u></td></tr>
<tr><td colspan="2"><u>Three months</u> -------------- AFTER DATE, WE, OR EITHER OF US, PROMISE TO PAY</td></tr>
<tr><td colspan="2">TO THE ORDER OF <u>The Bank of Baltimore</u> ----------------------------</td></tr>
<tr><td colspan="2"><u>Seven thousand five hundred xx/100</u>----------------- DOLLARS</td></tr>
</table>

WITH ATTORNEY'S FEES. NEGOTIABLE AND PAYABLE AT **INDUSTRIAL TRUST & SAVINGS BANK OF MUNCIE, IND.,** FOR VALUE RECEIVED. WITHOUT RELIEF FROM VALUATION OR APPRAISMENT LAWS. THE DRAWERS AND ENDORSERS SEVERALLY WAIVE PRESENTMENT FOR PAYMENT. PROTEST. NOTICE OF PROTEST AND NOTICE OF NON PAYMENT OF THIS NOTE WITH <u>10</u> PERCENT INTEREST AFTER DATE. AND TEN PERCENT INTEREST AFTER MATURITY UNTIL PAID.

John Olivo

Elaine Turk

1. Who owes the money?____

2. Who is to receive the money when it is due?_________________________________

3. Is this a long-term or a short-term loan?_________________________________

4. For how many months does the business have the use of the borrowed funds?___________

5. How much interest will the bank receive when the note is due? [Hint: The interest rate is an annual rate.]

____

17-D. A corporation issued $150,000 of 8 percent preferred stock and $300,000 of common stock. Profits for the year were $50,000. The board of directors decided to distribute all profits as dividends. Using this data, answer the following questions.

1. How much in dividends would the preferred stockholders earn?___________________

2. How much in dividends would the common stockholders earn? ___________________

3. What percentage return on their investment would preferred stockholders earn? ___________

4. What percentage return on their investment would common stockholders earn?___________

17-E. Steve Koranski owns a very profitable business. However, he used nearly all his retained earnings by plowing them back into the business. Each year he expanded operations, but cannot quite reach his dream of becoming a nationwide business. He has borrowed heavily from banks and believes there are no other major sources of cash. Then, he heard about venture capitalists.

1. Might a venture capitalist be interested in loaning Steve Koranski a large sum of cash to expand his

    business nationwide? Yes_______ No_______

    Why?____

    ____

2. What will a venture capitalist want to know about the business before considering loaning

    money?____

    ____

    ____

3. What might Steve Koranski have in common with many venture capitalists?___________

    ____

    ____

    ____

17-F. The following table shows average bank interest rates on business loans of one year or less for three different years. Using this data, answer the questions that follow.

Size of the Loan	Year #1	Year #2	Year #3
$ 1,000-$ 9,999	11.1 %	10.1 %	10.9%
$ 10,000-$ 99,999	11.0	9.9	10.4
$100,000-$499,999	10.7	9.6	9.8
$500,000-$999,999	10.4	9.4	9.5

1. If a business borrowed $15,000 in Year #2, how much would the interest rate have been?______________

2. If a business borrowed $8,000 for all of Year #3, how much interest would it have to pay on the loan?__________

3. Does it appear that interest rates go up every year?__________

4. Does it appear that interest rates go down as loans get larger?______________

17-G. The Moore Company and the Hunt Corporation have 50,000 shares of common stock ($100 par value), which they had both previously sold to stockholders. Each business needs $5 million to expand. The Moore Company obtained its $5 million by issuing an additional 50,000 shares of its common stock. The Hunt Corporation obtained its $5 million by issuing 5 percent, 20-year bonds with a face value of $5 million. For purposes of this problem, assume the stock and the bonds were sold for enough above par or face value to offset exactly the expenses of selling the stock and bonds.

Both corporations had the same operating profits before paying dividends and bond interest for the next three years as follows: first year, $500,000; second year, $600,000; third year, $250,000.

Assuming that all operating profits were paid out as dividends or bond interest, complete the report below:

	First Year	Second Year	Third Year
Moore Company			
Dividends paid to stockholders...... (1)	$__________	$__________	$__________
Dividends paid per share .... (2)	$__________	$__________	$__________
Hunt Corporation			
Interest paid to bondholders ...... (3)	$__________	$__________	$__________
Dividends paid to stockholders...... (4)	$__________	$__________	$__________
Dividends paid per share .... (5)	$__________	$__________	$__________

17-H. On July 1, 20--, the Acme Corporation issues (sells) $3 million of 8 1/2 percent, 30-year mortgage bonds. The assets pledged as security for the mortgage bond issue include the Acme Corporation's ten-year-old building and five acres of land. Each bond has a face value of $1,000, and the interest is payable semiannually. The First National Bank, New York City, is the trustee for the bondholders.

1. How many bonds were issued?______________

2. If you owned one of these bonds, how much interest would you receive every six months? ______________

3. What will be the total amount of interest paid to bondholders during the 30 years?______________

4. Must the interest be paid to bondholders before dividends can be paid to the stockholders?______________

5. Does each bondholder possess a share of ownership in the Acme Corporation?_______________

6. Who holds the mortgage?____

7. If the Acme Corporation failed to pay the interest on the bonds at the end of the sixth year, what might

   happen? ____

   ____

   ____

8. If the Acme Corporation should fail, what security do the bondholders have? _______________

   ____

   ____

17-I. The Wells Electric Company has outstanding $1 million in 8 percent cumulative preferred stock. (If a dividend is not paid one year on cumulative preferred stock, it accumulates the next year.) The company also has outstanding $1 million in 10 percent ordinary preferred stock, and $1 million in common stock. The net profits and losses in three successive years were $380,000 profit, $10,000 loss, and $400,000 profit. The corporation does not pay any dividends in years in which it operates at a loss. Complete the following form to show what dividends would be received by each class of stockholders (assume that the common stockholders received all of the profits remaining after the preferred stockholders were paid their dividends).

Class of Stockholders	First Year	Second Year	Third Year
8 percent cumulative- preferred stockholders	1. $_______	$_______	$_______
10 percent preferred stockholders	2. $_______	$_______	$_______
common stockholders	3. $_______	$_______	$_______

SMALL GROUP ACTIVITIES

Group Activity 1

Your teacher will place you into groups of three or more students in such a way that there will be an even number of groups. Each group will be numbered, such as one through four. The odd-numbered groups will play the role of entrepreneurs who own a business and need to borrow funds in order to expand. The even-numbered groups will be bankers who lend money. Facts about the business borrowers and the banking lenders follow.

The odd-numbered groups (entrepreneurs) own and operate a small corporation that has been somewhat successful since they started three years ago. The five owners have not had to borrow prior to their current need for $100,000. While the business made no profits during the first year, it did make a small profit the second year. As it nears the end of its third year, profits have increased somewhat over last year. Four of the five stockholders in this close corporation strongly believe that with the borrowed capital, they could expand the store and open a second one in an excellent new location. One of the stockholders, however, does not believe the new location is all that good.

The even-numbered banking groups will need to decide under what conditions they wish to loan money to the business. Each lending group must decide on what terms the loan should be made to this modestly successful firm. For example, what interest rate should be set in relation to the current average rate for such loans by banks? And for how many months should the loan last? The lending groups may also raise other questions. The lenders should interview the stockholders to gather as much additional information as possible.

The odd-numbered team members will meet to discuss how they can obtain the loan at the lowest rate for a maximum period of time. These groups must also discuss how to answer any questions they might be asked by the lenders. Each lender group needs to come up with a plan that is acceptable to their bank and earns a reasonable profit for it. Both teams should investigate the current interest rates for loans.

When both the lending teams and borrowing teams have arrived at a game plan, the two sides must meet and arrive at the loan conditions. Upon completion, the teams should report to the entire class the final borrowing arrangement and also discuss the negotiating styles that each of the teams used in order to arrive at the final agreement.

Group Activity 2

After your teacher has placed you into a group of three to five students, your group is to seek a venture capitalist to help you raise money for your two-year-old Internet company. The company has been rather successful at selling a variety of toys and games online that were popular over one hundred years ago. Your company was originally created to gain experience at starting an Internet business. You are proud of what you have learned but are not quite as proud of your results.

You do not know whether this current popularity of your products will continue for very long in the U.S. As a result, you want to find old toys and games and perhaps some unique new ones from other countries to expand your market worldwide. To do this, you will need to hire toy and game experts from other countries, enlarge your Web site, establish warehouses, and contract with shipping companies.

You may need as much as $1 million to succeed, and your local lenders are too cautious to loan you money. Thus, you are seeking a venture capitalist who might provide you with at least $500,000 to move ahead with your plan.

At least one of your team members should investigate whether there are other firms who compete with you in your business online or offline. Your team should also gather as much information as possible about (a) the names and addresses of venture capitalist firms, (b) the kinds of firms they have invested in, (c) the amounts that they typically provide, and (d) the kinds of things they look for before taking a chance with a company like yours. Each member of the team should also search your local area, the library, or the Internet for venture capitalists.

From the evidence that your team members obtain, develop an outline of a business plan that a venture capitalist might consider. Then select five venture capitalists of those identified who you think would most likely invest in your Internet company. Once this task is done, prepare one letter that might be sent to all of these venture capitalists together with a plan that outlines your need for funds.

Of course, you will not actually send the letter. Rather, you will share your letter with the class after reporting on the information you gathered, the venture capitalists you found, the five you selected, and other information you feel is important. Other teams will also present their reports. Discuss the results learned after hearing from all teams.

<table>
<tr><td rowspan="3">Chapter 18

Financial Services</td><td rowspan="3">Name _______________

Date _______________</td><td colspan="4" align="center">Scoring Record</td></tr>
<tr><td></td><td>Part A</td><td>Part B</td><td>Total</td></tr>
<tr><td>Perfect score</td><td>20</td><td>15</td><td>35</td></tr>
<tr><td></td><td></td><td>My score</td><td></td><td></td><td></td></tr>
</table>

Study Guide

Part A—*Directions:* Indicate your answer to each of the following questions by circling either yes or no in the Answers column.

		Answers	For Scoring
1.	Does a bank accept demand deposits as well as make commercial loans?	yes no	1. ______
2.	Are commercial loans made to individuals as well as to businesses?	yes no	2. ______
3.	Do commercial banks handle demand deposits, commercial loans, and consumer loans?	yes no	3. ______
4.	Do mutual savings banks specialize in handling long-term loans, such as mortgages?	yes no	4. ______
5.	Is "collateral" property that a borrower pledges to assure repayment of a loan?	yes no	5. ______
6.	Can new or less successful businesses usually obtain unsecured loans?	yes no	6. ______
7.	Is the prime rate the lowest rate of interest offered to the best-qualified borrowers?	yes no	7. ______
8.	With EFT transactions, can money be transferred by computer?	yes no	8. ______
9.	Can banks electronically transfer paychecks directly from the employer's bank account to the employees' bank accounts?	yes no	9. ______
10.	Does a certificate of deposit usually earn a lower interest rate than a savings account?	yes no	10. ______
11.	Does a certificate of deposit allow deposits and withdrawals at any time without financial penalties?	yes no	11. ______
12.	Can money market fund depositors withdraw funds at any time without penalty?	yes no	12. ______
13.	Does a mutual fund pool the money of many investors primarily for the purchase of stocks and bonds?	yes no	13. ______
14.	Are T-bills long-term securities that are sold to finance the cost of running the government?	yes no	14. ______
15.	Are treasury notes considered safe investments?	yes no	15. ______
16.	Do investors diversify to reduce risk?	yes no	16. ______
17.	Are investors who buy stock in newly developed corporations looking for maximum security?	yes no	17. ______
18.	Does a broker buy and sell corporate securities for customers?	yes no	18. ______
19.	Is NASDAQ the nation's first electronic stock market?	yes no	19. ______
20.	Can most skilled investors usually predict when the market will reach its high and low points?	yes no	20. ______

Part B—*Directions:* For each of the following statements, select the word, or group of words, that best completes the statement. In the Answers column, write the letter corresponding to the answer selected.

	Answers	For Scoring

1. Which service is NOT provided by commercial banks? (a) offer legal and tax advice, (b) provide bill-paying and payroll-preparation services, (c) collect promissory notes and sell insurance, (d) sell treasury notes and treasury bonds. .... _______ 1._______

2. Banking institutions that manage property for customers are known as (a) mortgage banks, (b) trust companies, (c) commercial banks, (d) mutual savings banks. _______ 2._______

3. All of the following are non-bank institutions *except* (a) stock brokerage firms, (b) savings and loan associations, (c) insurance companies, (d) credit unions. .. _______ 3._______

4. The endorsement "For Deposit Only, Big Blue Corporation" is known as a (a) blank endorsement, (b) full endorsement, (c) restrictive endorsement, (d) special endorsement. .... _______ 4._______

5. When you endorse a check, you should use a full endorsement when you want to (a) limit the use of the funds in some way, (b) transfer the rights to the funds to someone else, (c) allow anyone to cash the check, (d) deposit the funds. .... _______ 5._______

6. Which transaction *cannot* be handled by EFT? (a) ATM deposits, (b) direct deposits, (c) payroll preparation, (d) debit-card payments. .... _______ 6._______

7. With ATMs, bank customers (a) can make deposits but not withdrawals, (b) can make withdrawals but not deposits, (c) can make deposits and withdrawals and transfer funds, (d) can make deposits and withdrawals but cannot transfer funds. _______ 7._______

8. If your bank's ATM fee is $7.50 to withdraw $500 and you withdraw the money from a competitor's ATM that charges $9.00, by how much would your bank account be reduced? (a) $483.50, (b) $507.50, (c) $509.00, (d) $516.50. ...... _______ 8._______

9. Which statement is *incorrect* about CDs? (a) CDs can be purchased for periods ranging from three months to five years. (b) Interest is lost when CDs are withdrawn before the time stated. (c) Savings accounts usually pay a higher rate of interest than do CDs. (d) Interest rates vary in relation to the life of the CD. _______ 9._______

10. Which of the following investment instruments has the least amount of risk? (a) stocks, (b) mutual funds, (c) treasury notes, (d) bonds. .... _______ 10._______

11. For a person who wants to invest $5,000 for 10 years, the safest investment would be a (a) secured loan, (b) treasury bond, (c) mutual fund, (d) T-bill. ...... _______ 11._______

12. Which factor does NOT affect investment goals? (a) liquidity, (b) safety, (c) growth, (d) stock prices. .... _______ 12._______

13. To achieve a high degree of safety, investors will likely (a) accept smaller earnings on the investment, (b) earn higher earnings on the investment, (c) lose all of their investment, (d) lose some of their investment. .... _______ 13._______

14. Which rule should be followed when planning to invest? (a) Invest entirely in bonds if their interest rates are high. (b) Invest entirely in stocks if their market value is high. (c) Invest entirely in money market funds if their rates of return are high. (d) Spread your risks by investing in different bonds, stocks, and money market funds even though rates of return may not be as high. .... _______ 14._______

15. Which of the following is NOT a purpose of the Depository Institutions Deregulation and Monetary Act that was passed by Congress in 1980? (a) increase competition among financial institutions, (b) set stricter controls over financial institution activities, (c) provide flexibility in setting interest rates, (d) extend the geographic areas served. .... _______ 15._______

Directions: Study each controversial issue carefully. Follow the advice of your teacher before listing in the columns provided reasons why people might answer Yes or No. Your teacher may want you to work with a classmate, talk with others in your community to gather information, or use the library or Internet to gather facts.

18-1. Because financial institutions provide similar services, should all of the following be referred to as banks: commercial banks, mutual savings banks, savings and loan associations, and credit unions?

Reasons for "Yes"	Reasons for "No"

18-2. Because of the dangers involved, should blank endorsements no longer be accepted by businesses or banks?

Reasons for "Yes"	Reasons for "No"

PROBLEMS

18-A. Check whether the services described classify the financial institution as a bank or a non-bank.

Type of Service	Bank	Non-Bank
1. Offers time deposits and commercial loans	____	____
2. Offers consumer loans and demand deposits.	____	____
3. Offers time and demand deposits and consumer loans.	____	____
4. Offers demand deposits and commercial loans.	____	____
5. Offers checking accounts, consumer loans, and commercial loans. ...	____	____
6. Offers certificates of deposit and money market accounts.	____	____

18-B. Because computers are used extensively in banking, many EFT services are available. For each service below, list two advantages. Can you list any disadvantages?

1. Direct Deposit: Advantages:____

____

____

   Disadvantages:____

____

____

2. ATM: Advantages:____

____

____

   Disadvantages: ____

____

____

18-C. Check the appropriate column for the maturity date for each financial instrument purchased for its shortest life.

Financial Instrument	No Maturity Date	One Year Or Less	One Year Or More
1. Treasury bill	____	____	____
2. Certificate of deposit	____	____	____
3. Savings account	____	____	____
4. Treasury note	____	____	____
5. Treasury bond	____	____	____
6. Mutual fund	____	____	____
7. Money market fund	____	____	____

18-D. For each investment goal shown in the columns on the right, place a check mark in the column that would most likely represent the investment goal for each situation described.

		Liquidity	Safety	Growth
1.	Juan is 35, single, and a lawyer in a corporation.	___	___	___
2.	Martin is 22, single, and just started a new business.	___	___	___
3.	Jackie is 55, single, and a clerk.	___	___	___
4.	Wanda is 67, divorced, and a house cleaner.	___	___	___
5.	Jim and Laura are 48, have 2 teens, and operate a profitable partnership.	___	___	___
6.	Terry is 39, newly married, and just lost his job due to downsizing.	___	___	___

18-E. Below are three different types of mutual funds. Four individuals recently invested $5,000 each on the same day, divided among the different funds as shown. Their choice of investments strongly suggest their investment goals. First, calculate the percentage that each person invested in each fund. Then answer the questions that follow.

	Growth Fund	%	Money Market Fund	%	Bond Fund	%
Crowley	0		$3,500		$1,500	
Galvin	$4,000		0		$1,000	
Harriman	$2,500		0		$2,500	
Amanai	$1,000		$500		$3,500	
Student's name:						

1. What appears to be Crowley's primary investment goal or goals? ______________________________

____

2. What appears to be Galvin's primary investment goal or goals? ______________________________

____

3. What appears to be Harriman's primary investment goal or goals? ______________________________

____

4. What appears to be Amani's primary investment goal or goals? ______________________________

____

5. How would you invest the $5,000? ______________________________

____

18-F. A business needs checks written and endorsed. Assume you are the accountant for the business. Complete the tasks specified for each check below. Use correct procedures.

1. Write the following check to Harrison Brothers for $925.50.

The Collision Shop
425 Munson Avenue
Los Angeles, CA 90910

1205

____________________ 20 ________   72-2029/290

PAY TO THE
ORDER OF ____________________________________ $ ____________________

____ D O L L A R S

FOR CLASSROOM USE ONLY

THE FIRST NATIONAL BANK
ANYWHERE, CA 90343

MEMO ____________________

|:27629290|:   1205

2. Write the following check to Karen Anderson for $110.

The Collision Shop
425 Munson Avenue
Los Angeles, CA 90910

1206

____________________ 20 ________   72-2029/290

PAY TO THE
ORDER OF ____________________________________ $ ____________________

____ D O L L A R S

FOR CLASSROOM USE ONLY

THE FIRST NATIONAL BANK
ANYWHERE, CA 90343

MEMO ____________________

|:27629290|:   1206

3. Endorse the following check that will later be mailed to your bank for deposit in your business checking account.

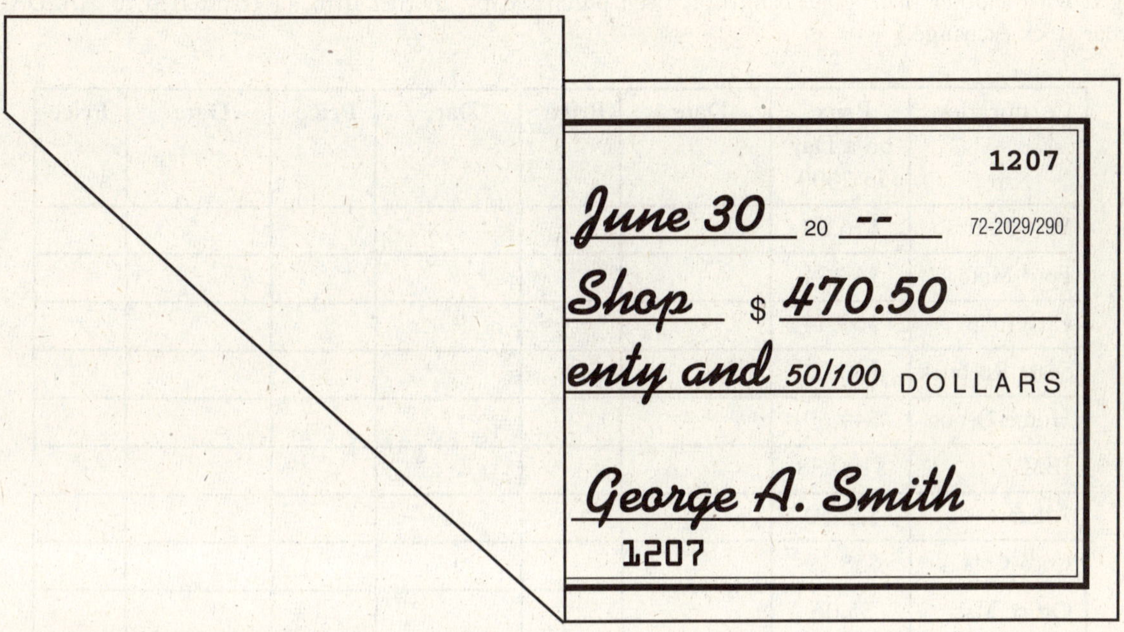

4. Endorse the following check that you are transferring to Maxine Wexton.

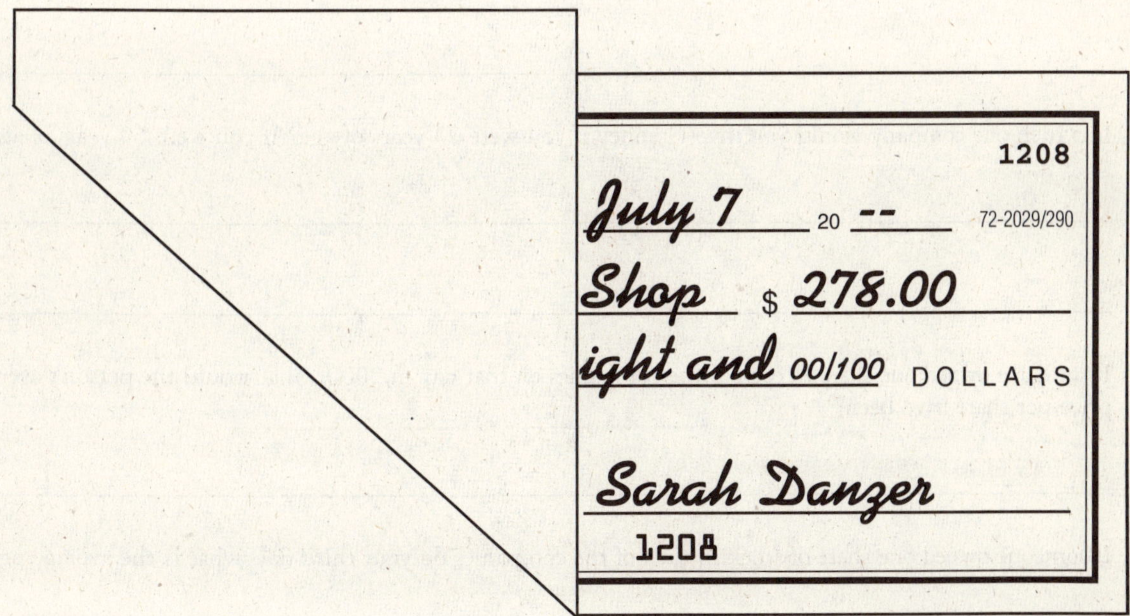

18-G. Below is a list of major American corporations and the cost per share of stock on a particular day in the year 2000. For each of the next three days, find the price of each stock by checking the New York Stock Exchange section of a newspaper or the Internet. In the columns below, record the date and share price for each day. From the stock listings, select the price shown in the columns labeled "last" for the common stock, not preferred (pfd) stock. Then answer the questions below. [If you cannot find a stock, omit it. It may have changed its name, merged with another firm, gone bankrupt, been purchased by another firm, or transferred to NASDAQ or another stock exchange.]

Corporation	Price on a Day in 2000	Date	Price	Date	Price	Date	Price
Wal-Mart	$56.88						
Ford Motor	$43.94						
Citigroup	$62.44						
Sears Roebuck	$33.00						
Home Depot	$49.69						
IBM	$109.88						
Allstate	$23.50						
Coca-Cola	$58.19						
Office Max	$5.06						
Quaker Oats	$76.00						

1. Which three stocks show the best overall gain since the year 2000?

2. Which three stocks show the least gain, or the greatest loss, since the year 2000?

3. In which one company would you invest money if you were 25 years of age? If you were 60 years of age?

4. If someone owned one share in each of the companies on that day in 2000, what would the person's average price per share have been?

5. If someone owned one share of stock in each of the companies on your third day, what is the average price?

6. Using your answers for questions 4 and 5, what would be the gain or loss in percent for those years?

SMALL GROUP ACTIVITIES

Group Activity 1

In teams of three people each, obtain from a nearby commercial bank, savings bank, and savings and loan association a complete list of the services offered to business customers. Be sure to obtain the fees that are charged for the services. Summarize the services and fees of the three financial institutions and analyze the information. You may now be asked to present a brief oral report to the class or a written report to your teacher.

Second, find three financial institutions on the Internet that provide checking accounts, savings accounts, and home mortgages. Obtain the fees that are charged for the services. Summarize the services and rates and analyze the information. You may now be asked to present an oral report to the class or a written report to your teacher.

Third, compare the services and fees between the three walk-in financial institutions in your community and those found on the Internet. Summarize the similarities of services and the differences. Identify the most significant differences between these different forms of financial institutions. Provide an opinion from your team under what circumstances a regular walk-in financial institution is better and under what conditions an online financial institution is better. Be sure to identify the advantages and disadvantages of each. Follow the instructions of your teacher for how to present your final report.

Group Activity 2

Many businesses and individuals simplify their investments by dealing with just one mutual fund company that offers many types of funds, such as money market accounts, bond funds, growth funds, and international funds. A mutual fund's family of funds permits investors to invest money in one or many funds to meet their investment goals.

Your teacher will divide the class into groups of three to five members. Your group is a new financial consulting firm. One of your customers is a small successful firm that wants to invest $90,000. The company's CEO told you that $25,000 must always be readily available during certain times of the year but should earn money. You will be given about a three-month notice before those funds will be needed. Half of the remaining funds should be in somewhat safe investments, while the remaining funds can be invested for growth purposes.

Your team is to select one mutual fund company from among the many that are available in which you can invest your customers' funds. *Caution:* Some mutual fund companies subtract a percentage of the amount to be invested as their service fees, while others do not. This fee may upset your customer. After you have selected a family of mutual funds, prepare a plan for investing the $90,000. When done, you should show the specific fund name, brief information about the past success of the fund, the amount to be invested in it, and an explanation of why you picked this particular fund to meet specific objectives. You may select more than three funds to meet the customer's requirements.

Fund information is available from many sources, including libraries, Internet sites, and stock brokerage firms. In particular, seek the ratings of funds from an organization called Morningstar that is available at stock brokerage firms and online (www.morningstar.com).

Prepare your information and present it as an oral or written report to your customer, as specified by your teacher. Your teacher, and possibly your class, will review your report and decide whether to accept it or ask you to improve it.

<table>
<tr><td rowspan="3">Chapter 19

Credit and Insurance</td><td>Name ________________</td><td colspan="4" align="center">Scoring Record</td></tr>
<tr><td rowspan="2">Date ________________</td><td>Part A</td><td>Part B</td><td>Part C</td><td>Total</td></tr>
<tr><td>Perfect score</td><td>20</td><td>10</td><td>5</td><td>35</td></tr>
<tr><td></td><td>My score</td><td></td><td></td><td></td><td></td></tr>
</table>

Study Guide

Part A—*Directions:* Indicate your answer to each of the following questions by circling either yes or no in the Answers column.

		Answers	For Scoring

1. Can credit card sales be made on the Internet without a customer's signature?   yes   no   1. ______

2. Can a bank charge a business a fee if the business accepts expired credit cards too often?   yes   no   2. ______

3. Is a major advantage to the business issuing its own credit card the convenience of operating the credit card system?   yes   no   3. ______

4. Can a debit card store financial, health, and credit information?   yes   no   4. ______

5. Are character, capacity, capital, and credit the four C's for determining credit-worthiness?   yes   no   5. ______

6. Is Dun & Bradstreet, Inc. an important source of information on the credit standing of retailers, wholesalers, and manufacturers?   yes   no   6. ______

7. Does an applicant have the right to know why credit was refused?   yes   no   7. ______

8. Are the two major objectives of a collection procedure to collect the amount due and to retain the goodwill of the customer?   yes   no   8. ______

9. Is a credit manager likely to skip the final collection step if the amount is small and the customer is financially unable to pay?   yes   no   9. ______

10. Does a firm's cash flow increase when its bad debts increase?   yes   no   10. ______

11. Is insurance most often purchased when a company faces the risk of non-financial losses?   yes   no   11. ______

12. Should businesses insure against every possible financial loss?   yes   no   12. ______

13. Should a business buy insurance to protect against the loss of records that are so valuable that the business could not operate without them?   yes   no   13. ______

14. Should a business be able to predict whether it will have specific losses and the amount of those losses during the year?   yes   no   14. ______

15. Is a risk defined as the uncertainty that a loss may occur?   yes   no   15. ______

16. Are insurance companies required by law to charge the same rates for a certain amount of insurance no matter what the level of risk?   yes   no   16. ______

17. Must the policyholder have an insurable interest in the property in order to purchase insurance?   yes   no   17. ______

18. When purchasing insurance, should the purchaser be concerned about the insurance company's reputation for paying claims in the event of a loss?   yes   no   18. ______

19. Does transportation insurance protect people if they are injured while traveling by air, automobile, or bus?   yes   no   19. ______

20. Are changes in fashion and styles considered non-insurable risks?   yes   no   20. ______

		Answers	For Scoring

1. An example of installment credit is a (a) manufacturer giving a retailer thirty days to pay for merchandise, (b) bank providing a business loan, (c) customer purchasing an automobile and agreeing to pay over a five-year period, (d) retailer holding a purchase until the last payment is made. .... _______ 1. _______

2. An advantage of a debit card for a bank is that (a) it doesn't have to send a transaction statement to its customers, (b) it doesn't have to bill and collect from customers, (c) it doesn't have to charge interest, (d) it doesn't have to charge a service fee. .... _______ 2. _______

3. What is the *best* single measure of whether to grant credit to an applicant? (a) Type of job held by the applicant. (b) Length of time applicant has held the job. (c) Total debts owed by the applicant. (d) Past credit-paying record of the applicant. .... _______ 3. _______

4. Under the Fair Credit Reporting Act, people (a) have the right to see their credit agency reports but do not have the right to have errors corrected, (b) have the right to see their credit agency reports and have errors corrected, (c) have the right to know why their credit application was rejected, (d) have the right to see their credit reports before credit agencies file them. .... _______ 4. _______

5. If the amount of accounts receivable for a business steadily increased over the last six months, but its credit sales remained about the same, bad debt losses are likely to (a) gradually disappear, (b) stay about the same, (c) increase, (d) decrease. .... _______ 5. _______

6. To pay claims, insurance companies use money collected from (a) the federal government, (b) the insured, (c) policyholders, (d) losses. .... _______ 6. _______

7. Most insurance contracts are purchased from (a) policyholders, (b) banks, (c) insurance actuaries, (d) insurance agents. .... _______ 7. _______

8. Organizations that provide an alternative to traditional health insurance include all of the following except (a) health and wellness centers, (b) preferred provider organizations (PPOs), (c) health maintenance organizations (HMOs), (d) all of the responses are correct. .... _______ 8. _______

9. Typical business insurance policies usually do not cover losses resulting from (a) burglaries and robberies, (b) international business operations, (c) the death of an executive, (d) injury to customers caused by the business's product. .... _______ 9. _______

10. Which of the following procedures should businesses consider using to protect important documents and records? (a) Make duplicate copies of all records. (b) Store copies in a separate location from originals. (c) Prepare and practice a disaster plan. (d) All of the responses. .... _______ 10. _______

Part C—*Directions:* In the Answers column, write the letter of the word or expression in Column I that most closely matches each statement in Column II.

Column I	Column II	Answers	For Scoring
A. Equal Credit Opportunity Act	1. Gives women the same credit rights as men.	_______	1. _______
B. insurance	2. A payment to the insurer for protection against a risk	_______	2. _______
C. Truth-in-Lending Act	3. Requires businesses to reveal the total cost of credit and finance charges on credit forms and statements.	_______	3. _______
D. actuaries	4. Gives individuals the right to check personal information appearing in credit agency files.	_______	4. _______
E. Fair Credit Reporting Act	5. Responsible for calculating the rates insurance companies must charge to cover losses and make a profit.	_______	5. _______
F. premium			

Name ____

Directions: Study each controversial issue carefully. Follow the advice of your teacher before listing in the columns provided reasons why people might answer Yes or No. Your teacher may want you to work with a classmate, talk with others in your community to gather information, or use the library or Internet to gather facts.

19-1. Consumers have the right to review their credit records under the Fair Credit Reporting Act, even though few do until a problem arises. Consequently, should credit reporting agencies be required to mail to consumers a copy of all information in their credit file every few years?

Reasons for "Yes"	Reasons for "No"

19-2. In many states, insurance companies are allowed to cancel property and liability insurance contracts if they believe the risk has increased. This means that people who have had an expensive claim on their auto insurance or have received a couple of tickets while driving may have their insurance cancelled. Should states pass laws to require insurance companies to continue to offer automobile insurance to people who pay their premiums, even if the level of risk has increased?

Reasons for "Yes"	Reasons for "No"

PROBLEMS

19-A. Check whether each situation described below calls for a business credit card, bank credit card, or bank debit card.

Situation	Business Credit Card	Bank Credit Card	Bank Debit Card
1. A shopper used one card to buy goods at three different stores.	____	____	____
2. A shopper used a plastic card to buy groceries, but first checked his bank account balance.	____	____	____
3. A retailer withdrew $200 in cash from an automatic teller machine to place in cash registers at the start of the day.	____	____	____
4. A businessperson used a card to pay for a client's luncheon.	____	____	____
5. A shopper used a card to purchase items from advertisements the store enclosed with each month's statement.	____	____	____

19-B. Joel Bender has applied for credit to buy a car on the installment plan. He possesses certain characteristics that might affect his request for credit.

1. Classify each characteristic on the form below.

	Character	Capacity	Capital	Conditions
a. Has a steady, high-paying job.	____	____	____	____
b. Does not have much money in cash savings of any kind.	____	____	____	____
c. Owns a nice home.	____	____	____	____
d. Poor credit record—rarely pays bills on time.	____	____	____	____
e. Frequently loses jobs because of excessive absenteeism.	____	____	____	____
f. A recession is affecting his employer's business.	____	____	____	____

2. Is Joel Bender a good candidate for obtaining the credit he desires? _______________

   Reasons for your answer: ____

   ____

   ____

19-C. The annual sales and the loss on bad debts in each of five business firms are given below. For each firm, determine what percent of the sales is represented by the loss on bad debts.

Business	Sales	Loss on Bad Debts	Percent
Hart Company	$300,000	$ 3,000	________
Cable & Cable	200,000	1,000	________
Bell Corporation	400,000	3,600	________
Wahl Appliances	500,000	7,500	________
Eastern Corporation	600,000	12,000	________

19-D. On the next page is a credit application form. Use the following information to complete the form. Leave blank any item for which information is not provided.

The applicant is Arnold Prince, 41, who lives at 15 Oak Lane, Atlanta, GA 30315-5391. His home telephone number is 404-555-6842, and his social security number is 057-28-8375. Mr. Prince is married, has two children, and has owned his own home for five years. His monthly mortgage payment is $1,250.

The applicant has worked for Cabinets, Inc. (2183 Pine St., Atlanta, GA) as a carpenter and earns an average of $52,000 a year. The company makes kitchen cabinets that are sold to contractors. The business phone number is 404-555-5921. Prior to obtaining his job five years ago, Mr. Prince worked for the Long Lumber Co. in Atlanta on Worth Avenue. He was with the company two years.

Arnold Prince's wife, Marilyn, aged 38, is not currently working for an employer. Her social security number is 061-21-7451.

The Princes have their checking and savings accounts at the same bank: First National Bank, Main Street, Atlanta. The checking account number is 57918 and the money market account number is 57-302. They have a charge account, No. B-78-3564, at Wiley's Department Store with a $115 balance. They buy all their gas for the family car using a Stahl credit card, No. 214-35-892, which they just paid in full. The Princes are requesting $2,500 of credit and would like two credit cards. Sign for Marilyn and Arnold Prince using today's date.

Kramer's Application for Credit

☐ **Individual Account**—Complete sections A, B, C, E. You may designate one authorized user, for whose payments you will be responsible, by writing only his/her name and relationship in section D.

☐ **Joint Account**—Complete sections A through E.

Section A—Tell us about yourself

LAST NAME	FIRST NAME	MIDDLE		SOCIAL SECURITY NO.	AGE

HOME ADDRESS	CITY	STATE	ZIP CODE	HOME PHONE ( )	NO. OF DEPENDENTS

☐ OWN ☐ ROOM & BOARD ☐ LIVE WITH PARENTS ☐ RENT FURNISHED ☐ RENT UNFURNISHED ☐ MOBILE HOME ☐ OTHER | TIME AT THIS ADDRESS YRS. MOS. | MONTHLY RENT/MORTGAGE $

PREVIOUS HOME ADDRESS (IF LESS THAN 3 YEARS AT PRESENT ADDRESS)	TIME AT PREVIOUS ADDRESS YRS. MOS.

NAME AND ADDRESS OF NEAREST RELATIVE NOT LIVING WITH APPLICANT	RELATIVE HOME PHONE ( )

Section B—Tell us about your employment

BUSINESS OR EMPLOYER	TYPE OF BUSINESS	BUSINESS PHONE ( ) EXT.

BUSINESS ADDRESS	CITY	STATE	ZIP CODE	EDUCATION ☐ GRADUATE ☐ COLLEGE ☐ HIGH SCHOOL ☐ ELEMENTARY

POSITION OR TITLE	HOW LONG WITH THIS EMPLOYER? YRS. MOS.	ANNUAL SALARY $

PREVIOUS BUSINESS/EMPLOYER (IF LESS THAN 3 YEARS AT THIS JOB)	HOW LONG? YRS. MOS.	POSITION OR TITLE

OTHER INCOME: ALIMONY, CHILD SUPPORT, OR SEPARATE MAINTENANCE INCOME NEED NOT BE REVEALED IF YOU DO NOT WISH TO HAVE IT CONSIDERED AS A BASIS FOR REPAYING THIS OBLIGATION.	ANNUAL AMOUNT $	SOURCE

Section C—Tell us about your credit and banking relationships

BANK REFERENCES—NAMES OF BANKS AND BRANCH LOCATIONS	ACCOUNT NUMBERS	BALANCE
1.		$
2.		$

CREDIT REFERENCES—ACCOUNTS WITH DEPT. STORES, BANK CARDS, OIL COMPANIES	ACCOUNT NUMBERS	BALANCE
1.		$
2.		$

OUTSTANDING LOANS (NAME OF CREDITOR/CREDIT UNION/FINANCE COMPANY)

OTHER CREDIT REFERENCES	HAVE YOU EVER HAD ANOTHER KRAMER'S ACCOUNT?	ACCOUNT NO. (IF KNOWN)

Section D—Information regarding joint applicant or authorized user

LAST NAME	FIRST NAME	MIDDLE		SOCIAL SECURITY NO.	AGE

BUSINESS OR EMPLOYER	TYPE OF BUSINESS	BUSINESS PHONE ( ) EXT.

BUSINESS ADDRESS	CITY	STATE	ZIP CODE	EDUCATION ☐ GRADUATE ☐ COLLEGE ☐ HIGH SCHOOL ☐ ELEMENTARY

POSITION OR TITLE	HOW LONG WITH THIS EMPLOYER? YRS. MOS.	ANNUAL SALARY $

RELATIONSHIP TO APPLICANT	OTHER INCOME: ALIMONY, CHILD SUPPORT, OR SEPARATE MAINTENANCE INCOME NEED NOT BE REVEALED IF YOU DO NOT WISH TO HAVE IT CONSIDERED AS A BASIS FOR REPAYING THIS OBLIGATION.	ANNUAL AMOUNT $	SOURCE

Section E—Optional Accountguard Credit Insurance Plan

Please enroll me in the Accountguard Credit Insurance Plan providing the coverages described and at the cost set forth on the reverse. I understand it is not required to obtain credit and will not be provided unless I sign below and pay the additional cost disclosed on the reverse.

☐ YES __________, I want ____/____/____ ☐ NO __________, I do not want Accountguard Credit Insurance
     initial   birthdate   initial

Section F—Please sign here and on reverse side

I (We) understand that you may investigate my (our) credit record and may report information concerning the credit experience of the Account for individual and joint accountholders and authorized users to consumer reporting agencies and others.

If Applicant signs on behalf of Joint Applicant, Applicant represents that he or she is authorized to make this application.

I (We) agree to terms of the **RETAIL INSTALLMENT CREDIT AGREEMENT** on reverse side.

X ____
APPLICANT'S SIGNATURE   DATE

X ____
JOINT APPLICANT'S SIGNATURE   DATE

19-E. Your credit manager handed you the report below. Study it and answer the following questions.

Comparative Analysis of Past-Due Accounts

Days Past Due	Current Month	Percent	Prior Month	Percent	Increase or (Decrease)
1-30	$2,580,300	______	$1,335,000	________	$________
31-60	393,800	______	171,200	________	________
61-90	330,700	______	346,100	________	________
Over 90	94,500	______	49,500	________	________
	$________	100.0%	$________	100.0%	$________

1. Complete the report.

2. By what percent did past-due accounts increase over last month?________________________________

3. Should the credit manager be concerned? Yes ______ No ______

   Explain: ____

   ____

   ____

4. What are two possible reasons for the changes that have occurred?

   a. ____

   b. ____

19-F. The Autocity Taxi Company owns and operates a fleet of 100 taxis. It pays an annual insurance premium of $960 per taxi. Thirty percent of the premium pays for liability and medical payments coverage while 70 percent provides collision and comprehensive coverage. During the past five years, Autocity has had the following record of losses covered by collision and comprehensive insurance:

Year 1 $75,000
Year 2 $52,000
Year 3 $43,000
Year 4 $68,000
Year 5 $74,000

Autocity is considering dropping its coverage for collision and comprehensive and putting the money it saves into an account to pay for damage to its taxis.

1. If Autocity had followed its plan for the past five years, how much money could have been saved?

   ____

   ____

2. What other factors should Autocity consider before deciding to drop the insurance coverage?

   ____

   ____

19-G. The Monumental Insurance Company sells life insurance. Premiums for each $1,000 of ordinary life insurance are shown in the following table. The smallest policy the company sells is for $5,000 coverage. Premiums may be paid once a year (annually), twice a year (semiannually), or four times a year (quarterly). Study the table and answer the following questions.

Age Nearest Birthday	Premiums		
	Annually	Semiannually	Quarterly
25	$10.13	$5.27	$2.74
26	$10.50	$5.46	$2.84
27	$10.86	$5.65	$2.93
28	$11.26	$5.86	$3.04
29	$11.68	$6.07	$3.15
30	$12.07	$6.28	$3.26
31	$12.47	$6.48	$3.37
32	$12.90	$6.71	$3.48
33	$13.34	$6.94	$3.60
34	$13.81	$7.18	$3.73
35	$14.30	$7.44	$3.86

1. What is the quarterly premium for Beth Williams? She purchased a $50,000 policy at age 34.

   ____

2. What is the semiannual premium for John VanDyke? He purchased a $20,000 policy at age 25.

   ____

3. What is the annual premium for Earl McCauley? He purchased a $35,000 policy at age 28.

   ____

4. What is the yearly premium for Alice Evans, who purchased a $15,000 policy at age 30, but pays premiums quarterly? ____________________________

5. If Alice Evans paid premiums annually rather than quarterly, how much would she save yearly?

   ____

6. Give a reason why total premiums are less if paid once a year than premiums paid four times a year.

   ____

19-H. Identify the following risks as normally being insurable or non-insurable by placing a check mark in the appropriate column.

	Insurable	Non-Insurable
1. Due to a cold and rainy summer season, a clothing store, unable to sell much of its inventory of swimwear, cannot pay the supplier.	____	____
2. Because of improper storage procedures, a manufacturer finds that a large quantity of the raw materials used in production has been damaged and cannot be used.	____	____
3. A trucking company has had a very large contract with a wholesaler for the past five years. During the last six months, several of the older trucks have had an unusual number of breakdowns resulting in problems delivering the wholesaler's orders. As a result, the wholesaler has refused to sign a new contract with the trucking company.	____	____
4. An insurance company has computer records of all policies and stores them in a vault in another city to protect against loss in case of fire or other damage to its headquarters building. However, the company would still face a significant expense if the original records were destroyed.	____	____
5. A company had just purchased several new vehicles that were parked on the street waiting to be serviced before they were picked up by the company's salespeople. During the night, an uninsured driver lost control of his car while driving by the vehicles. Three of the vehicles had major damage while two others had minor damage.	____	____

SMALL GROUP ACTIVITIES

Group Activity 1

Your teacher will divide the class into three to five teams. Each team is to obtain a list of commercial banks in your geographic area. Then select several preferred banks to contact. However, before contacting any bank, the team leaders should meet and agree on which banks each team will select. The result will be that not more than one team contacts any one bank. Your team will identify and make arrangements for meeting with a bank representative. A meeting time and date should be established early.

Your main topic is: What are the procedures, policies, and problems that arise when a new business sets up and operates a credit card system that involves a national credit card company such as Visa or Master Card? You will want your banker to explain and show how a credit card account system is established and maintained for small businesses. Prior to the meeting, the team must meet to prepare and discuss a set of key questions that you will ask on the topic. For example, you may wish to know the specific kinds of problems that most often occur with new businesses regarding credit card accounts. Your banker may wish to see the questions in advance.

Work out the meeting date and time with the banker. The banker may prefer that you go to the bank where you can be shown forms, policies, electronic equipment, and procedures that the bank uses in working with business credit card accounts. Helpful brochures may also be available.

After your visit, be prepared to make a report to the class. Summarize the most important points learned. Other teams will also present their reports. Comparisons among the teams will allow you to better understand the importance of banks to everyone and how banks might have different approaches to achieving their goal of serving entrepreneurs. When finished, prepare a special note of thanks and give it to your teacher to review. Then send it to the banker.

Group Activity 2

Risks pose important concerns to businesspeople. The business that does an effective job of managing risks has a better chance of being successful than those that do not manage risks effectively. For this activity, your class needs to be divided into teams of three or four students. Each team will review business magazines, newspapers, and Internet sites that provide general business information. Each team should collect as many examples as possible of reports of risks businesses have faced. Write a two- or three-sentence description of each example on a note card.

When the examples have been collected, each team should prepare a poster with the following heading across the top of the poster—Insurable, Non-Insurable—and the following headings on the left side of the poster—Managed Successfully, Managed Unsuccessfully. The result will be four categories on the poster. Now, as a team, decide into which category each note card should be placed and write the category name on the back of the card.

Each team, in turn, should read the information on their note cards to the other teams. The first team to identify the correct category receives a point. (In case of a disagreement, your teacher will identify the correct category.) After all teams have read their note cards, tally the team points and identify the team with the most points.

As a final activity, look at the two categories titled "managed unsuccessfully." The entire class should discuss the risks described and decide how the business could have responded better to each of the risks.

Study Guide

Part A—*Directions:* Indicate your answer to each of the following questions by circling either yes or no in the Answers column.

		Answers		For Scoring

1. Is it possible for companies to spend several million dollars to develop and manufacture one new product? .... yes no 1. _______
2. Do nearly 90 percent of new products developed by businesses survive in the market for at least five years? .... yes no 2. _______
3. Are most of the products you will be using in 10 years currently for sale on the market? .... yes no 3. _______
4. For a company to survive, must it continually search for ways to improve even its most successful products? .... yes no 4. _______
5. Should companies rely on scientists and engineers for their new product ideas? yes no 5. _______
6. Are customers reliable sources of product development information? .... yes no 6. _______
7. Is research that is done without a specific product in mind known as pure research? .... yes no 7. _______
8. Should research and testing on new products be conducted before the product is produced and marketed? .... yes no 8. _______
9. Is manufacturing a form of production that turns raw and semifinished materials into finished products? .... yes no 9. _______
10. Does manufacturing require the use of assembly lines and mass production? .. yes no 10. _______
11. Is the conversion of iron ore into steel an example of continuous processing? . yes no 11. _______
12. Has the assembly line concept changed significantly since Henry Ford used the idea to produce cars? .... yes no 12. _______
13. Should a company that uses a large quantity of raw materials attempt to locate close to the source of those materials? .... yes no 13. _______
14. Should customer location be the most important factor in deciding where to locate a new production facility? .... yes no 14. _______
15. Do some cities offer reduced tax rates or even remove some taxes in order to encourage new businesses to locate there? .... yes no 15. _______
16. Are the three important production planning activities inventory management, human resource planning, and production scheduling? .... yes no 16. _______
17. Have the quality management ideas of Dr. W. Edwards Deming failed to improve the competitiveness of U. S. businesses? .... yes no 17. _______
18. Do robots now complete just the most complex and difficult production processes? .... yes no 18. _______
19. Have service businesses grown at a slower rate than manufacturing businesses? yes no 19. _______
20. Does the quality of a service usually depend on who provides the service? ...... yes no 20. _______

Part B—*Directions:* For each of the following statements, select the word, or group of words, that best completes the statement. In the Answers column, write the letter corresponding to the answer selected.

		Answers	For Scoring

1. The process of creating or improving a product is known as (a) marketing, (b) pure research, (c) logistics, (d) product development. .... ________ 1. ________
2. A consumer panel is made up of people who (a) do not know the company, (b) have worked for the competitor, (c) sell products to the company's customers, (d) have bought or are likely to buy the company's products. .... ________ 2. ________
3. Substituting plastics for metal parts in an automobile to reduce weight and improve efficiency is a product design improvement resulting from (a) marketing research, (b) applied research, (c) pure research, (d) advertising research. .. ________ 3. ________
4. Research in fiber optics conducted for the purpose of increasing the amount of voice and data communications that can move on the same transmission line is an example of (a) pure research, (b) product research, (c) applied research, (d) experimental research. .... ________ 4. ________
5. Which of the following businesses would be *least* likely to locate close to the source of raw materials? (a) furniture manufacturer, (b) steel mill, (c) soft drink bottler, (d) all of the businesses listed would need to locate close to sources of raw materials. .... ________ 5. ________
6. The American management expert W. Edwards Deming suggested that the most important goal for businesses is (a) reducing costs, (b) underpricing the competition, (c) effective marketing, (d) quality. .... ________ 6. ________
7. The United States is changing from the world's leading manufacturing economy to the leading (a) marketing economy, (b) agriculture economy, (c) production economy, (d) service economy. .... ________ 7. ________
8. Which of the following is an example of a service business? (a) an equipment rental business, (b) an insurance agency, (c) a home cleaning business, (d) all are examples of service businesses. .... ________ 8. ________
9. A difference between a product and a service is (a) a service is intangible and a product is tangible, (b) a service can be separated from the person supplying it and a product cannot, (c) the quality of a service depends on the manufacturer, (d) a service can be stored or held longer than a product. .... ________ 9. ________
10. Scheduling fewer lifeguards at a swimming pool during a particularly cool summer is an example of (a) matching supply and demand, (b) matching cost and price, (c) overemphasizing personnel decisions, (d) a poor marketing decision. ________ 10. ________

Part C—*Directions:* In the Answers column, write the letter of the word or expression Column I that most closely matches each statement in Column II.

Column I	Column II	Answers	For Scoring
A. Custom manufacturing	1. Short production runs to make batches of different products.	________	1. ________
B. Mass production	2. A large number of products are produced, each of which is identical to the next.	________	2. ________
C. Continuous processing	3. Raw materials constantly move through equipment that converts them into a more usable form.	________	3. ________
D. Repetitive process	4. The design and building of a product to meet the specific needs of a purchaser.	________	4. ________
E. Intermittent process	5. Modules are assembled in the same way over and over to produce the finished product.	________	5. ________

Name _______________________________

Directions: Study each controversial issue carefully. Follow the advice of your teacher before listing in the columns provided reasons why people might answer Yes or No. Your teacher may want you to work with a classmate, talk with others in your community to gather information, or use the library or Internet to gather facts.

20-1. If a company's research discovers a way to build a safer product but the change makes the product much more expensive and difficult to use, should the company produce and market the safer product?

Reasons for "Yes"	Reasons for "No"

20-2. If the United States continues to change from a manufacturing economy to a service economy, will wages and the standard of living for most citizens decline?

Reasons for "Yes"	Reasons for "No"

PROBLEMS

20-A. One consumer products firm spent $2,300,000 on research in a recent year. Those dollars were divided among several types of research as follows:

Consumer research	25%
Pure research	40%
Applied research	35%

1. If the company's research budget was 6 percent of the total sales for the year, what was the amount of the

    company's sales? $__________________

2. Calculate the amount spent on each type of research.

    a. Consumer research $__________________

    b. Pure research $__________________

    c. Applied research $__________________

3. In the space below, construct a bar graph that shows the percentage of the total research budget spent on

    each type of research.

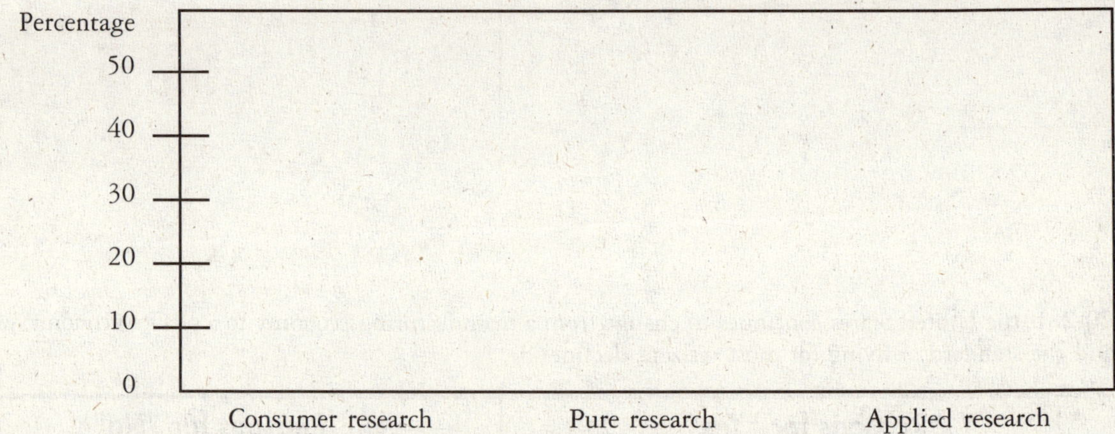

20-B. Jackson and Smith, Inc., is considering building a new factory. They have limited the choice of location to three states. One of the factors they are considering is the taxes and fees they will have to pay in each state. They have collected the following information:

Tax or Fee	State #1	State #2	State #3
Corporate income tax	3%	6%	10%
Property tax	$35/1,000	$30/1,000	$25/1,000
Annual corporation fee	$1,000	$0	$250
Annual license fees	$100	$1,000	$3,000

If the company plans to build a $6,000,000 plant and estimates a net income the first year of $360,000, compute the total cost of taxes and fees for the first year in each state.

	State 1	State 2	State 3
Corporate income tax			
Property tax			
Annual corporation fee			
Annual license fees			
Total			

20-C. The Raydon Company is planning an important change in one of its products. Management has identified the following steps that need to be completed and the estimated time it will take to complete each step:

1.	Review of old product by consumer panel	14 days
2.	Product design	70 days
3.	Product development	40 days
4.	Developing manufacturing facilities	60 days
5.	Test marketing	90 days
6.	Production and distribution	30 days

The Raydon Company is beginning the process on March 15. Assume that each step must be completed before the next step is started. Identify the date each step will be completed and the earliest date customers will be able to buy the new product.

Step   Date Completed

1. _______________

2. _______________

3. _______________

4. _______________

5. _______________

6. _______________

7. Date product available for sale: _______________

20-D. You and your friend are planning to start a service business. The business will provide pet and plant care for people while they are on vacation. For each of the following characteristics of service businesses, a customer need is identified. In the column on the right, describe one thing your business will do to ensure that your business will be able to meet that specific customer need.

Characteristic	Specific Customer Need	What will your business do to meet that customer need?
1. Form	Some people have exotic plants requiring special care.	
2. Availability	People want to be certain that you will deliver the promised services, so they don't have to worry while on vacation.	
3. Quality	Pet owners want their pets to receive attention and to follow their accustomed schedule.	
4. Timing	Some pet owners need to find a place to leave their pets for an afternoon or evening on very short notice.	

20-E. An automobile manufacturer asked a marketing research firm to survey prospective new car buyers. One of the questions asked the respondents to identify the factor that was most important to them when purchasing a new car. The responses are summarized in the following table:

Factor	Number of Responses	% of Total
Price	210	_____
Styling	480	_____
Brand name	365	_____
Reputation of dealer	240	_____
Special accessories	245	_____
Fuel economy	400	_____
Other	60	_____
Total respondents	_____	

1. Complete the table by calculating the total number of people responding to the survey and the percentage of respondents who selected each of the factors as most important.
2. After reviewing the results, make two specific written recommendations to the automobile manufacturer to help in the design of cars for the types of people surveyed.

Recommendation #1:

____

____

____

____

Recommendation #2:

____

____

____

____

20-F. Often, to enhance a service business, a company will offer products associated with the service. For each of the service businesses listed below, think of at least one product offered by the business. Write the product on the space provided.

Service Business   **Product Offered**

1. Dog groomer   _______________________________

2. Hair salon   _______________________________

3. Carpet cleaners   _______________________________

4. Internet service provider   _______________________________

5. Dentist   _______________________________

Conversely, businesses that sell products often offer services to complement their products. Think of at least five products that include a free service. Write your answers on the spaces provided.

Product   **Service Provided**

1. _______________________   _______________________________

2. _______________________   _______________________________

3. _______________________   _______________________________

4. _______________________   _______________________________

5. _______________________   _______________________________

SMALL GROUP ACTIVITIES

Group Activity 1

With instructions from your teacher, divide into groups of four or five students. In your group, read the following scenario and answer the questions.

Companies regularly work to identify new products that they can introduce to consumers. Those products can result from pure or applied research, from the study of consumer needs, and from the recommendations of customers or company employees. Many new product ideas are developed creatively when businesspeople think about problems and needs.

For each of the categories listed below, identify an existing product that appears to have been developed to fit that category. List that product or its description in the second column. Then in the third column, try to develop a new product idea that fits the criteria.

Criteria	Current Product	New Product Idea
1. Making a household task easier	______________	______________
2. A new recreational activity	______________	______________
3. A new use for an old product	______________	______________
4. A product related to a holiday or a special event	______________	______________
5. A product that uses new technology ..	______________	______________
6. A product that makes it easier to use another product	______________	______________
7. A product designed to reduce the chance of accident or injury	______________	______________

Group Activity 2

With instructions from your teacher, divide into groups so that the number of students per group equals the number of groups formed. You are preparing to conduct a customer panel on some aspect of your high school experience. Your teacher will give each group a topic. Spend about 10-15 minutes brainstorming questions to ask about your topic. When your teacher signals time, he or she will select a group to be the consumer panel leader. The other groups will act as the panels. Spend the remaining time in the panels discussing the chosen topic. Save about 10 minutes at the end of the period to have each panel report their findings.

<table>
<tr><td>Chapter 21</td><td rowspan="2">Name ___________________

Date ___________________</td><td colspan="5">Scoring Record</td></tr>
<tr><td>Nature and Scope of Marketing</td><td></td><td>Part A</td><td>Part B</td><td>Part C</td><td>Total</td></tr>
<tr><td rowspan="2"></td><td></td><td>Perfect score</td><td>20</td><td>10</td><td>5</td><td>35</td></tr>
<tr><td></td><td>My score</td><td></td><td></td><td></td><td></td></tr>
</table>

Study Guide

Part A—*Directions:* Indicate your answer to each of the following questions by circling either yes or no in the Answers column.

		Answers	For Scoring
1.	Do people make decisions in their daily lives that influence supply and demand?	yes no	1. _______
2.	Do marketing activities help to match production and consumption in our private enterprise economy?	yes no	2. _______
3.	Is marketing defined as the transporting of products from producers to consumers?	yes no	3. _______
4.	Are retailers and wholesalers involved in marketing?	yes no	4. _______
5.	Are jobs that involve customer service and credit services types of marketing jobs?	yes no	5. _______
6.	Does approximately half of every dollar consumers spend go to pay the cost of marketing activities?	yes no	6. _______
7.	Do firms that are production-oriented pay most attention to decisions about what and how to produce?	yes no	7. _______
8.	Do firms that are customer-oriented emphasize widespread distribution and promotion in order to sell the products produced?	yes no	8. _______
9.	Should a company that has adopted the marketing concept have a marketing manager as a part of top management?	yes no	9. _______
10.	Does selecting a market involve determining whom to serve and where to serve?	yes no	10. _______
11.	Is a good target market made up of people with needs that are very different from those of other people in the same target market?	yes no	11. _______
12.	Do marketers group customers by characteristics such as age, gender, family status, education, income, and occupation?	yes no	12. _______
13.	Is the marketing mix a blend of all decisions related to the four elements of marketing?	yes no	13. _______
14.	Do companies that market the same product usually use the same marketing mix?	yes no	14. _______
15.	Is a product most profitable during the introductory stage of the product life cycle?	yes no	15. _______
16.	Can some companies move a product out of the decline stage of the product life cycle by finding new uses for the product?	yes no	16. _______
17.	Can the same product be both an industrial good and a consumer good?	yes no	17. _______
18.	Do consumers believe that most brands of shopping goods are quite similar?	yes no	18. _______
19.	Are unsought goods products that consumers do not shop for because they have no strong need for them?	yes no	19. _______
20.	Do many of the complaints consumers have about businesses today involve marketing activities?	yes no	20. _______

		Answers	For Scoring

1. The goal of effective marketing is to (a) create and maintain satisfying exchange relationships, (b) successfully sell the products produced, (c) find the right price to make a profit, (d) distribute products as efficiently as possible. .... ______ 1. ______

2. What percentage of all people employed in the United States work in a marketing job or a marketing business? (a) less than 10 percent, (b) well over 30 percent, (c) about 50 percent, (d) nearly 90 percent. .... ______ 2. ______

3. Which of the major marketing activities is involved in holding goods until they are needed by consumers? (a) buying, (b) transporting, (c) storing, (d) grading and valuing. .... ______ 3. ______

4. An attractive market is one that has (a) few existing competitors, (b) a large number of customers with a need for the product, (c) customers with sufficient money to spend on such a product, (d) all of the responses are part of an attractive market. .... ______ 4. ______

5. Companies that direct their activities at satisfying the needs of consumers are (a) customer-oriented, (b) sales-oriented, (c) production-oriented, (d) competition-oriented. .... ______ 5. ______

6. Groups of customers with similar needs are known as (a) final consumers, (b) industrial consumers, (c) marketing mixes, (d) target markets. .... ______ 6. ______

7. If you bought a computer, which of the following items that came with your computer can be considered part of the product? (a) the hard drive, (b) the software installed in it, (c) the technical support provided by the company, (d) all of these are part of the product. .... ______ 7. ______

8. Which of the following is NOT an element of the marketing mix? (a) people, (b) product, (c) place, (d) price .... ______ 8. ______

9. The product life cycle stage in which sales are highest is (a) introduction, (b) growth, (c) maturity, (d) decline. .... ______ 9. ______

10. Whether a product is an industrial good or a consumer good is based on (a) who uses the product, (b) what kind of company makes the product, (c) the type of marketing activities used, (d) the price of the product. .... ______ 10. ______

Column I	Column II	Answers	For Scoring
A. Convenience goods	1. Products used by another business.	______	1. ______
B. Shopping goods	2. Products among which consumers see important differences in terms of prices and features of different brands.	______	2. ______
C. Specialty goods	3. Products that many consumers do not feel a strong need for, such as life insurance, encyclopedias, and funeral services.	______	3. ______
D. Unsought goods	4. Inexpensive items that consumers purchase regularly.	______	4. ______
E. Industrial goods	5. Particular products that consumers insist on having and are willing to search for.	______	5. ______

     Name ___________________________________

Directions: Study each controversial issue carefully. Follow the advice of your teacher before listing in the columns provided reasons why people might answer Yes or No. Your teacher may want you to work with a classmate, talk with others in your community to gather information, or use the library or Internet to gather facts.

21-1. Does marketing cause people to purchase products and services they really don't want or need?

Reasons for "Yes"	Reasons for "No"

21-2. Are most businesses today customer-oriented?

Reasons for "Yes"	Reasons for "No"

PROBLEMS

21-A. Marketing- oriented firms attempt to identify target markets before they sell their products. For most products, there will be several groups of potential customers. Each group will have different needs and will want a different marketing mix.

For each of the products listed below, describe two unique target markets for the product. Then describe the marketing mix that would be needed to satisfy each of the target markets.

Product	Description of Target Market	Description of Marketing Mix
Automobile	#1	#1
	#2	#2
Motel	#1	#1
	#2	#2

21-B. Marketing managers make decisions about each of the elements of the marketing mix— product, price, place, and promotion. For each of the marketing decisions listed below, decide which element is most related to the decision. Place a check mark in the appropriate column to indicate your answer.

Marketing Decision	Product	Price	Promotion	Place
1. A new package will be used for the product.	___	___	___	___
2. We will sell two albums for $12.	___	___	___	___
3. A display of the new shoes will be built inside the store entrance.	___	___	___	___
4. A discount of 2 percent will be given if payment is received in 30 days.	___	___	___	___
5. We will begin advertising our product on television.	___	___	___	___
6. A wholesaler will sell the product to retailers.	___	___	___	___
7. If the goods are sent by air, they will get to the store sooner.	___	___	___	___
8. We must improve the quality to satisfy the customer.	___	___	___	___
9. We will open a store in the new shopping center.	___	___	___	___
10. We will provide more training for our salespeople.	___	___	___	___

21-C. Some goods are marketed directly from the producer to the consumer. Ask your relatives and neighbors what purchases they have recently made directly from the producer. Report in the following space those items purchased and place a check mark in the appropriate column to indicate the method used.

Item Purchased	By Mail or Internet	By Going to the Producer	By Having the Producer or a Salesperson Come to the Consumer
1. _________________	___	___	___
2. _________________	___	___	___
3. _________________	___	___	___
4. _________________	___	___	___
5. _________________	___	___	___
6. _________________	___	___	___

21-D. In a survey of 400 business executives, the respondents identified the marketing activities that were performed in their businesses. The activities and the number of executives who said the activity was performed in their business are:

Marketing Activity	Number of Businesses in Which It Is Performed
Buying	341
Selling	386
Transporting	236
Storing	337
Financing	222
Researching	163
Risk taking	332
Grading and valuing	342

1. List the marketing activities in rank order according to the number of firms that perform each activity:

a. ___________________________   e. ___________________________

b. ___________________________   f. ___________________________

c. ___________________________   g. ___________________________

d. ___________________________   h. ___________________________

2. How many additional firms are involved in storing activities than are involved in financing activities? _________

3. What percentage of total firms are involved in risk-taking activities? ___________

4. What percentage of the firms conduct research as a part of their marketing efforts? ___________

5. Why do you believe that the highest-rated marketing activity is selling, while research is the lowest-rated activity? ____

____

____

21-E. For each of the following descriptions of competition, identify whether the product is in the introduction, growth, maturity, or decline stage of the product life cycle.

Description	Life-Cycle Stage
1. Several brands of a product are available and new brands are being introduced. Profits are excellent for the brands already on the market.	_____________
2. A company is attempting to improve its product. It is losing sales because a new, much improved product has been introduced by a competitor. Sales are not very good and many competitors are losing money.	_____________
3. Many customers have purchased the product and find it to be quite satisfying. Because of a very profitable market in the past, many businesses have brands that are competing for a share of the market. A great deal of money is spent on promotion by the companies, but customers are not very loyal to one brand.	_____________
4. Some customers are excited about a new product that they believe offers real advantages compared to other products they have been buying. However, only one brand is currently available and it is very high priced—so most customers continue to buy the products they are used to. If the company cannot find new customers quickly, it will be unable to make a profit.	_____________
5. Sales are the highest they have ever been in the market, but companies are having a difficult time making a profit. Costs are increasing as companies try hard to convince customers their brand is best. It seems that while businesses work hard to attract customers, the customers really don't seem to recognize important differences among the many brands.	_____________

21-F. Products can be classified as either industrial or consumer goods, depending on who buys the product and how they will use it. It is also possible for the same product to fit within any of the four consumer goods classifications, depending on how important the product is to the consumers and whether they are willing to shop and compare products and brands. In the following activity, match the letter of the goods classification in Column 1 with the description of the product use in Column 2. Place the letter of the correct response in Column 3.

Goods Classification

A. Industrial good
B. Convenience good
C. Shopping good
D. Specialty good
E. Unsought good

Description of Product Use

1. A recent college graduate has saved enough money to make a down payment on a new car. She will be able to afford a car of no more than $11,000. In order to make the best decision, she reads a popular consumer magazine that rates the major brands. She asks several co-workers about their experiences with three brands she is considering. When she has decided on a model, she visits two dealers to compare prices. .... _______

2. An insurance company is replacing ten cars in its fleet. The purchasing agent contacts three manufacturers and provides specifications for the ten cars. When bids are received, the company selects the lowest bid and makes the purchase. .... _______

3. A 50-year-old man has purchased a new car every four years for the past twenty years. He used to spend a great deal of time shopping and comparing and was not brand loyal. However, he has been quite satisfied with his last two cars, which were both the same brand. So this year he has decided to go to his local dealer and buy the latest model of that brand. _______

4. A mother is filling her shopping cart at the grocery store. For some products, she compares prices and nutritional content before making her buying decision. But now she needs to buy diapers and wipes for her baby. She has been satisfied with the brand she normally buys, and she can't see any particular difference between her brand and others, so she just grabs her usual brand and heads for the checkout line. .... _______

5. A college student has just moved to a new apartment that is five miles from campus. To get to campus for classes, most students choose to ride a bicycle, take the bus, or buy an automobile. Because the student does not have a garage or parking space, she decides it will be most convenient to ride the bus each day. .... _______

Answer

SMALL GROUP ACTIVITIES

Group Activity 1

With instructions from your teacher, divide into groups of four or five students. Your group is assigned the job of coming up with an idea for a fund-raising activity for your school. After you have decided on the activity, your task is to plan how you will market the fund-raising activity, using all four elements of the marketing mix. Be prepared to present your ideas to the class.

Group Activity 2

With instructions from your teacher, divide into groups of four or five students. Complete the following chart, describing the marketing activities that have to be completed for each product or service listed and, if possible, who is responsible for completing each activity. Be prepared to present your list to the class.

Marketing Activity	Crest Toothpaste	Alpo Dog Food	Gold's Gym	American Airlines
Buying				
Selling				
Transporting				
Storing				
Financing				
Researching				
Risk taking				
Grading & valuing				

<table>
<tr><td rowspan="3">Chapter 22

Product Development and Distribution</td><td colspan="6" align="center">Scoring Record</td></tr>
<tr><td rowspan="2">Name ___________

Date ___________</td><td></td><td>Part A</td><td>Part B</td><td>Part C</td><td>Total</td></tr>
<tr><td>Perfect score</td><td>20</td><td>10</td><td>5</td><td>35</td></tr>
<tr><td colspan="2">My score</td><td></td><td></td><td></td><td></td></tr>
</table>

Study Guide

Part A—*Directions:* Indicate your answer to each of the following questions by circling either yes or no in the Answers column.

		Answers	For Scoring
1.	Do businesspeople and consumers have the same perceptions of a product?	yes no	1. _______
2.	Do businesses study their target markets to decide what basic, enhanced, and extended products to produce?	yes no	2. _______
3.	If a business decides to offer its product in a variety of sizes, would it be expanding its product line?	yes no	3. _______
4.	If you are satisfied with one product from a company, are you likely to have confidence in a different product sold under the same brand?	yes no	4. _______
5.	Does our economic system rely on the successful exchange of products and services between businesses and consumers?	yes no	5. _______
6.	Do differences between the offerings of businesses and the requirements of consumers create an economic discrepancy?	yes no	6. _______
7.	Are businesses that participate in activities that transfer goods and services from the producer to the user called marketing channels?	yes no	7. _______
8.	Are producers and consumers the most common types of channel members? ..	yes no	8. _______
9.	Does the shortest distribution channel include a retailer?	yes no	9. _______
10.	Will a manufacturer need fewer salespeople if a channel of distribution includes retailers rather than going directly to consumers?	yes no	10. _______
11.	Is it illegal to have more than one wholesaler in a channel of distribution?	yes no	11. _______
12.	Does one business own the organizations at other levels of a channel of distribution in an administered channel?	yes no	12. _______
13.	Is it possible for the same product to be sold through several different channels of distribution at the same time?	yes no	13. _______
14.	Will the channel of distribution usually be short for a product that requires special handling?	yes no	14. _______
15.	Are railroads responsible for handling over half of the volume of products shipped in the United States?	yes no	15. _______
16.	Are trucks frequently used for short-distance shipping?	yes no	16. _______
17.	Is air shipping used primarily for small, high value, or perishable items?	yes no	17. _______
18.	Though air transport is one of the most expensive means of transporting goods, are more products continually being shipped by air?	yes no	18. _______
19.	Can the bar codes on products and packages be used to track the products during shipment?	yes no	19. _______
20.	Is a distribution center a building used to store large quantities of products until they can be sold?	yes no	20. _______

	Answers	For Scoring

1. Which of the following is NOT one of the levels of product design? (a) extended product, (b) basic product, (c) expanded product, (d) enhanced product. ______ 1: ______

2. An extended product is (a) the physical product in its simplest form, (b) a product that offers different features and options for the consumer, (c) a product that includes additional features that are not part of the physical product, (d) both a and b. ______ 2. ______

3. A group of similar products with obvious variations in the design and quality is a (a) basic product, (b) product line, (c) enhanced product, (d) tangible product. ______ 3. ______

4. Two important product mix decisions are (a) packaging and branding, (b) pricing and advertising, (c) size and location, (d) transportation and storage. ______ 4. ______

5. A brand (a) always indicates quality, (b) often plays a major role in buying decisions, (c) helps protect a product from breakage, (d) makes a product easier to use. ______ 5. ______

6. An example of an economic discrepancy is (a) a farmer harvests tomatoes and sells them immediately to customers at a roadside stand, (b) a small furniture manufacturer produces only the products that customers order, (c) a bank is open from 9 a.m. to 5 p.m. but many customers do not get off from work until 5:30 p.m., (d) all of the responses. ______ 6. ______

7. Which type of channel member primarily works with other channel members rather than with the final consumer? (a) producer, (b) wholesaler, (c) retailer, (d) end user. ______ 7. ______

8. Which of the following is an example of a direct channel of distribution? (a) producer to retailer, (b) retailer to consumer, (c) producer to consumer, (d) wholesaler to retailer. ______ 8. ______

9. Combining telephone sales with computer technology is a popular method of direct sales known as (a) telemarketing, (b) computer sales, (c) infomercials, (d) teledistribution. ______ 9. ______

10. A channel of distribution in which one organization takes a leadership position to benefit all channel members is (a) a direct channel, (b) an administered channel, (c) an integrated channel, (d) none of the responses. ______ 10. ______

	For Scoring

1. A _____________ consists of all attributes, both _____________ and _____________, that customers receive in exchange for the purchase price. 1. ______

2. A ___________________ is the complete set of all products a business offers to a market. It can have _____________, _____________, or _____________. 2. ______

3. When a producer cannot or chooses not to perform all of the ___________________, the need for an _____________ channel of distribution arises. 3. ______

4. The most commonly used methods of _________________ goods are by railroad, _____________, and _____________. 4. ______

5. A _____________________ is a large building designed to accumulate and _____________ products efficiently. 5. ______

Directions: Study each controversial issue carefully. Follow the advice of your teacher before listing in the columns provided reasons why people might answer Yes or No. Your teacher may want you to work with a classmate, talk with others in your community to gather information, or use the library or Internet to gather facts.

22-1. Have manufacturers/producers exceeded reasonable limits in offering a wide variety of products and services?

Reasons for "Yes"	Reasons for "No"

22-2. Do wholesalers deserve some type of government protection to keep them from being forced out of channels of distribution by large producers or retailers?

Reasons for "Yes"	Reasons for "No"

PROBLEMS

22-A. For the following products and services, complete the chart below describing the features of the basic product, enhanced product, and extended product. The first row is filled in as an example.

Product	Basic Features	Enhanced Features	Extended Features
Car wash service	Wash and wax	Vacuuming, air freshener	Services in your driveway, detailing
Refrigerator			
Automobile			
Dog grooming service			
Fitness center			
Personal computer			

22-B. A brand is a name, symbol, word, or design that identifies a product, service, or company. Although producers want customers to make pleasant associations with their brands, often brands help customers avoid products and services as well as seek the products out. Based on your shopping experience, list five brands that you use regularly and five brands that you usually choose not to purchase. List your reasons for your answers.

Brands I Purchase   **Reasons**

1. ____________   ________________________________
2. ____________   ________________________________
3. ____________   ________________________________
4. ____________   ________________________________
5. ____________   ________________________________

Brands I Avoid   **Reasons**

1. ____________   ________________________________
2. ____________   ________________________________
3. ____________   ________________________________
4. ____________   ________________________________
5. ____________   ________________________________

22-C. A channel member is often used to reduce the number of transactions that must occur in a channel of distribution. The charts below show how including a retailer reduces the number of transactions needed to move products between producers and consumers.

1. Draw lines between the producers and consumers in the following chart to show the transactions that must occur if each consumer buys each producer's product. Two transactions are shown as examples.

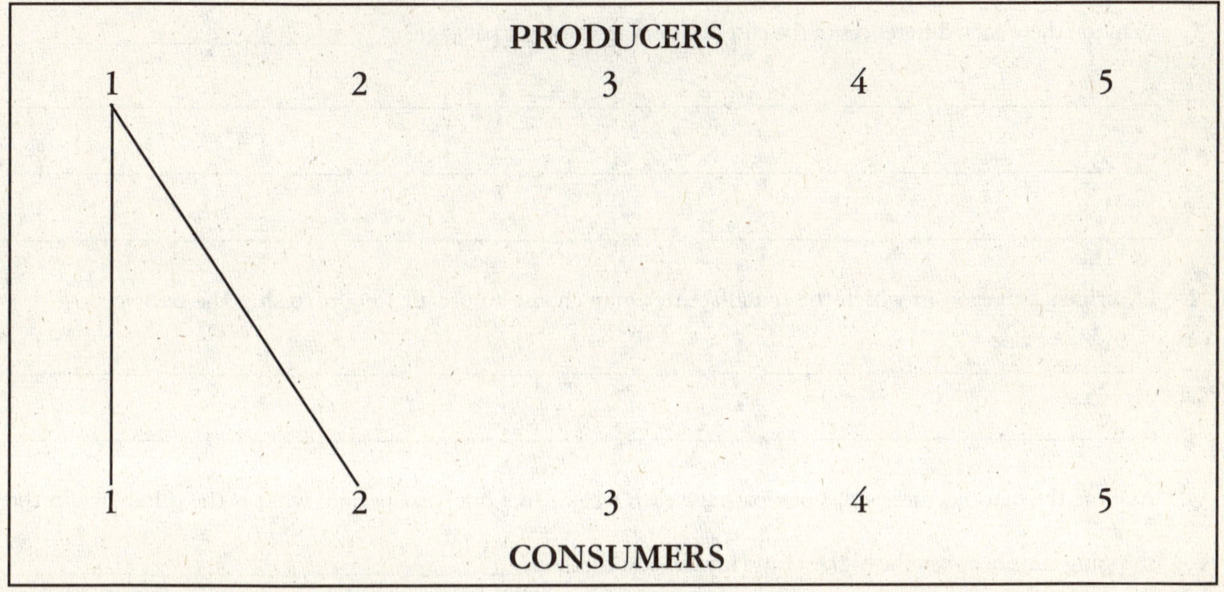

2. Now draw lines indicating the transactions that need to be made if a retailer is used. Each consumer again buys every product, and all products are sold by the retailer. An example is shown for two transactions.

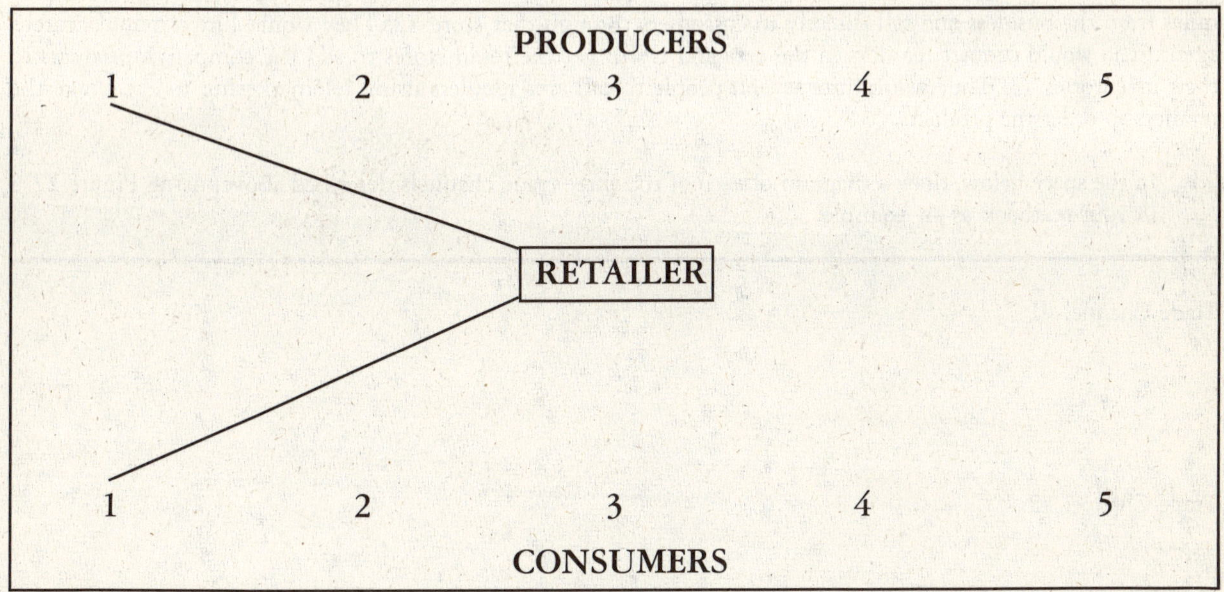

3. How many transactions were needed when no retailer was present? ________________________________

4. How many transactions were needed when the retailer was used? ________________________________

5. In addition to reducing the number of buying and selling transactions, what benefits result from the retailer entering the marketing channel? ________________________________

____

22-D. A manufacturer regularly makes shipments to a retailer located 800 miles away. The shipment weighs 50 pounds. The following chart shows the cost of shipment using several methods.

Carrier	Cost
Bus	$18.75
Parcel service	9.50
Air freight	42.00
Truck	28.50

1. Why are there such differences in the cost of shipping the same package? _______________

   ____

   ____

   ____

2. Describe a situation in which the manufacturer may choose to use air freight to ship the package.

   ____

   ____

3. Assume the manufacturer ships one package each week. In a one-year period, what is the difference in the

   shipping costs between the highest- and lowest-cost method? _______________

22-E. A small business will soon open to produce high-quality leather wallets, purses, and related accessories. For at least the first three years of the business, the owners plan to sell the products only within a fifty-mile radius of the business's location. The owners are trying to decide on the most appropriate distribution channel and are evaluating three choices: (1) They would open one retail outlet in a large shopping center located ten miles from the business and sell directly to customers through that store. (2) They would hire a manufacturer's agent, who would contact retailers in the area and try to get the retail stores to add the company's products to their inventories. (3) They would hire several people to call area retailers using telemarketing to encourage the retailers to order the products.

1. In the space below, draw a diagram of each of the three trade channels described above, using Figure 22-3 in your textbook as an example.

Trade Channel #1

Trade Channel #2

Trade Channel #3

2. Write a brief statement describing each channel.

**Trade
Channel**   Evaluation

1   ____

      ____

      ____

2   ____

      ____

      ____

3   ____

      ____

      ____

SMALL GROUP ACTIVITIES

Group Activity 1

With instructions from your teacher, divide into small groups and answer the following questions.

A company that operates a distribution center is considering the purchase of an automated product-storage system. The system moves packages on metal tracks to storage bins through the use of robots that load and unload the packages from the bins. The system will cost $380,000 and will require two people to operate it. It is expected the salary of each of the two people will average $25,000 a year.

Currently, packages in the distribution system are handled by 15 employees using handcarts. Each employee has a handcart, which costs $100 each and must be replaced every three years. The average employee salary is $15,000 a year.

1. Using only equipment and employee costs, compare the company's costs of the automated system and the current system for the next four years. Assume that the company will buy each employee a new handcart in Year 1.

Year	Automated System	Current System
1	$ _______	$ _______
2	$ _______	$ _______
3	$ _______	$ _______
4	$ _______	$ _______
Total Cost	$ _______	$ _______

2. In addition to the equipment and employee costs, list four other factors the company should consider in deciding whether to purchase the automated system.

1. ____

2. ____

3. ____

4. ____

Group Activity 2

With directions from your teacher, divide into groups and answer the following questions.

Identify three retail stores in your community that fit into each of the categories listed below. Then describe the differences you found among the categories of retail stores.

A store that offers a broad variety of many products:

_____________________ _____________________ _____________________

A store that offers a large variety of a few products:

_____________________ _____________________ _____________________

A store that offers many products with limited variety:

_____________________ _____________________ _____________________

A store that offers limited products and variety:

_____________________ _____________________ _____________________

Be prepared to share your choices with the class.

<table>
<tr><td rowspan="3">Chapter 23

Pricing and Promotion</td><td rowspan="3">Name _______________

Date _______________</td><td colspan="5" align="center">Scoring Record</td></tr>
<tr><td></td><td>Part A</td><td>Part B</td><td>Part C</td><td>Total</td></tr>
<tr><td>Perfect score</td><td>20</td><td>10</td><td>5</td><td>35</td></tr>
<tr><td></td><td></td><td>My score</td><td></td><td></td><td></td><td></td></tr>
</table>

Study Guide

Part A—*Directions:* Indicate your answer to each of the following questions by circling either yes or no in the Answers column.

		Answers	For Scoring
1.	Should products be priced so that buyers consider them a good value for the money?	yes no	1. ______
2.	Are these the four decisions businesses must make when planning a purchase: what to purchase, when to purchase, how much to purchase, and what to do with the goods after the purchase?	yes no	2. ______
3.	Are customers' needs the most important consideration for businesses when they make purchases?	yes no	3. ______
4.	Do companies that sell to other businesses often extend credit to their customers?	yes no	4. ______
5.	Are discounts offered by suppliers to their business customers subtracted from the selling price?	yes no	5. ______
6.	For a product, is the price charged to the final consumer the cost of goods sold?	yes no	6. ______
7.	Is markup the same as profit?	yes no	7. ______
8.	Does setting an extremely high price for a product ensure a profit for the business?	yes no	8. ______
9.	When stated in dollars and cents, are markup and margin identical?	yes no	9. ______
10.	Does a business determine the price that will earn a specific profit by adding the costs of producing the product to the target profit?	yes no	10. ______
11.	Is promotion the primary marketing activity used to communicate with prospective customers?	yes no	11. ______
12.	Does advertising include both paid and non-paid promotion?	yes no	12. ______
13.	Is more money spent on advertising each year than is spent on any other type of promotion?	yes no	13. ______
14.	Are billboards a type of mass-media advertising?	yes no	14. ______
15.	Would a business with a loyal group of customers and a product that has been on the market a long time likely have to spend more money on advertising than a business with a very complex product?	yes no	15. ______
16.	Should salespeople deal with all customers in the same way when selling the company's products and services?	yes no	16. ______
17.	Are amusement, friendship, and fear all examples of buying motives?	yes no	17. ______
18.	Should salespeople discourage customers from handling or using the product to avoid damage or injury?	yes no	18. ______
19.	Should a salesperson encourage a customer to ask questions and identify any objections during the sales presentation?	yes no	19. ______
20.	Are coupons an effective method of increasing a product's sales for a short period of time?	yes no	20. ______

		Answers	For Scoring

1. The business buying decision includes (a) what and when to purchase, (b) from whom to purchase, (c) how much to purchase, (d) all of the responses. ....   1. ______

2. A discount given to the buyer for ordering or taking delivery of goods in advance of the normal buying period is a (a) quantity discount, (b) cash discount, (c) seasonal discount, (d) trade discount. ....   2. ______

3. If a product sells for $40, the operating expenses are $23, and the cost of goods sold is $24, what is the net profit or loss? (a) a loss of $7, (b) a profit of $87, (c) a profit of $1, (d) a profit of $17. ....   3. ______

4. If customers carefully compare prices among several businesses, a business should probably use which method of pricing? (a) pricing to meet competition, (b) pricing to earn a specific profit, (c) pricing based on consumer demand, (d) pricing to sell more merchandise. ....   4. ______

5. The primary difference between advertising and selling is that advertising is (a) expensive, (b) impersonal, (c) able to reach fewer people at one time, (d) all of the responses. ....   5. ______

6. Which of the following is NOT a form of advertising media? (a) publications, (b) mass media, (c) salespeople, (d) displays. ....   6. ______

7. A large one-time expenditure for advertising should be used when the business (a) has very little money, (b) is promoting a successful product, (c) has a great deal of competition, (d) is introducing a new product. ....   7. ______

8. For many salespeople, the most difficult part of the selling process is (a) presenting and demonstrating the product, (b) answering customer questions, (c) closing the sale, (d) suggestion selling. ....   8. ______

9. Window displays, layouts for newspaper advertisements, and sales presentation materials provided by manufacturers to retailers are all examples of (a) publicity, (b) dealer aids, (c) advertising support, (d) promotional materials. ....   9. ______

10. The legal requirement that advertisers be able to prove their claims about their products is called (a) corrective advertising, (b) cease and desist order, (c) substantiation, (d) full disclosure. ....   10. ______

Part C—*Directions:* In the Answers column, write the letter of the word or expression in Column I that most closely matches each statement in Column II.

Column I	Column II	Answers	For Scoring
A. Cost of Goods Sold B. Trade Discount C. Cash Discount D. Selling Price E. Net Profit	1. The actual price customers pay for the product or service.	______	1. ______
	2. The difference between the selling price and all costs and expenses of the business.	______	2. ______
	3. A price reduction that manufacturers give to their channel partners in exchange for additional services.	______	3. ______
	4. The cost to produce the product or buy it for resale.	______	4. ______
	5. A price reduction given for paying by a certain date.	______	5. ______

Directions: Study each controversial issue carefully. Follow the advice of your teacher before listing in the columns provided reasons why people might answer Yes or No. Your teacher may want you to work with a classmate, talk with others in your community to gather information, or use the library or Internet to gather facts.

23-1. If a business is facing increasing prices and inflation, should it cut the quality of the products and services sold in order to prevent major increases in the prices it charges to customers?

Reasons for "Yes"	Reasons for "No"

23-2. Returned merchandise represents a major cost for businesses, which they often pass on to consumers in the form of higher prices. Should businesses tighten up their rules for returning merchandise to help control costs?

Reasons for "Yes"	Reasons for "No"

PROBLEMS

23-A. One of the problems in operating a retail business is deciding how many brands of an item should be stocked. Before making a decision, managers like to know how many different brands and sizes are stocked by competing business firms. Visit a supermarket and a small convenience store and count the number of brands and different package sizes stocked for each item listed below. Record your answers in the appropriate spaces on the form.

Item	Supermarket		Convenience Store	
	Number of Brands	Number of Package Sizes	Number of Brands	Number of Package Sizes
Sugar				
Canned peaches				
Frozen pizza				
Gelatin dessert				
Milk				

1. Why do you believe there are differences in the number of brands and package sizes carried by the supermarket and the convenience store? ____

____

____

____

2. Why do you believe that more brands and package sizes are available for some products than for others?

____

____

____

____

23-B. A store that sells children's clothing had 120 items returned during one season.

Number of Items Returned	Reasons	Percent of Total
a. 40	a. Wrong size	a. ___________________
b. 10	b. Child did not like it	b. ___________________
c. 3	c. Defective merchandise	c. ___________________
d. 45	d. Shrunk when washed	d. ___________________
e. 20	e. Changed mind	e. ___________________
f. 2	f. Salesperson gave incorrect information	f. ___________________
Total 120		100%

1. Complete the chart by determining the percentage of total returned items represented by each of the reasons.

2. If you were the owner of this store, what might you do to reduce the number of returns?

____

____

23-C. Calculate the missing amounts in the chart:

	Cost of Merchandise	Operating Expenses	Markup	Net Profit	% Markup on Price	Selling Price
A.	$34.00	$12.00	______	$2.00	______	______
B.	$ 1.20	______	$ 1.20	$ .07	______	______
C.	______	$ 7.50	______	$2.50	______	$ 13.50
D.	______	$62.75	$85.55	______	______	$327.95
E.	$ .60	$ .25	$ .30	______	______	______
F.	$ 6.00	$ 2.50	______	______	40%	______

23-D. Most businesses provide accurate and honest information to prospective customers when advertising and selling products. Businesspeople know that if customers discover that purchases were made as a result of incorrect or inaccurate information, those customers will be dissatisfied and probably will not buy from the business again. However, a few businesses continue to use unethical practices in advertising and selling. Five advertisements used by those types of businesses are summarized below. For each advertisement, explain why it is unfair and misleading to consumers.

1. An advertisement of a year-end sale says, "Everything in the store reduced." However, many of the most popular items are not put on sale. ____

____

____

2. An advertisement for toothpaste tells prospective buyers that another company's toothpaste is inferior to the advertiser's product. However, there is no proof of the advertised claims. _______________________

____

____

3. A baseball player is used in a testimonial for a brand of auto tires. The player had never used the tires before the advertisement was made. ____

____

____

4. An advertisement for furniture says, "Three rooms of furniture for $200." The furniture is of poor construction and is mismatched or out of date. The ad gives no information on quality or style. ________________

____

____

5. A stereo company sends an announcement to people telling them they have won a free stereo. When the winners come into the store to claim their prize, they are not allowed to take it unless they sign a contract to buy 200 compact discs at very high prices. ____

____

____

23-E. Do you have the characteristics necessary to be a good salesperson? While it is difficult to identify what makes a good salesperson, *some* personal characteristics are very important. Rate yourself on the following checklist to see how many of the characteristics you already have. Be honest with yourself. Place a check mark in the column that best describes you.

Personal Characteristics	Usually	Sometimes	Seldom
1. I am concerned about the feelings of others.	____	____	____
2. I take time to help others when they have problems.	____	____	____
3. I listen to other people without interrupting.	____	____	____
4. I believe other people's opinions are as important as mine.	____	____	____
5. I am a happy person.	____	____	____
6. I enjoy the things I do.	____	____	____
7. I think most of my problems can be solved.	____	____	____
8. I like to learn about things—how they are made and how they work.	____	____	____
9. When I meet people, I try to learn their names and something about them.	____	____	____
10. I like to talk to people about themselves, not about me.	____	____	____
11. I don't like to hurt other people's feelings.	____	____	____
12. I can say the right thing at the right time.	____	____	____
13. When I find a job I like, I enjoy working until it is finished.	____	____	____
14. I like to plan my day before I begin it.	____	____	____
15. I am good at solving problems when they occur.	____	____	____
16. I am concerned about the way other people think I look.	____	____	____
17. When I talk with people, they understand what I say.	____	____	____
18. When I tell people something, they can believe me.	____	____	____
19. If I promise to do something, I will try to finish it.	____	____	____
20. Friendship and trust are important to me.	____	____	____

If most of your check marks are in the Usually column, you already have many of the personal characteristics needed by salespeople. If you checked Sometimes or Seldom on some items, you can begin planning ways to improve those characteristics.

23-F. Some companies plan the amount they will spend on advertising by developing an estimate of the sales for the year and then setting the advertising budget as a percentage of the estimated sales. In the following table, Column 1 lists the planned sales for the year and Column 2 provides the percentage of sales the company plans to spend on advertising. Calculate each company's advertising budget by completing Column 3.

Column 4 lists the actual sales achieved by each company during the year and Column 5 shows the actual amount spent on advertising for the year. Complete the chart by calculating the percentage of sales spent on advertising by each firm and list the answers in Column 6.

	Column 1 Bud. Sales	Column 2 Adv. Perct.	Column 3 Bud. Adv.	Column 4 Act. Sales	Column 5 Act. Adv.	Column 6 Adv. Perct.
A.	$ 950,000	3 %	__________	$1,100,000	$ 32,000	__________
B.	230,000	11 %	__________	210,000	25,500	__________
C.	6,600,000	1.5%	__________	6,950,000	105,500	__________
D.	155,250	10 %	__________	158,000	15,800	__________
E.	2,850,500	5.5%	__________	2,860,000	171,600	__________

SMALL GROUP ACTIVITIES

Group Activity 1

With the help of your teacher, divide into groups of three to five students to work on the following problem.

1. Some types of products are most effectively sold through full-service stores where customers can receive help from knowledgeable salespeople. Others can be sold easily through self-service merchandising. In your groups, review the following list of products. For those that typically would require full-service selling, place an F in the blank space after the item. For those that could be effectively sold through self-service merchandising, place an S in the blank space.

Product	Full- or Self-Service	Store
automobiles	F	Car Max
diamond rings		
magazines		
camera lenses		
fresh fruits and vegetables		
children's games		
television sets		
school supplies		

2. Together, write a brief explanation for why your group feels it is possible to sell the items you marked with an S with self-service merchandising, while the other items will require full-service selling.

3. Retail stores are constantly changing. Relying on the personal experience and knowledge of all group members, think of either a full-service store that would sell the product you indicated as self-service or a self-service store that would sell the product you indicated was full-service. Place your answers in the third column of the table. An example is provided to help you get started.

Group Activity 2

In groups of three to five students, consider the following problem.

Individuals are motivated to buy for different reasons. Buying motives are the reasons people buy. Some common buying motives are listed on the next page. For each buying motive in the column on the left, your group should think of one product and one service that someone would buy to satisfy that buying motive. An example is provided for you.

Be prepared to share your answers with the class.

Buying Motive	Product	Service
Status	Mercedes Benz automobile	House cleaning service
Appetite	_________________	_________________
Comfort	_________________	_________________
Desire for bargains	_________________	_________________
Recognition	_________________	_________________
Ease of use	_________________	_________________
Love of beauty	_________________	_________________
Amusement	_________________	_________________
Desire for good health	_________________	_________________
Friendship	_________________	_________________
Affection	_________________	_________________
Wealth	_________________	_________________
Enjoyment	_________________	_________________
Pride of ownership	_________________	_________________
Fear	_________________	_________________

Name _______________________________

Date _______________________________

Scoring Record

	Part A	Part B	Part C	Total
Perfect score	20	10	5	35
My score				

Study Guide

Part A—*Directions:* Indicate your answer to each of the following questions by circling either yes or no in the Answers column.

		Answers	For Scoring
1.	Of all the resources used by a business, are people the most important to the success of the business?	yes no	1. _______
2.	Are human resources managers the only managers who work with people?	yes no	2. _______
3.	Are acquiring, developing, and compensating employees some of the major activities of the human resources department?	yes no	3. _______
4.	Are human resources activities unnecessary in small companies?	yes no	4. _______
5.	Does the productivity of employees compared to the expenses of wages and benefits determine whether a company will be profitable or not?	yes no	5. _______
6.	Are companies required by law to provide such benefits as social security, Medicare, vacation, and life insurance?	yes no	6. _______
7.	Are the training responsibilities of human resources completed once orientation training has been provided to new employees?	yes no	7. _______
8.	Do participants in a 360-degree feedback program sign their feedback forms, so that the employee being evaluated will know whom to consult about areas that need improvement?	yes no	8. _______
9.	Do employee assistance programs often help employees with non-work related problems?	yes no	9. _______
10.	Is the first step in hiring a new employee establishing the need for a new hire?	yes no	10. _______
11.	Is the job specification a form sent to the human resources department requesting that a position be filled?	yes no	11. _______
12.	Do companies normally give current employees the first opportunity to apply for open positions in the company?	yes no	12. _______
13.	Are employment agencies businesses that actively recruit, evaluate, and help people prepare for and locate jobs?	yes no	13. _______
14.	Is it possible for job applicants to use the Internet to submit their resumes to prospective employers?	yes no	14. _______
15.	To be legal, must tests administered to job applicants measure only characteristics important for success on the job?	yes no	15. _______
16.	Do some companies allow work teams to interview job applicants?	yes no	16. _______
17.	Is transferring an employee to another job generally a form of punishment?	yes no	17. _______
18.	Is a layoff the release of an employee from the company due to inappropriate work behavior?	yes no	18. _______
19.	Do exit interviews provide an opportunity to learn about the causes of employee turnover?	yes no	19. _______
20.	Do time-based wage plans reward employees who provide extra effort or do outstanding work?	yes no	20. _______

Part B—*Directions:* For each of the following statements, select the word, or group of words, that best completes the statement. In the Answers column, write the letter corresponding to the answer selected.

	Answers	For Scoring

1. Human resources activities include (a) employment, (b) wages and benefits, (c) performance improvement, (d) all these activities are human resources activities. .... _______ 1. _______

2. A very formal set of relationships exists between management and employees if the company has (a) a high wage rate, (b) an employee assistance program, (c) a labor union, (d) a human resources department. .... _______ 2. _______

3. The first step in processing applicants for a job is (a) interviewing the applicants, (b) reviewing applications to eliminate unqualified applicants, (c) checking an applicant's references, (d) administering knowledge and skill tests. ..... _______ 3. _______

4. The advancement of an employee within a company to a position with more authority and responsibility is (a) employee turnover, (b) an employee transfer, (c) a promotion, (d) a layoff. .... _______ 4. _______

5. The extent to which people enter and leave employment in a business during a year is known as (a) layoffs, (b) the application process, (c) transfers and terminations, (d) employment turnover. .... _______ 5. _______

6. The money and other benefits people receive for work is called (a) wages, (b) salary, (c) compensation, (d) employee assistance. .... _______ 6. _______

7. Employee benefits (a) can significantly increase the total compensation an employee receives, (b) are offered only to salaried employees, (c) are also called bonuses, (d) all of the answers are correct. .... _______ 7. _______

8. Regular payments made to employees after their retirement are (a) profit sharing, (b) cafeteria payments, (c) bonuses, (d) pensions. .... _______ 8. _______

9. A minimum wage was established by the (a) Fair Labor Standards Act, (b) Occupational Safety and Health Act, (c) Social Security Act, (d) Workers' Compensation Act. .... _______ 9. _______

10. In order to qualify for unemployment insurance, a worker must (a) not be responsible for losing the job, (b) be discharged from the job, (c) be eligible for employment under the Americans with Disabilities Act, (d) pass a test of complex job requirements. .... _______ 10. _______

Part C—*Directions:* In the Answers column, write the letter of the word or expression in Column I that most closely matches each statement in Column II.

Column I	Column II	Answers	For Scoring
A. Promotion	1. Wage system based on the number of units an employee produces.	_______	1. _______
B. Discharge	2. The advancement of an employee within a company to a position with more authority and responsibility.	_______	2. _______
C. Transfer	3. Payment for performance that exceeds a standard.	_______	3. _______
D. Piece-rate	4. The release of an employee from the company due to inappropriate work behavior.	_______	4. _______
E. Bonus	5. The assignment of an employee to another job in the company that involves the same types of responsibilities and authority.	_______	5. _______

Directions: Study each controversial issue carefully. Follow the advice of your teacher before listing in the columns provided reasons why people might answer Yes or No. Your teacher may want you to work with a classmate, talk with others in your community to gather information, or use the library or Internet to gather facts.

24-1. If there is a major conflict between the needs of a company and the needs of employees, should employees in the human resources department take the side of the business?

Reasons for "Yes"	Reasons for "No"

24-2. Are laws such as the Occupational Safety and Health Act and the Americans with Disabilities Act examples of too much government interference in business operations?

Reasons for "Yes"	Reasons for "No"

PROBLEMS

24-A. The following items describe steps to be taken in hiring employees. Number the steps to show the correct order for completing the employment procedures. The first step should be the first activity completed, the second step should be the second activity, and so forth.

__________   A.   Review applicant applications to eliminate those that do not meet minimum qualifications.

__________   B.   Have applicants fill out an application form.

__________   C.   Administer skills and knowledge tests.

__________   D.   Hire the most qualified applicant.

__________   E.   Establish a need to hire an employee and request one.

__________   F.   An HR employee conducts a general interview with applicants.

__________   G.   Provide orientation and initial training.

__________   H.   Check the applicants' references, education, and past work experience.

__________   I.   Prepare a job description and job specification.

__________   J.   A department manager or work team interviews the applicants.

__________   K.   Recruit applicants for the opening.

24-B. The human resources manager asked you to prepare a report on the employee turnover in the manufacturing industry over the last eight years. Use the data and the firm below to figure out the percentage of employee turnover.

Year No.	Average Number of Employees During the Year	Number of Employees Who Terminated Their Employment During the Year	Percentage of Employee Turnover
1	3,125	100	
1	3,125	100	
1	3,125	100	
1	3,125	100	
1	3,125	100	
1	3,125	100	
1	3,125	100	
1	3,125	100	

24-C. Obtain the classified section of a newspaper and clip an example of an employment advertisement that contains appropriate information for potential applicants. Next, clip an example of an ad that does not contain appropriate information. Attach both ads to this page in the space provided below. Below the ads, write why you believe the ads are good or poor.

Good employment ad	Poor employment ad

____

____

____

24-D. The Storeze Company employs six salespeople to sell its products. Last year, each salesperson sold the following amounts:

Salesperson	Amount of Sales	Straight Salary	Commission	Salary and Bonus
Jackson	$569,000			
Klein	$630,000			
Drase	$520,500			
Teng	$605,200			
Russo	$723,000			
Astor	$502,600			
Total Salary Costs				

The company is considering several pay plans. Salespeople are currently paid a straight salary of $27,000 a year. Proposed pay plans are (1) a straight commission of 4.5 percent on all sales, and (2) a salary of $20,000 plus a bonus of 9 percent on all sales above $500,000.

1. Complete the table on the previous page to show the salary of each salesperson for the three pay plans. Also compute the cost of each plan for the company.

2. Write a recommendation for the company in which you justify one of the plans based on this chart's information.____

____

____

____

____

____

____

____

24-E. Complete the following chart illustrating the costs of fringe benefits for six companies.

Company	Total Payroll	Fringe Benefit % of Total Payroll	Fringe Benefit Costs	Total Payroll and Benefits
A	$960,000	32.00%		
B		28.50%		$1,350,000
C	$495,000		$170,775	
D		30.00%	$36,500	
E	$827,600			$910,000
F		25.00%		$1,500,000

24-F. If you are currently employed, use your job duties to complete the following Job Specification Form. If you are not employed, interview a family member or friend who has a job and use that information to complete the form.

Job Specification Form

Company: _________________________   Department: _________________________
Job Title: _________________________   Rate of Pay: From _________ to _________

Previous Job in Organization: ____
Next Job in Organization: ____
Supervisor's Job Title: ____

QUALIFICATIONS
Education:

Experience:

Physical Requirements:

Specific Skills or Abilities Required:

Training Provided:

JOB REQUIREMENTS
Major Job Tasks:

Specific Job Duties:

Number of Work Hours Required per Week:
     Maximum_________   Minimum_________
Normal Work Schedule:
     Daily:

     Weekly:

Employee Benefits Provided:
     Vacation:

     Insurance:

     Other:

SMALL GROUP ACTIVITIES

With instructions from your teacher, divide into small groups and participate in the following activities.

New students in your school are similar to new employees in an organization. To help new employees adjust to the new work environment, many businesses offer new employee orientation sessions to acquaint a new hire with the policies and procedures of the business.

Group Activity 1

You have been asked by your principal to develop an orientation session for new students. Within your group, outline the information that should be included in this orientation session.

Group Activity 2

Your principal has also asked you to develop questions for a follow-up interview with new students that will be conducted four to six weeks after the student enrolls. Develop a list of potential questions or discussion topics that would be appropriate to ask the new students.

Group Activity 3

Occasionally, students transfer from your school to another school during the school year. Develop a list of potential questions or discussion topics that would be appropriate to ask transferring students during an exit interview. Be prepared to share and discuss your answers with the class.

<table>
<tr><td rowspan="4">Chapter 25

Employee and Organizational Development</td><td colspan="6" align="center">Scoring Record</td></tr>
<tr><td rowspan="2">Name ______________</td><td></td><td>Part A</td><td>Part B</td><td>Part C</td><td>Total</td></tr>
<tr><td>Perfect score</td><td>20</td><td>10</td><td>5</td><td>35</td></tr>
<tr><td>Date ______________</td><td>My score</td><td></td><td></td><td></td><td></td></tr>
</table>

Study Guide

Part A—*Directions:* Indicate your answer to each of the following questions by circling either yes or no in the Answers column.

		Answers	For Scoring
1.	Were a number of companies forced to restructure and downsize in the 1990s?	yes no	1. ______
2.	Is job security the likelihood that a worker will continue to be employed by the same company in the future?	yes no	2. ______
3.	Is organizational development a term used to describe programs that match the long-term career planning of employees with the employment needs of the business?	yes no	3. ______
4.	Is an important objective of organizational development to improve work processes?	yes no	4. ______
5.	Is the reason a previously successful business fails likely to be the inability to change?	yes no	5. ______
6.	Is affirming the organization's mission and goals the first step in planning and implementing an organizational development program?	yes no	6. ______
7.	Are customer service standards specific statements of the expected results from critical business activities?	yes no	7. ______
8.	Is it easier to create change in an organization when only the employees who are affected by the change are informed of the change?	yes no	8. ______
9.	Are organizational changes successful if they are not accepted as the new culture of the organization?	yes no	9. ______
10.	Are most employees concerned only with the amount of their paycheck and benefits?	yes no	10. ______
11.	Is job design making a job more interesting by adding variety to the tasks?	yes no	11. ______
12.	Should companies enlarge jobs to reduce the number of employees needed?	yes no	12. ______
13.	Do the company and the employees benefit if the company trains employees for more than one job in the company, even though they typically perform only one?	yes no	13. ______
14.	Do managers who practice job enrichment allow their employees to make decisions about their work?	yes no	14. ______
15.	In the past, did many companies terminate employees who were not needed, without considering future employment needs?	yes no	15. ______
16.	Must career paths move an employee from an entry-level position into management?	yes no	16. ______
17.	Is it necessary for the human resources department to make long-term projections about the company's employment needs?	yes no	17. ______
18.	Should each job in a company be part of a career path?	yes no	18. ______
19.	Should companies develop training programs to prepare employees for new job requirements before the need arises?	yes no	19. ______
20.	In a performance evaluation meeting, should the employee and manager discuss the employee's strengths as well as areas needing improvement?	yes no	20. ______

	Answers	For Scoring

1. When human resources departments help employees match their long-term employment needs with those of the business, they are involved in (a) organizational development, (b) restructuring, (c) career planning, (d) employee evaluation. ...... ______ 1. ______
2. When employees are encouraged to participate in important decision making in the business, they are involved in (a) cross training, (b) job design, (c) job enrichment, (d) labor relations. .... ______ 2. ______
3. In the past, the attitude of many companies toward employees was (a) you have a job for life, (b) if you are not needed, you will be terminated, (c) we will hire only part-time employees, (d) we will give you regular promotions. .... ______ 3. ______
4. Which of the following is needed for an effective career development program? (a) career paths, (b) effective employee evaluation, (c) employee training, (d) all of the responses. .... ______ 4. ______
5. Traditional career paths moved employees (a) into other companies, (b) into dead-end jobs, (c) toward management positions, (d) into highly technical positions. .. ______ 5. ______
6. A performance evaluation conference should include (a) a discussion of the employee's strengths and areas that need improvement, (b) a focused discussion on the employee's performance, (c) a scheduled time for the discussion, (d) all of the responses are correct. .... ______ 6. ______
7. Providing regular and positive feedback on progress, allowing practice time, explaining why as well as how something is done, and relating to knowledge the employee has already developed are characteristics of (a) an effective training program, (b) a career pathway scheme, (c) a performance review, (d) a career development program. .... ______ 7. ______
8. Which of the following might indicate a need for training? (a) employee conflicts, (b) new technology, (c) customer dissatisfaction, (d) all of these responses. ______ 8. ______
9. The level of employment that requires extensive understanding of the operations of a specific company or industry is (a) an entry-level occupation, (b) a specialist occupation, (c) a team leader, (d) an executive/entrepreneur. .... ______ 9. ______
10. A career portfolio should include (a) examples of school projects you completed, (b) checklists of competencies you have mastered, (c) performance reviews from employers, (d) all of these responses. .... ______ 10. ______

Column I	Column II	Answers	For Scoring
A. Career plan B. Portfolio C. Career path D. Job enrichment E. Job design	1. An organized collection of information and materials developed to represent an employee, his or her preparation and accomplishments..	______	1. ______
	2. A progression of related jobs with increasing skill requirements and responsibility.	______	2. ______
	3. Giving employees the authority to make meaningful decisions about their work.	______	3. ______
	4. Identifies the jobs that are part of the employee's career path, the training and development needed to advance along the career path, and a tentative schedule.	______	4. ______
	5. The kinds of tasks that make up a job and the way workers perform these tasks in doing their jobs.	______	5. ______

          Name ________________________

Directions: Study each controversial issue carefully. Follow the advice of your teacher before listing in the columns provided reasons why people might answer Yes or No. Your teacher may want you to work with a classmate, talk with others in your community to gather information, or use the library or Internet to gather facts.

25-1. Employee work teams are often given the responsibility to schedule work, assign responsibilities to team members, schedule vacations, and even hire and fire members of the work team. Should employees in non-managerial positions be given these responsibilities and authority over their peers?

Reasons for "Yes"	Reasons for "No"

25-2. When employees are hired in many Japanese firms, they usually remain with the company for as long as they choose, provided they perform effectively. Should U.S. companies adopt a philosophy like those Japanese firms?

Reasons for "Yes"	Reasons for "No"

PROBLEMS

25-A. Using the Internet, business magazines, or newspapers, locate an article about a business facing a problem requiring major change. Use the list of indicators in Figure 25-1 in the textbook to guide your research. Read the article and write a one-paragraph description of the problem.

     Assume you are a manager in charge of organizational development for an organization facing the problem you described. Follow the steps for planning and implementing an organizational development program listed in the chapter to describe how you would solve the problem. Prepare a two-page report describing the solution and the procedure you would follow.

25-B. A recent survey was completed of 823 employees involved in work teams that are responsible for the day-to-day decisions for their work areas. When asked what were the barriers to developing effective work teams, they listed the following factors:

Barrier	% of Respondents	No. of Respondents
Insufficient training	54%	_____
Supervisor resistance	47%	_____
Incompatible policies	47%	_____
Lack of planning	40%	_____
Lack of management support	31%	_____
Lack of recognition	24%	_____

1. Complete the chart by calculating the number of employees who identified each of the barriers. Then prepare a bar chart that illustrates the findings from the survey.

Barriers to Effective Teams

	insufficient training	supervisor resistance	incompatible policies	lack of planning	lack of mgt. support	lack of recognition
60%						
50%						
40%						
30%						
20%						
10%						
0%						

2. Prepare three recommendations for managers on what the company should do to increase the chances that the work teams will be effective.

____

____

____

25-C. Conduct a survey of five people who have worked full-time for less than two years and five people who have worked full-time for more than ten years. Ask each person the following questions:

	Very Important	Somewhat Important	Uncertain	Somewhat Unimportant	Very Unimportant
1. How important is job security to you?	_______	_______	_______	_______	_______
2. How important is employee involvement in critical work decisions to you?	_______	_______	_______	_______	_______

After you have completed the surveys, prepare a bar graph to illustrate your results, comparing the responses of the two groups. Then combine your results with the results of your classmates. Discuss the findings and the implications for organizational development in businesses.

25-D. Traditional career paths in business have evolved from an entry-level position requiring limited amounts of education and experience to management positions requiring advanced education and experience. Today, new career paths are available allowing those employees who do not choose a career in management to advance into more specialized careers with greater responsibilities.

Using the classified advertising of a newspaper or an Internet site that provides job listings, identify three different jobs that you believe would form a career ladder that would move a person from entry level to a management position. Complete the chart on the left with the required information for each job. Then prepare another career ladder to identify a sequence of jobs leading to greater responsibility but not into management. Complete the chart on the right with the required information.

When you have completed the two career ladders, list the advantages and disadvantages of a management versus a non-management career path based on the information you collected.

Management Career Ladder	Non-Management Career Ladder

Beginning Job:
 	
  Job title:
 	
  Major duties:
 	
  Education:
 	
  Experience:
	Beginning Job:
	
	  Job title:
	
	  Major duties:
	
	  Education:
	
	  Experience:

2nd Level:
 	
  Job title:
 	
  Major duties:
 	
  Education:
 	
  Experience:
	2nd Level:
	
	  Job title:
	
	  Major duties:
	
	  Education:
	
	  Experience:

3rd Level:
 	
  Job title:
 	
  Major duties:
 	
  Education:
 	
  Experience:
	3rd Level:
	
	  Job title:
	
	  Major duties:
	
	  Education:
	
	  Experience:

25-E. International business opportunities are expanding and offer exciting and rewarding opportunities for people who carefully plan and prepare for international careers. That preparation may take several years and a number of jobs as well as the appropriate education, training, and experience.

Using the library or the Internet, research a career area that can lead to a job in international business. Choose one area you would like to investigate and develop a career path for yourself beginning now. If possible, identify jobs in the career path that fit each of the five employment levels described in Chapter 25. List additional education you will need, special training required, and amount and type of work experience needed to qualify for each job. Prepare this information in both written form and on a timeline for presentation to your class.

Career Area in International Business ____

Entry-Level Job ___________________________________

Education Required   **Special Training Required**   **Experience Required**

Career-Level Job ___________________________________

Education Required   **Special Training Required**   **Experience Required**

Specialist Job ___________________________________

Education Required   **Special Training Required**   **Experience Required**

Supervisor/Management Job ___________________________________

Education Required   **Special Training Required**   **Experience Required**

Executive/Entrepreneur Job ___________________________________

Education Required   **Special Training Required**   **Experience Required**

SMALL GROUP ACTIVITIES

Group Activity 1

When a supervisor conducts an evaluation conference with an employee to review the employee's performance, it should be a positive experience. Discussion should focus on the employee's performance, not on the employee. The supervisor should identify ways the employee can improve and what will happen if improvement occurs. The employee should be encouraged to do a good job.

In each of the following examples, an area for employee improvement is identified. In your group, discuss how you would talk to the employee about the concern. Then prepare a three- to five-minute role play script demonstrating how a successful evaluation conference could be held between an employee and supervisor related to the specific employee performance issue. Select members from your team to role play each of the scenarios for the other teams. Then discuss the approaches to the evaluation conference demonstrated by each team.

1. An employee responsible for preparing customer invoices has a record of errors in totaling the amounts on the invoices. Each invoice is double-checked before it is mailed, so the errors are found and corrected before they are mailed. Since the employee has a large number of invoices to complete each day, it appears he hurries, knowing someone else will correct the mistakes.

   Your team's plan: ____

   ____

   ____

2. An employee is responsible for operating a machine that punches holes through metal plates one inch thick. A safety shield is supposed to be lowered in place each time the punch is operated. The employee has found that more plates can be punched if the shield is not used. You know that if the employee's hands are caught in the press, a serious injury will result.

   Your team's plan: ____

   ____

   ____

3. The employee is having trouble organizing her work. She is very effective when she is organized but spends a great deal of time finding materials and supplies and determining how she will do the job.

   Your team's plan: ____

   ____

   ____

4. The employee seems to be very shy around co-workers. He seldom speaks to them, does not sit with them at lunch, and seldom goes on breaks with anyone he works with. It does not seem to affect the quality of the work he does by himself, but he is not as effective when he works with others.

   Your team's plan: ____

   ____

   ____

Group Activity 2

Often, training needs can be identified from the areas where employees are not performing as well as expected. Review each of the four situations in Small Group Activity 1 above. Your team should review the scenario and, for each, identify a specific training need. Then your team should outline the training procedures you believe would be most effective in improving employee performance.

	Training Need	Recommended Training Procedures
1.		
2.		
3.		
4.		